Find us online

▶ GOV.UK – Simpler, clearer, faster

GOV.UK is the best place to find government services and information for

- car drivers
- motorcyclists
- driving licences
- driving and riding tests
- towing a caravan or trailer
- medical rules
- driving and riding for a living
- online services.

Visit **www.gov.uk** and try it out.

You can also find contact details for DVSA and other motoring agencies like DVLA at **www.gov.uk**

You'll notice that links to **GOV.UK**, the UK's new central government site, don't always take you to a specific page. This is because this new kind of site constantly adapts to what people really search for and so such static links would quickly go out of date. Try it out. Simply search what you need from your preferred search site or from **www.gov.uk** and you should find what you're looking for. You can give feedback to the Government Digital Service from the website.

Message from Lesley Young, the Chief Driving Examiner

Learning to ride is an exciting experience. As with getting to grips with any new skill, you may be nervous and it may be challenging at first. Before long, though, you'll be ready to take the step towards getting your full motorcycle licence and enjoying the freedom that comes with it.

A sound understanding of riding theory will help you to reach that stage and carry on improving right through your riding life. Understanding and practice come together in a safe and responsible rider, so my advice is to get at least some practical lessons with an approved training body under your belt while you're studying for your theory test. It helps to make the theory meaningful, and that helps it to stick.

And you'll be glad of that on the day of your theory test!

I wish you safe riding for life.

Lesley Young
Chief Driving Examiner

Contents

Introduction

About the theory test

In this section, you'll learn about

- how to use this book
- getting started
- the theory test
- after the theory test
- using the questions and answers sections
- using this book to learn and revise.

How to use this book

To prove that you have the right knowledge, understanding and attitude to be a safe and responsible rider, you'll need to pass the theory test.

It includes

- a multiple choice test, to assess your knowledge of riding theory
- a hazard perception test, to assess your hazard recognition skills.

This book contains hundreds of questions, which are very similar to the questions you'll be asked in the test and cover the same topics. It's easy to read, and explains why the answers are correct. References to the source material also appear with each question.

Everyone learns in different ways, so this book has features to help you understand riding theory whatever kind of learner you are, including

- bite-size chunks of information, which are easier to understand at your own pace
- lots of photographs and images to illustrate what you're learning
- fourteen topic-specific case studies and six mixed-topic ones, just like those you'll get in the test
- things to discuss and practise with your trainer, to put your learning about each topic into practice
- meeting the standards, to help you understand how each topic relates to the National Standard for Riding.

This book is designed to help you learn about the theory of riding and to practise for the test. To prepare thoroughly, you should also study the source materials that the questions are taken from. These are

The Official Highway Code
Know Your Traffic Signs
The Official DVSA Guide to Riding – the essential skills

There's always more you can learn, so keep your knowledge up to date throughout your riding career.

Getting started

Applying for your licence

You must have a valid provisional driving licence before you can ride on the road.

Licences are issued by the Driver and Vehicle Licensing Agency (DVLA). You'll need to fill in application form D1, which you can download from **www.gov.uk** or collect from any post office. In Northern Ireland, the issuing authority is the Driver and Vehicle Agency (DVA; online at **nidirect.gov.uk/motoring**) and the form is a DL1. For more information, see **nidirect.gov.uk/information-and-services/motoring/learners-and-new-drivers**

Send your form to the appropriate office, as shown on the form. You must enclose the required passport-type photographs, as all provisional licences are now photocard licences.

When you receive your provisional licence, check that all the details are correct before you ride on the road. If you need to contact DVLA, the telephone number is 0300 790 6801. (DVA's telephone number is 0300 200 7861.)

Residency requirements

You can't take a test or get a full licence unless you're normally resident in the United Kingdom. Normal residence means the place where you live because of personal or occupational (work) ties. However, if you moved to the United Kingdom having recently been permanently resident in another state of the EC/EEA (European Economic Area), you must have been normally resident in the UK for 185 days in the 12 months before your application for a driving test or full driving licence.

Compulsory basic training

Before you take your practical motorcycle tests, you must hold a valid compulsory basic training (CBT) course certificate of completion (DL196). This doesn't apply to riders upgrading from one A category to another; for example, upgrading from category A1 to category A. CBT courses can be given only by training bodies approved by DVSA. These are checked regularly to make sure that there's a high standard of instruction.

The course will include classroom training and practical skills training. You can find out about CBT courses from

- DVSA (visit **www.gov.uk** or call 0115 936 6547)
- the Safe Driving for Life website (**safedrivingforlife.info**)
- your motorcycle dealer
- your local road safety officer, by contacting your local council.

DVSA also produces *The Official DVSA Guide to Learning to Ride* (see pages 11 and 22 for further details), which will give you details about the course.

⊙ About the theory test

You'll take the theory test on-screen in two parts. It's designed to test your knowledge of riding theory – in particular, the rules of the road and best riding practice.

The first part is a series of multiple choice questions. Some multiple choice questions will be presented as a case study. More information about this part of the test is given on pages 17–19. The revision questions are given in the main part of the book, beginning on page 30.

Each question has references to the learning materials; for example

RES s8, HC r162–163, KYTS p32

RES s indicates the section within *The Official DVSA Guide to Riding – the essential skills.*

HC r/HC p indicates the rule or page in *The Official Highway Code.*

KYTS p indicates the page in *Know Your Traffic Signs.*

The second part of the theory test is the hazard perception part. More information about this is given on pages 19–20.

Can I take the practical test first?

No. You must pass your theory test before you can book a practical test.

Does everyone have to take the theory test?

All motorcycle test candidates have to pass the theory test before a booking for a practical test will be accepted. However, you won't have to take a theory test if you want to take an A1 small motorcycle test and hold a full moped licence obtained by passing both a theory and practical moped test or if you're upgrading your motorcycle licence from an A1 to A2 or A2 to category A under the progressive access rules.

If you want to take a practical motorcycle test under the direct access rules then you do need a valid motorcycle theory test pass certificate.

If you have any questions about whether you need to take a theory test, write to DVSA theory test enquiries, PO Box 381, Manchester M50 3UW. Tel 0300 200 1122 or email **customercare@pearson.com**

For Northern Ireland, contact the Driver Licensing Division, County Hall, Castlerock Road, Coleraine, BT51 3TB. Tel 0300 200 7861.

Foreign licence holders: if you hold a foreign licence issued outside the EC/EEA, first check with DVLA (Tel 0300 790 6801; for Northern Ireland call 0300 200 7861), to see whether you can exchange your licence. If you can't, you'll need to apply for a provisional licence, then take a theory test and a practical test.

❯ Preparing for your theory test

Although you must pass your theory test before you can take your practical tests, it's best to start studying for your theory test as soon as possible – but don't actually take it until you have some practical experience of riding.

To prepare for the multiple choice part of the theory test, DVSA strongly recommends that you study the books from which the theory test questions are taken, as well as the questions you'll find in this book.

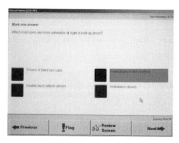

It's important that you study, not just to pass the test, but to become a safer rider.

The Official Highway Code This is essential reading for all road users. It contains the very latest rules of the road and up-to-date legislation, as well as advice on road safety and best practice.

Know Your Traffic Signs This contains most of the signs and road markings that you're likely to see.

The Official DVSA Guide to Riding – the essential skills This is the official reference book, giving practical advice and best practice for all riders.

The Official DVSA Guide to Learning to Ride This gives full details of basic machine handling for compulsory basic training and the full practical test syllabus.

These books will help you to answer the questions correctly and will also help you when studying for your practical tests. The information in them will be relevant throughout your riding life, so make sure you always have an up-to-date copy.

⊙ Other study aids

The Official DVSA Theory Test for Motorcyclists (DVD-ROM) This is an alternative way of preparing for the multiple choice part of the theory test. It contains all the revision questions and answers, and also allows you to take mock tests.

The Official DVSA Guide to Hazard Perception (DVD-ROM) We strongly recommend that you use this, preferably with your riding trainer, to prepare for the hazard perception part of the test. The DVD-ROM is packed with useful tips, quizzes and expert advice. It also includes more than 100 interactive hazard perception clips, which you can use to test yourself and see if you're ready to take the real test.

Better Biking – the Official DVSA Training Aid (DVD) This DVD gives expert advice on improving your skills. It covers all the key skills, including negotiating bends, junctions and roundabouts. An ideal solo ride is demonstrated to show the standard of riding for which you should be aiming.

The Official DVSA Highway Code iPhone App All the latest rules of the road and traffic signs at your fingertips.

The Official DVSA Hazard Perception Practice iOS App A simple and convenient way to prepare for your hazard perception test on the go. The app is compatible with both iPhone and iPad, and contains 14 official interactive DVSA practice clips.

You can buy official DVSA learning materials online at **safedrivingforlife.info/shop** or by calling our expert publications team on **0333 200 2401**. The team can give you advice about learning materials and how to prepare for the tests and beyond. They can also help you select a suitable learning material if you have a special need; for example, if you have a learning disability or English isn't your first language.

DVSA publications are also available from book shops and online retailers. DVSA apps can be downloaded from the iOS App Store and eBooks are available from your device's eBook store.

Why do the questions change?

To make sure that all candidates are being tested fairly, questions and video clips are under continuous review. Some questions may be changed as a result of customer feedback. They may also be altered because of changes to legislation, and DVSA publications are updated so that the revision questions reflect these changes.

Can I take a mock test?

You can take mock tests for the multiple choice part of the theory test online at **safedrivingforlife.info/practicetheorytest**

The theory test

❯ Booking your theory test

Visit **www.gov.uk** to book your theory test online (for Northern Ireland, use **nidirect.gov.uk/motoring**).

If you have any special needs for the theory test, call 0300 200 1122 (0845 600 6700 for Northern Ireland). If you're a Welsh speaker, call 0300 200 1133.

If you have hearing or speech difficulties and use a minicom machine, call 0300 200 1166.

You'll need your

- DVLA or DVA driving licence number
- credit or debit card details (if you do this over the phone, the card holder must book the test). We accept Mastercard, Visa, Delta and Visa Electron.

You'll be given a booking number and you'll receive an appointment email on the same day if you book online.

If you book over the phone and don't provide an email address, you'll receive an appointment letter within 10 days.

Where can I take the test?

There are over 150 theory test centres throughout England, Scotland and Wales, and six in Northern Ireland. Most people have a test centre within 20 miles of their home, but this will depend on the density of population in your area. To find your nearest test centre, please visit **www.gov.uk**

What should I do if I don't receive an acknowledgement?

If you don't receive an acknowledgement within the time specified, please visit **www.gov.uk** or telephone the booking office to check that an appointment has been made. We can't take responsibility for postal delays. If you miss your test appointment, you'll lose your fee.

When are test centres open?

Test centres are usually open on weekdays, some evenings and some Saturdays.

How do I cancel or postpone my test?

You can cancel or postpone your test online by visiting **www.gov.uk** or by telephone. You should contact the booking office at least **three clear working days** before your test date, otherwise you'll lose your fee.

Short-notice cancellation and rebooking (not refund) is permitted in the following circumstances:

- if you're ill or injured and have a supporting medical certificate
- if you've been affected by a bereavement
- if you're sitting school examinations.

Booking by post If you prefer to book by post, you'll need to fill in an application form. The form can be downloaded from **www.gov.uk**, or your riding trainer may have one.

You should normally receive confirmation of your appointment within 10 days of posting your application form. This will be by email if you've provided an email address or by post if not.

If you need support for special needs, please turn to page 16.

⊗ Taking your theory test

Arriving at the test centre You must make sure that when you arrive at the test centre you have all the relevant documents with you. If you don't have them, you won't be able to take your test and you'll lose your fee.

You'll need

- your signed photocard licence, or
- your signed driving licence and valid passport (your passport doesn't have to be British).

No other form of identification is acceptable in England, Wales or Scotland.

Other forms of identification may be acceptable in Northern Ireland; please check **nidirect.gov.uk/motoring** or your appointment letter.

All documents must be original. We can't accept photocopies.

The test centre staff will check your documents and make sure that you take the right category of test.

Remember, if you don't bring your documents your test will be cancelled and you'll lose your fee.

Make sure you arrive in plenty of time so that you aren't rushed. If you arrive after the session has started, you may not be allowed to take the test.

Watch the 'Theory test explained' video on DVSA's YouTube channel. This explains how to prepare for the theory test, what to expect on the day and what you need to do to pass.

⊗ **youtube.com/dvsagovuk**

Languages other than English

In Wales, and at theory test centres on the Welsh borders, you can take your theory test with Welsh text on-screen. A voiceover can also be provided in Welsh.

All Great Britain driving test candidates must take their theory test in either English or Welsh. Unless you're taking the test in Northern Ireland

- no voiceovers will be provided in any other language
- translators cannot attend the test with you to translate it from English into any other language.

Provision for special needs

Every effort is made to ensure that the theory test can be taken by all candidates.

It's important that you state your needs when you book your test so that the necessary arrangements can be made.

Reading difficulties There's an English-language voiceover on a headset to help you if you have reading difficulties or dyslexia.

You can ask for up to twice the normal time to take the multiple choice part of the test.

You'll be asked to provide a letter from a suitable independent person who knows about your reading ability, such as a teacher or employer. Please check with the Special Needs section (call on the normal booking number; see page 13) if you're unsure who to ask.

We can't guarantee to return any original documents, so please send copies only.

Hearing difficulties If you're deaf or have other hearing difficulties, the multiple choice part and the introduction to the hazard perception part of the test can be delivered in British Sign Language (BSL) by an on-screen signer.

A BSL interpreter, signer or lip speaker can be provided if requested at the time of booking. If you have any other requirements, please call the Special Needs section on the normal booking number (see page 13).

Physical disabilities If you have a physical disability that would make it difficult for you to use a touch-screen system or a mouse button in the theory test, we may be able to make special arrangements for you to use a different method if you let us know when you book your test.

Multiple choice questions

The first part of the theory test consists of 50 multiple choice questions. Some of these will be in the form of a case study. You select your answers for this part of the test by touching the screen or using the mouse.

Before you start, you'll be given the chance to work through a practice session for up to 15 minutes to get used to the system. Staff at the test centre will be available to help you if you have any difficulties.

The questions will cover a variety of topics relating to road safety, the environment and documents. Only one question will appear on the screen at a time, and you'll be asked to mark one correct answer.

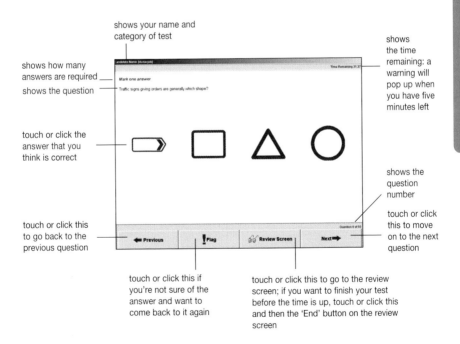

shows your name and category of test

shows the time remaining: a warning will pop up when you have five minutes left

shows how many answers are required

shows the question

touch or click the answer that you think is correct

shows the question number

touch or click this to move on to the next question

touch or click this to go back to the previous question

touch or click this if you're not sure of the answer and want to come back to it again

touch or click this to go to the review screen; if you want to finish your test before the time is up, touch or click this and then the 'End' button on the review screen

To answer, you need to touch or click the box beside the answer you think is correct. If you change your mind and don't want that answer to be selected, touch or click it again. You can then choose another answer.

Take your time and read the questions carefully. You're given 57 minutes for this part of the test, so relax and don't rush. Some questions will take longer to answer than others, but there are no trick questions. The time remaining is displayed on the screen.

You may be allowed extra time to complete the test if you have special needs and you let us know when you book your test.

You'll be able to move backwards and forwards through the questions and you can also 'flag' questions you'd like to look at again. It's easy to change your answer if you want to.

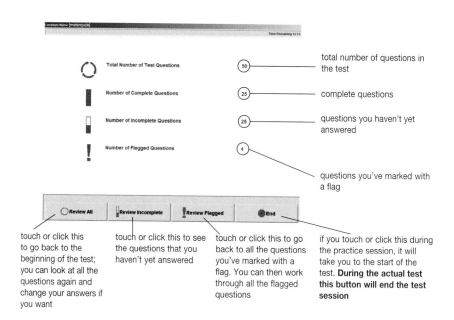

total number of questions in the test

complete questions

questions you haven't yet answered

questions you've marked with a flag

touch or click this to go back to the beginning of the test; you can look at all the questions again and change your answers if you want

touch or click this to see the questions that you haven't yet answered

touch or click this to go back to all the questions you've marked with a flag. You can then work through all the flagged questions

if you touch or click this during the practice session, it will take you to the start of the test. **During the actual test this button will end the test session**

Try to answer all the questions. If you're well prepared, you shouldn't find them difficult.

Before you finish this part of the test, if you have time, you can use the 'review' feature to check your answers. If you want to finish your test before the full time, touch or click the 'review' button and then the 'end' button on the review screen. When you touch or click the review button, you'll see the screen on the previous page.

Case studies

Some of the multiple choice questions will be presented as part of a case study. Case studies are designed to test

- knowledge (recall of facts)
- comprehension (understanding)
- application (practical use of knowledge and understanding).

This is done by creating a set of circumstances that you may encounter in a real-life situation. You'll then be asked some questions relating to the scenario, and you'll have to decide how you would react or behave in each case. For an example of a case study, see page 460.

The case studies at the end of each section in this book set out scenarios and then ask you relevant questions. This is to help you test your knowledge in a format similar to the case studies in the theory test. However, the layout isn't the same as the theory test screens.

Hazard perception

After you've finished the multiple choice part, there's a break of up to three minutes before you start the hazard perception part of the test. You can't leave your seat during this break. This part of the test is a series of computer-generated image (CGI) video clips, shown from a rider's point of view. You'll be using a mouse for this part of the theory test.

Before you start this part of the test, you'll be shown a short CGI video that explains how the test works and gives you a chance to see a sample clip. This will help you to understand what you need to do. You can play this video again if you wish.

During the hazard perception part of the test, you'll be shown 14 CGI video clips. Each clip contains one or more developing hazards. You should press the mouse button **as soon as you see** a hazard developing that may need you, the rider, to take some action, such as changing speed or direction.

The earlier you notice a developing hazard and make a response, the higher your score. There are 15 hazards for which you can score points.

Your response won't change what happens in the scene in any way. However, a red flag will appear on the bottom of the screen to show that your response has been noted.

Before each clip starts, there'll be a 10-second pause to allow you to see the new road situation.

The hazard perception part of the test lasts about 20 minutes. For this part of the test no extra time is available, and you can't repeat any of the clips – you don't get a second chance to see a hazard when you're riding on the road.

⊘ Trial questions

We're constantly checking the questions and clips to help us decide whether to use them in future tests. After the hazard perception part of the test, you may be asked to try a few trial questions and clips. You don't have to do these if you don't want to, and if you answer them they won't count towards your final score.

⊘ Customer satisfaction survey

We want to make sure our customers are completely satisfied with the service they receive. At the end of your test you'll be shown some questions designed to give us information about you and how happy you are with the service you received from us.

Your answers will be treated in the strictest confidence. They aren't part of the test and they won't affect your final score or be used for marketing purposes. You'll be asked if you want to complete the survey, but you don't have to.

> The result

You should receive your result at the test centre within 10 minutes of completing the test.

You'll be given a score for each part of the test (the multiple choice part and the hazard perception part). You'll need to pass both parts to pass the theory test. If you fail one of the parts, you'll have to take the whole test again.

Why do I have to retake both parts of the test if I only fail one?

It's really only one test. The theory test has always included questions relating to hazard awareness – the second part simply tests the same skills in a more effective way. The two parts are only presented separately in the theory test because different scoring methods are used.

What's the pass mark?

To pass the multiple choice part of the theory test, you must answer at least 43 out of 50 questions correctly. For learner car drivers and motorcyclists, the pass mark for the hazard perception part is 44 out of 75.

If I don't pass, when can I take the test again?

If you fail your test, you've shown that you're not fully prepared. You'll have to wait at least three clear working days before you can take the theory test again.

Good preparation will save you both time and money.

After the theory test

When you pass your theory test, you'll be given a certificate. Keep this safe, as you'll need it when you go for your practical test.

The certificate is valid for two years from the date of your test. This means that you have to take and pass the practical test within this two-year period. If you don't, you'll have to take and pass the theory test again before you can book your practical test.

Your practical tests

Your next step is to prepare for and take your practical tests. To help you, *The Official DVSA Guide to Learning to Ride* has details of the Module 1 off-road and Module 2 on-road practical tests. As well as giving the full test syllabus, it explains the skills that you should show and the faults that you should avoid when taking your tests.

Please refer to the back of this book for information about other publications that will help you prepare for your practical tests.

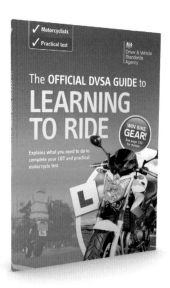

If this is your first full licence and you get six penalty points in the first two years of riding, your licence will be revoked and you'll have to go right back to the beginning and retake your theory test. **Don't risk it; ride safely.**

Using the questions and answers sections

Sections 1 to 14 contain the revision questions for the multiple choice part of the theory test. These are very similar to the questions you'll be asked in the test and cover the same topics.

The questions are in the left-hand column with a choice of answers below.

For easy reference, the questions are divided into topics. Although this isn't how you'll find them in your test, it's helpful if you want to look at particular subjects.

At the start of each topic, before the questions, there are a few pages of useful information to help you learn more about each topic.

On the right-hand side of the page, there's a brief explanation to help you understand the question. There'll also be some advice on correct riding procedures and some short references to the relevant source materials. These refer to the books listed on page 9.

The correct answers are at the back of the book, in section 16.

Case study pr
Alertness

The morning is clear and fine,
You're riding your motorcycle
dipped headlights.
There's an unmarked junctic
right shoulder before turnin
in the road.
Later, a school crossing pa
children are crossing.

Don't just learn the answers; it's important that you know why they're correct. To help you do this, there's a short scenario at the end of each question section, with five questions to answer. This will give you an idea of how the case study part of the theory test will assess your understanding of the subject covered. This knowledge will help you with your practical skills and prepare you to become a safe and confident rider.

Taking exams or tests is rarely a pleasant experience, but you can make your test less stressful by being confident that you have the knowledge to answer the questions correctly.

Make studying more enjoyable by involving friends and relations. Take part in a question-and-answer game. Test those 'experienced' riders who've had their licence a while: they might learn something too!

Some of the questions in this book won't be relevant to Northern Ireland theory tests. These questions are marked as follows: **NI EXEMPT**

Best wishes for your theory test. Once you're on the road, remember what you've learnt and be prepared to keep learning.

Using this book to learn and revise

We're all different. We like different foods, listen to different music and learn in different ways.

This book is designed to help you learn the important information that you'll need for the theory test in a variety of different formats, so you can find a way of learning that works best for you.

Features

> A summary, at the start of each section, of what you'll learn.

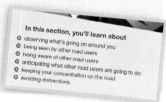

> All the key information presented in bite-size chunks with clear headings.

> Images to help you relate the information to the real world.

> Diagrams and tables to help make information clear and summarise key points.

Links and QR codes to online videos and interactive activities, to further increase your knowledge and skills. Scan the QR code on your smartphone (you'll need a QR code reader app) to access the online content.

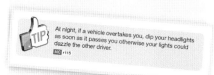

Links to other relevant publications, like *The Official Highway Code* and *The Official DVSA Guide to Riding – the essential skills*.

Tips containing useful extra information about riding safely.

A summary, at the end of each section, of what you'll need to know and be able to do to meet the National Standard for Riding.

Pages for your own notes, with suggested things to think about.

Ideas to discuss with your riding trainer and practise when riding.

Self-assessment – revision questions like the ones you'll get in the test.

Case studies showing how the information might work in practice, and related questions.

The theory test is just one part of the process of learning to ride. You need to learn the facts, but it's important to understand how they relate to real riding.

The combination of knowing rider theory and having good practical riding skills won't only help you pass your test; it will also make you a safer rider for life.

⊚ What kind of learner are YOU?

Ask yourself these questions

- Why are you doing this? What's motivating you?
- How have you learned best in the past? What helped you to remember what you needed to know?
- What are your strengths and weaknesses as a learner?

Think about the way that you learn best. You could try any combination of the following ideas.

I remember what I see or read

- Create flashcards with important facts or statistics
- Make diagrams and charts
- Use mind maps
- Use colour coding
- Watch the DVSA short films
- Make your own notes
- Cross-reference information using a variety of books, eg *The Official Highway Code*
- Draw your own diagrams to show key information.

I remember best when I physically do something

- Short study sessions
- Do things – create models or diagrams; make lists
- Use props
- Try the interactive activities
- Watch and copy what your riding trainer does
- Mime or act out different riding moves.

I remember what I hear

- Repeat rules out loud
- Use a voice recorder to make recordings of key information
- Work with others and discuss things
- Watch and listen to the DVSA video content.

Top tips

Remember your motivation

Think about the reason you're learning to ride. Is it for independence? For work? To ride a dream motorcycle? Remind yourself, from time to time, of your motivation for learning. Don't give up!

Relate to your personal experience

Information is more memorable when it's linked to what you already know. Try to picture yourself in the position of the rider. The case studies throughout the book can help you think about how the ideas would work in real life.

Use mnemonics

Mnemonics are little sayings, stories or techniques that help you remember something. A classic example is 'Richard Of York Gave Battle In Vain', which you can use to remember the colours of the rainbow (red, orange, yellow, green, blue, indigo, violet). You can use similar techniques to memorise statistics, facts or information to help you ride safely.

Question format

However you choose to learn the content, make certain you're familiar with the format of the test and how the questions will be presented. Go through the self-assessment questions in each chapter and see if you can answer them. Mark any you struggle with and try them again at a later date.

Plan your study

Set yourself timelines and targets. Try to set aside dedicated time for study, when you're feeling awake and are unlikely to be interrupted. The environment in which you study is important – try to find an area where you can concentrate.

Getting help

Think about the people you can speak with to ask questions, get advice or share experiences about riding – such as your riding trainer, parents, friends or colleagues at work.

Taking your test

Don't rush into the theory test before you're ready. You need to be confident with the information, and have enough practical experience to give you a deep understanding of the information too.

Section one
Alertness

In this section, you'll learn about

- observing what's going on around you
- being seen by other road users
- being aware of other road users
- anticipating what other road users are going to do
- keeping your concentration on the road
- avoiding distractions.

Alertness

Being alert to what's going on around you is vital to riding safely and will help you to avoid dangerous situations.

> Observation and awareness

It's important to be aware of what's happening around you while you're riding, including

- other road users
- pedestrians
- signs and road markings
- weather conditions
- the area you're riding through.

Keep scanning the road ahead and to the sides, and assess the changing situations as you ride.

Before you move off, you should

 use your mirrors or look around to check how your actions will affect traffic behind you

 signal, if necessary

 take a final look behind to check your **blind spots**.

HC r159–161 RES s6

blind spot
the area behind you that you're unable to see in the mirrors

'lifesaver' check
the 'lifesaver' is a last check over the shoulder into the blind spot to make sure nothing unexpected is happening before committing yourself to a manoeuvre

Getting a clear view

If your elbows obstruct your view in the mirrors, you may be able to fit mirrors with longer stems to get an unobstructed view. Having mirrors fitted to both sides of your motorcycle will give you the best view of the road behind.

Looking over your shoulder before manoeuvring may also warn other drivers that you may be about to change lane, direction or speed. Don't forget your **'lifesaver' check**.

If your view is blocked by parked cars when you're coming out of a junction, move forward slowly and carefully until you have a clear view.

Watch the 'Test your awareness' TFL video.

> **youtube.com/ watch?v=Ahg6qcgoay4**

Overtaking

Observation is particularly important when you're overtaking another vehicle. Make sure you can see the road ahead clearly, looking out for

- vehicles coming towards you
- whether you're near a junction – vehicles could come out of the junction while you're overtaking

- whether the road gets narrower – there may not be enough space for you to overtake
- bends or dips in the road, which will make it difficult for you to see traffic coming towards you
- road signs that mean you **MUST NOT** overtake.

Before you overtake, check that

- it's safe, legal and necessary
- you have enough time to complete the overtaking manoeuvre.

HC r162–163, 165 **RES** s8 **KYTS** p64

Being seen by others

Other road users can find it difficult to see motorcyclists, so it's important to make sure you can be seen as clearly as possible.

- Wear a light or brightly coloured helmet and fluorescent clothing or strips.
- Use dipped headlights, even in good daylight, to make yourself easy to see.
- At night, reflective clothing or strips make you visible from a longer distance.
- Where you can't be seen, such as at a hump bridge, you may need to use your horn.

HC r86–87, r115

If you're following a large vehicle, stay well back. This will help the driver to see you in their mirrors. Staying back will also help you see the road ahead much more clearly. This is especially important if you're planning to overtake the vehicle.

HC r164

Remember, if you can't see a large vehicle's mirrors, the driver can't see you.

❯ Anticipation

Anticipation can help you to avoid problems and incidents so that you can ride more safely. For example, a 'give way' sign warns you that a junction is ahead, so you can slow down in good time.

Look at the road signs and markings: these give you information about hazards.

You should

- follow their advice
- slow down if necessary.

RES s7 **KYTS** p10, 62

Circles
give orders

Triangles
give warnings

Rectangles
give information

When turning right onto a **dual carriageway**, check that the **central reservation** is wide enough for your vehicle to stop in. Do this in case you have to wait before joining the traffic. If there's not enough space for your vehicle, only emerge when it's clear both to the right and left.

Definition

dual carriageway
a road that has a central reservation to separate the carriageways

central reservation
an area of land that separates opposing lanes of traffic

If you're approaching traffic lights that have been green for some time, be prepared to stop because they may change.

Road conditions will affect how easy it is to anticipate what might happen. It's more difficult when

- the weather is very wet or windy
- the light is poor
- the traffic volume is heavy
- the route you're riding is new to you.

In these conditions, you need to be particularly aware of what's happening around you.
RES s8

Anticipating what other road users might do

Watch other road users. Try to anticipate their actions so that you're ready if you need to slow down or change direction.

Be aware of more vulnerable road users. Watch out for

pedestrians approaching a crossing, especially young, older or disabled people who may need more time to cross the road

cyclists – always pass slowly and leave plenty of room, especially if the cyclist is young and may have little experience of dealing with traffic

horses, which may be startled by the noise of your motorcycle – pass them slowly and leave plenty of room.

HC r204–218 **RES** s10

Always be ready to stop

However well prepared you are, you may still have to stop quickly in an emergency. Keep both hands on the handlebars as you brake to keep control of your motorcycle.

RES s6, 10

❯ Staying focused

Riding safely takes a lot of concentration – as well as controlling the motorcycle, you need to be aware of what's happening on the road and what could happen next. Stay focused on riding and try not to get distracted.

Always plan your journey so that you

- know which route you need to take
- have regular rest stops.

Avoiding tiredness

You won't be able to concentrate properly if you're tired. It can also be difficult to concentrate if you're riding on a road that isn't very interesting, such as a motorway. Together, boredom and tiredness could make you feel sleepy, especially at night, so

- don't ride continuously for more than two hours
- if you start to feel drowsy, leave at the next exit. Find a safe and legal place to stop and take a break.

Stop in a safe place and have a cup of coffee or another caffeinated drink. Remember that this is only a short-term solution: it isn't a substitute for proper rest. If possible, take a short nap.

HC r91, 262 **RES** s1, 11

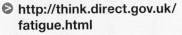
See the Think! road safety website for more information about riding when tired.

● **http://think.direct.gov.uk/ fatigue.html**

Keeping warm

It's just as easy to lose concentration if you're cold. Proper motorcycle clothing will keep you warm and will also help to protect you if you're involved in a road traffic incident.

Distraction

It's easy to be distracted by devices such as hands-free phones, intercom systems or music players because your concentration is divided between the road ahead and what you're hearing.

Losing your concentration, or just taking your eyes off the road for a second, could be disastrous. At 60 mph, your motorcycle will travel 27 metres in one second.

HC r149–150 **RES** s1

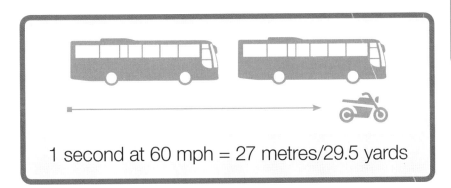
1 second at 60 mph = 27 metres/29.5 yards

Watch DVSA's 'Out of time' video to find out more about the risks of distraction.

> **youtube.com/safedrivingforlifeinfo**

Don't listen to music through an earpiece while you're riding, and make sure you switch off your phone and any hands-free kits. Wait until you're parked in a safe place before you

- retrieve any messages
- make any calls
- send or receive texts
- go online.

If you're riding on a motorway, you should leave the motorway and stop in a safe place before using your phone or programming a navigation system.

RES s1, 16, 18

You could also be distracted by something that has happened on the road, such as an incident on the other side of a motorway. Don't slow down or try to see what's happening; continue with your journey and keep your concentration on your riding.

Meeting the standards

The National Standard for Riding sets out the skills, knowledge and understanding that DVSA believes are required to be a safe and responsible rider. If you know, understand and are able to do the things described in the standard, then you'll not only be in a great position to pass your test but will also be well on your way to becoming a safe rider for life.

You can view the National Standard for Riding at **www.gov.uk**

You must be able to

decide if you're fit to ride. You shouldn't be

- too tired
- too ill
- too emotional
- under the influence of drugs or alcohol

keep concentrating and avoid being distracted

be aware of what's around you (nearby and far away) at all times

ride at such a speed that you can always stop in the clear space ahead of you.

You must know and understand

how these can make you tired

- a poor seating position
- bad posture
- too much noise
- lack of protective clothing

what can distract you. For example

- talking to pillion passengers
- using a sat-nav system

and how to manage these distractions

how helmets and visors may affect your field of vision and how to allow for this

how to read the road ahead and be prepared for the unexpected.

> Notes

You can use this page to make your own notes or diagrams about the key points you need to remember.

Think about

- Which clues can you use to help you anticipate what other road users might do? For example, a filling station at the side of the road could mean traffic slowing down to pull in, or vehicles pulling out.
- Why is it important to keep well back from large vehicles?
- What might you use to plan a long journey, and how would you make sure you took breaks at suitable points?
- Can you find a way to remind yourself to switch off your phone or put it to voicemail before you begin riding?

Your notes

Things to discuss and practise with your trainer

These are just a few examples of what you could discuss and practise with your trainer. Read more about alertness to come up with your own ideas.

Discuss with your trainer

- the 'lifesaver' check. What is it and when should you make it?
- what you need to take into account before overtaking, eg road markings, bends, etc
- what could distract you while riding, eg music via an earpiece, etc.

Practise with your trainer

- seeing and being seen when emerging from junctions, especially when your view is obstructed by parked cars
- turning right onto dual carriageways with different widths of central reservation
- riding at night, to get used to
  - using your dipped and main-beam headlights
  - coping with the lights from approaching vehicles
  - wearing the appropriate clothing to be seen.

You're about to turn right. What should you do just before you turn?

☐ Give the correct signal

☑ Take a lifesaver glance over your shoulder

☐ Select the correct gear

☐ Get in position ready for the turn

When you're turning right, plan your approach to the junction. Signal and select the correct gear in good time. Just before you turn, take a lifesaver glance for a final check behind and to the side of you.

What is the 'lifesaver' when riding a motorcycle?

☐ A certificate every motorcyclist must have

☐ A final rearward glance before changing direction

☐ A part of the motorcycle tool kit

☐ A mirror fitted to check blind spots

This action makes you aware of what's happening behind and alongside you. The lifesaver glance should be timed so that you still have time to react if it isn't safe to perform the manoeuvre.

You see road signs showing a sharp bend ahead. What should you do?

☐ Continue at the same speed

☐ Slow down as you go around the bend

☐ Slow down as you come out of the bend

☐ Slow down before the bend

Always look for any advance warning of hazards, such as road signs and hazard warning lines. Use this information to plan ahead and to help you avoid the need for late, harsh braking. Your motorcycle should be upright and moving in a straight line when you brake. This will help you keep maximum control when dealing with the hazard.

You're riding at night and are dazzled by the headlights of an oncoming car. What should you do?

☐ Slow down or stop

☐ Close your eyes

☐ Flash your headlights

☐ Turn your head away

If you're dazzled by the headlights of an approaching vehicle, slow down or stop until your eyes have adjusted. A dirty or scratched visor could make the dazzle worse and further impair your vision.

1.5 · Mark one answer · RES s5

When riding, your shoulders can obstruct the view in your mirrors. How can you overcome this?

☐ Indicate earlier than normal

☐ Fit smaller mirrors

☐ Extend the mirror arms

☐ Brake earlier than normal

It's essential that you have a clear view all around. Adjust your mirrors to give you the best view of the road behind. If your body obscures the view, try fitting mirrors with longer stems.

1.6 · Mark one answer · RES s1, HC r149

When may motorcyclists use a mobile phone?

☐ When they're carrying a pillion passenger

☐ When they're parked in a safe place

☐ When they're riding an automatic motorcycle

☐ When they're riding on quiet roads

It's important that you're in full control at all times. Even using a hands-free phone kit can distract your attention from the road. If you need to use a mobile phone, stop in a safe and convenient place before making the call.

1.7 · Mark one answer · RES s13, HC r115

You're riding at night. You have your headlights on main beam. Another vehicle is overtaking you. When should you dip your headlights?

☐ When the other vehicle signals to overtake

☐ As soon as the other vehicle moves out to overtake

☐ As soon as the other vehicle passes you

☐ After the other vehicle pulls in front of you

At night, you should dip your headlights to avoid dazzling oncoming drivers or those ahead of you. If you're being overtaken, dip your headlights as the other vehicle comes past. When you switch to dipped beam, your view of the road ahead will be reduced, so look ahead for hazards on your side of the road before you do so.

1.8 · Mark one answer · RES s6, HC r159

How should you move off safely from a parked position?

☐ Signal if other drivers will need to slow down

☐ Leave your motorcycle on its stand until the road is clear

☐ Give an arm signal as well as using your indicators

☐ Look over your shoulder for a final check

Before you move off from the side of the road, you should take a final look over your shoulder to check your blind spot. This will help you to see any road user who isn't visible in your mirrors.

1.9

You become cold when riding your motorcycle. How will this affect you?

☐ You'll be more alert

☐ You'll be more relaxed

☐ You'll react more quickly

☐ You'll lose concentration

It can be difficult to keep warm when riding a motorcycle. It's well worth buying good-quality motorcycle clothing, which will help to keep you warm and is essential for your safety. If you become very cold while riding, you'll find it difficult to concentrate on the road.

1.10

You're riding at night and are dazzled by the lights of an approaching vehicle. What should you do?

☐ Switch off your headlights

☐ Switch to main beam

☐ Slow down and stop if necessary

☐ Flash your headlights

If your view of the road ahead is restricted because you're being dazzled by approaching headlights, slow down and, if you need to, pull over and stop.

1.11

You should always check your blind spots before doing what?

☐ Moving off

☐ Slowing down

☐ Changing gear

☐ Giving a signal

Your blind spots are the areas behind and to either side of you that aren't covered by your mirrors. You should always check the relevant side when there's a risk of a hazard that isn't visible in your mirrors.

1.12

Blind spots should be checked before you do what?

☐ Give a signal

☐ Apply the brakes

☐ Change direction

☐ Give an arm signal

The areas that aren't covered by your mirrors are called blind spots. They should always be checked before changing direction. This check is so important that it's called the 'lifesaver'.

1.13
Mark one answer
RES s8, HC r133

When should you check the blind spots?

- [ ] Before changing gear
- [ ] Before giving signals
- [ ] Before slowing down
- [ ] Before changing lanes

The areas that aren't covered by your mirrors are called blind spots. Other vehicles may be hidden in these areas. Before changing lanes, you should make sure it's safe by checking the blind spot on the side you intend to move. This is called a lifesaver check.

1.14
Mark one answer
RES s8

Why can it be helpful to have mirrors fitted on each side of your motorcycle?

- [ ] To judge the gap when filtering in traffic
- [ ] To give protection when riding in poor weather
- [ ] To make your motorcycle appear larger to other drivers
- [ ] To give you the best view of the road behind

When riding on the road, you need to know as much about following traffic as you can. A mirror fitted on each side of your motorcycle will help give you the best view of the road behind.

1.15
Mark one answer
RES s8

What does the term 'lifesaver' mean?

- [x] A final rearward glance
- [ ] An approved safety helmet
- [ ] A reflective jacket
- [ ] The two-second rule

There are areas behind and to either side of you that aren't visible in your mirrors. These are known as blind spots. Just before turning or changing direction, you should look around to check that there's nothing hazardous in the blind spot. This check is known as a 'lifesaver'.

1.16
Mark one answer
RES s14

You're about to emerge from a junction. Your pillion passenger tells you it's clear. When should you rely on their judgement?

- [ ] Never; you should always look for yourself
- [ ] When the roads are very busy
- [ ] When the roads are very quiet
- [ ] Only when they're a qualified rider

Your passenger may be inexperienced in judging traffic situations, may have a poor view or may not have seen a potential hazard. You're responsible for your own safety and that of your passenger. Always make your own checks to be sure it's safe to pull out.

45

1.17   Mark one answer   RES s8, HC r161

What must you do before stopping normally?

☐ Put both feet down
☐ Select first gear
☑ Use your mirrors
☐ Move into neutral

Check your mirrors before slowing down or stopping, as there could be vehicles close behind you. If necessary, turn and look behind before stopping.

1.18   Mark one answer   RES s8

Why should you check over your shoulder before you change lanes in busy, moving traffic?

☐ To avoid having to give a signal
☐ Mirrors don't cover blind spots
☐ So traffic ahead will make room for you
☐ So your balance won't be affected

Before changing lanes, make sure there's a safe gap to move into. Looking over your shoulder allows you to check the area not covered by your mirrors, where a vehicle could be hidden from view. It also warns following drivers that you want to change lanes.

1.19   Mark one answer   RES s8

You've been waiting for some time to make a right turn into a side road. What should you do just before you make the turn?

☐ Move close to the kerb
☐ Select a higher gear
☐ Make a lifesaver check
☐ Wave to the oncoming traffic

Remember your lifesaver glance before you start to turn. If you've been waiting for some time and a queue has built up behind you, a vehicle further back may try to overtake. In this situation, it's especially important to look out for other motorcycles, which may be approaching at speed.

1.20   Mark one answer   RES s9, HC r173

You're turning right onto a dual carriageway. What should you do before emerging?

☐ Stop, and then select a very low gear
☐ Position in the left gutter of the side road
☐ Check the width of the central reservation
☐ Check that there's enough room for vehicles behind you

Before emerging right onto a dual carriageway, make sure that the central reservation is wide enough to protect your vehicle. If it isn't, you should treat it as one road and check that it's clear in both directions before pulling out.

1.21
Mark one answer
RES s5

What should you do when riding a motorcycle you've never ridden before?

☐ Ask someone to ride with you for the first time

☐ Just ride, as all the controls and switches are the same

☐ Leave your gloves behind, so the switches can be operated more easily

☑ Make sure you know where all the controls and switches are

While control layouts are generally similar, different makes and models have subtle differences in the position and operation of the switches. Before you ride any motorcycle, make sure you're familiar with the layout of all the controls and switches.

1.22
Mark one answer
RES s9, HC r184

You're turning right at a large roundabout. What should you do before you cross a lane to reach your exit?

☐ Take a lifesaver glance over your right shoulder

☐ Put on your right indicator

☑ Take a lifesaver glance over your left shoulder

☐ Cancel the left indicator

On busy roundabouts, traffic may be moving very quickly and changing lanes suddenly. You need to be aware of what's happening all around you. Before crossing lanes to the left, make sure you take a lifesaver glance to the left. This gives you time to react if it isn't safe to make the manoeuvre.

1.23
Mark one answer
RES s9, HC r184

You're positioned to turn right on a multi-lane roundabout. What should you do before moving to a lane on your left?

☐ Take a lifesaver glance over your right shoulder

☐ Cancel the left signal

☐ Signal to the right

☑ Take a lifesaver glance over your left shoulder

Before you change lane you need to know whether it's safe to do so. A lifesaver glance in the direction you want to move will allow you to check your mirrors' blind spots. Your life could depend on knowing where other vehicles are.

1.24 — Mark one answer — RES s9, HC r184

You're turning right on a multi-lane roundabout. When should you take a lifesaver glance over your left shoulder?

☐ After moving into the left-hand lane
☐ After leaving the roundabout
☐ Before signalling to the right
☑ Before moving into the left-hand lane

The 'lifesaver' is essential to motorcyclists and does exactly what it says: it could save your life. Its purpose is to check the blind spot that isn't covered by your mirrors. Learn and understand how and when you should use it.

1.25 — Mark one answer — RES s11, HC r282

You see an incident on the other side of the motorway. What should you do?

☐ Leave the motorway at the next exit
☐ Stop and cross the carriageway to help
☑ Concentrate on what's happening ahead
☐ Place a warning triangle in the road

Always concentrate on the road ahead. Try not to be distracted by an incident on the other side of the road. Many motorway collisions occur due to traffic slowing down because drivers are looking at something on the other side of the road.

1.26 — Mark one answer — RES s8, HC r159–161

What should you do before making a U-turn?

☐ Give an arm signal as well as using your indicators
☐ Check signs to see that U-turns are permitted
☑ Look over your shoulder for a final check
☐ Select a higher gear than normal

If you have to make a U-turn, slow down and ensure that the road is clear in both directions. Make sure that the road is wide enough for you to carry out the manoeuvre safely.

1.27

Mark one answer

RES s7, HC r112, 206

What should you do as you approach this bridge?

You should slow down and be cautious. The bridge is narrow and there may not be enough room for you to pass an oncoming vehicle at this point. Also, there's no footpath, so be aware of pedestrians in the road.

- [ ] Move to the right
- [x] Slow down
- [ ] Change gear
- [ ] Keep to 30 mph

1.28

Mark one answer

RES s8, HC r163, 166

In which of these situations should you avoid overtaking?

- [ ] Just after a bend
- [ ] In a one-way street
- [ ] On a 30 mph road
- [ ] Approaching a dip in the road

As you begin to think about overtaking, ask yourself whether it's really necessary. If you can't see well ahead, stay back and wait for a safer place to pull out.

1.29

Mark one answer

RES s8, HC r162–167, KYTS p63

What does this road marking mean?

In this picture, the road marking shows that overtaking drivers or riders need to return to the left before they reach the hatch markings ahead. The hatch markings are designed to separate opposing streams of traffic; for example, approaching some junctions or dual carriageways.

- [ ] Traffic should use the hard shoulder
- [ ] The road bends to the left
- [x] Overtaking traffic should move back to the left
- [ ] It's safe to overtake

Mark one answer RES s1, HC r149, 270

Your mobile phone rings while you're travelling. What should you do?

☐ Stop immediately

☐ Answer it immediately

☐ Ignore it

☐ Pull up at the nearest kerb

It's illegal to use a hand-held mobile or similar device when driving or riding, except in a genuine emergency. The safest option is to switch off your mobile phone before you set off, and use a message service. If you've forgotten to switch your phone off and it rings, you should ignore it. When you've stopped in a safe place, you can see who called and return the call if necessary.

1.31 Mark one answer RES s7, KYTS p68

Why are these yellow lines painted across the road?

These lines are often found on the approach to a roundabout or a dangerous junction. They give you extra warning to adjust your speed. Look well ahead and do this in good time.

☐ To help you choose the correct lane

☐ To help you keep the correct separation distance

☑ To make you aware of your speed

☐ To tell you the distance to the roundabout

1.32 Mark one answer RES s7, HC r175–176

What should you do when you're approaching traffic lights that have been on green for some time?

☐ Accelerate hard

☐ Maintain your speed

☑ Be ready to stop

☐ Brake hard

The longer traffic lights have been on green, the sooner they'll change. Allow for this as you approach traffic lights that you know have been on green for a while. They're likely to change soon, so you should be prepared to stop.

1.33   Mark one answer   RES s6

What should you do before stopping?

☐ Sound the horn

☑ Use the mirrors

☐ Select a higher gear

☐ Flash the headlights

Before pulling up, check the mirrors to see what's happening behind you. Also assess what's ahead and make sure you give the correct signal if it will help other road users.

1.34   Mark one answer   RES s10, HC r221

You're following a large vehicle. Why should you stay a safe distance behind it?

☐ You'll be able to corner more quickly

☐ You'll help the large vehicle to stop more easily

☑ You'll allow the driver to see you in their mirrors

☐ You'll keep out of the wind better

If you're following a large vehicle but are so close to it that you can't see its exterior mirrors, the driver won't be able to see you. Keeping well back will also allow you to see the road ahead by looking past on either side of the large vehicle.

1.35   Mark one answer   RES s10, HC r161

When you see a hazard ahead, you should use the mirrors. Why is this?

☐ Because you'll need to accelerate out of danger

☑ To assess how your actions will affect following traffic

☐ Because you'll need to brake sharply to a stop

☐ To check what's happening on the road ahead

You should be constantly scanning the road for clues about what's going to happen next. Check your mirrors regularly, particularly as soon as you spot a hazard. What's happening behind may affect your response to hazards ahead.

1.36   Mark one answer   RES s9

You're waiting to turn right at the end of a road. Your view is obstructed by parked vehicles. What should you do?

☑ Stop and then move forward slowly and carefully for a clear view

☐ Move quickly to where you can see so you only block traffic from one direction

☐ Wait for a pedestrian to let you know when it's safe for you to emerge

☐ Turn your vehicle around immediately and find another junction to use

At junctions, your view is often restricted by buildings, trees or parked cars. You need to be able to see in order to judge a safe gap. Edge forward slowly and keep looking all the time. Don't cause other road users to change speed or direction as you emerge.

> Case study practice – 1
Alertness

The morning is clear and fine, but very cold.

You're riding your motorcycle and using dipped headlights.

There's an unmarked junction. You look over your right shoulder before turning right. Ahead, there's a dip in the road.

Later, a school crossing patrol signals you to stop while children are crossing.

1.1 Why would you be using your headlights?
Mark **one** answer

☐ To help you see the road ahead
☐ To help you to be seen by others
☐ To help you see other road users
☐ To help others see the road ahead

RES s4 **HC** r86

1.2 Why did you look over your right shoulder?
Mark **one** answer

☐ Because the junction is unmarked
☐ Because your mirrors are broken
☐ Because your mirrors have blind spots
☐ Because your indicators are flashing slowly

RES s8 **HC** r180

1.3 What should you guard against on this journey?

Mark **one** answer

- ☐ Losing your way after turning right
- ☐ Running out of fuel
- ☐ Rushing to keep an appointment
- ☐ Getting cold and losing concentration

RES s4

1.4 After you've turned right, how would the road feature affect you?

Mark **one** answer

- ☐ It would obstruct your view of the road
- ☐ It would increase your fuel consumption
- ☐ It would improve your brake function
- ☐ It would cause more wear on your tyres

RES s8

1.5 How must you react to the school crossing patrol?

Mark **one** answer

- ☐ Stop your motorcycle and wait patiently
- ☐ Stop the engine and get off your motorcycle
- ☐ Ride past, keeping within the speed limit
- ☐ Park on the left and switch on your hazard warning lights

RES s8 **HC** r105, p105

Section two
Attitude

In this section, you'll learn about

- showing consideration and courtesy to other road users
- how to follow other road users safely
- giving priority to emergency vehicles, buses and pedestrians.

Attitude

Safe riding is all about developing the correct attitude and approach to road safety, together with a sound knowledge of riding techniques.

However modern, fast or expensive your motorcycle, it's you, the rider, who determines how safe it is.

❯ Good manners on the road

Be considerate to other road users. Other types of vehicle, cyclists and horse riders have just as much right to use the road as you. If you ride in a competitive way, you'll make the road less safe for everyone using it.

RES s1

It's also important to be patient with other road users. Unfortunately, not everyone obeys the rules. Try to be calm and tolerant, however difficult it seems. For instance, if someone pulls out in front of you at a junction, slow down and don't get annoyed with them.

HC r147 **RES** s1

Helping other road users

You can help other road users know what you're planning to do by signalling correctly and moving to the correct position at junctions. For instance, if you want to turn right, get into the right-hand lane well before the junction. A badly positioned vehicle could obstruct traffic behind it.

HC r143 **RES** s8, 9

If you're riding slowly, consider the other road users behind you. If there's a queue, pull over as soon as you can do so safely and let the traffic pass. Think how you would feel if you were one of the road users following behind you. They may not be as patient as you are.

HC r169 RES s10

If a large vehicle is trying to overtake you but is taking a long time, slow down and let it pass. It will need more time to pass you than a car would.

HC r168 RES s8

If you're travelling at the speed limit and a driver comes up behind flashing their headlights or trying to overtake, keep a steady course and allow them to overtake. Don't try to stop them – they could become more frustrated.

HC r168 RES s8, 11

Using your horn and lights

Only sound your horn if there's danger and you need to let others know you're there. Don't sound it through impatience.

HC r112 RES s5, 6, 10

At night, don't dazzle other road users. Dip your lights when you're

following another vehicle

meeting another vehicle coming towards you.

HC r114 RES s13

You should only flash your headlights to show other road users you're there. It's not a signal to show priority, impatience or to greet others.

`HC` r110–111 `RES` s6, 10

Animals on the road

Horses can be frightened easily and a rider could lose control of their horse. When passing horses

- keep your speed right down
- give them plenty of room.

`HC` r214–215 `RES` s10

See the Think! road safety website for more information about horses on the road.

❯ **http://think.direct.gov.uk/ horses.html**

Take care if there are animals, such as sheep, on the road. If the road is blocked by animals, or if you're asked to, stop and switch off your engine until the road is clear.

`HC` r214

❯ Following safely

Riding too closely behind another vehicle – known as tailgating – is

- intimidating and distracting for the road user in front
- very dangerous, as it could cause an incident if the vehicle stops suddenly.

`RES` s10

Travelling too closely to another vehicle also means that you can see less of the road ahead, so keep well back, especially from large vehicles. You'll be able to see further down the road and spot any hazards ahead more easily.

`RES` s8, 10

Section two Attitude

Keep a safe distance from the vehicle in front.

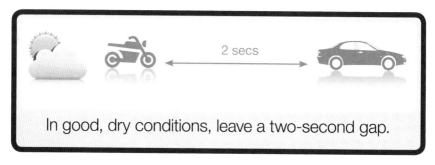

In good, dry conditions, leave a two-second gap.

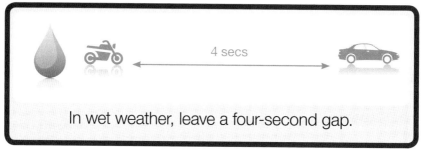

In wet weather, leave a four-second gap.

HC r126 **RES** s8, 10, 11

 Use a fixed point, like a road sign, to help you measure the gap between you and the vehicle in front.

See section 4, Safety margins, for more information about the amount of space to leave between you and the vehicle in front.

Keeping well back also allows

- the road user in front to see you in their mirrors
- traffic emerging from junctions ahead to see you more easily.

RES s8, 10

When you're following large vehicles, you may see them move to the centre of the road before turning left – this is because they need more room to manoeuvre. Keep well back and don't try to pass on the left as the rear of the vehicle will cut in.

If the road user behind is following too closely, gradually increase the gap between you and the vehicle in front. This will give you a greater safety margin. If another road user cuts in front of you, drop back until you've restored your safety margin.

HC r168

> Giving priority to others

Who has priority on the road at any time can vary. Sometimes traffic going in one direction is given priority, and this is shown by a road sign. Having priority doesn't mean you can demand right of way. Be careful: the driver coming towards you may not have seen or understood the road sign.

Priority over
oncoming
vehicles

Emergency vehicles

Always give priority to emergency vehicles. It's important for them to move quickly through traffic because someone's life might depend on it. Pull over to let them through as soon as you can do so safely.

HC r219 **RES** s8

As well as fire, police and ambulance services, other emergency services (including those shown here) use a blue flashing light.

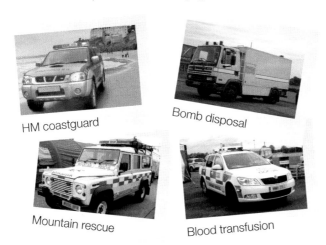

HM coastguard

Bomb disposal

Mountain rescue

Blood transfusion

Doctors' vehicles may use green flashing lights when answering an emergency call.

Watch the 'Blue light aware' video to find out more about how to help emergency vehicles get through traffic.

> **motoringassist.com/bluelightaware**

Priority for buses

Give priority to buses pulling out from bus stops, as long as you can do so safely. In some areas, bus lanes allow buses to proceed quickly through traffic. Be aware of road signs and markings so that you don't use bus lanes while they're in operation, unless permitted to do so.

HC r223 **RES** s7, 8, 10

Unmarked crossroads

At unmarked crossroads, no-one has priority. Slow down, look both ways and only emerge into the junction when you can do so safely.

Pedestrian crossings

Be particularly careful around pedestrian crossings so that you're ready to stop if necessary.

Type of crossing	What you need to be aware of
Zebra crossing 	Watch out for pedestrians at or approaching a zebra crossing. • Be ready to slow down and stop. • Be patient if they cross slowly. • Don't encourage them to cross by waving or flashing your headlights – there may be another vehicle coming. **HC** r195 **RES** s8
Pelican crossing 	If you're approaching a pelican crossing and the amber light is flashing • give way to pedestrians on the crossing • don't move off until the crossing is clear. **HC** r196–198 **RES** s8

Type of crossing	What you need to be aware of
Puffin crossing 	Puffin crossings are electronically controlled. Sensors ensure that the red light shows until the pedestrian has safely crossed the road. These crossings don't have a flashing amber light; they have a steady amber light, like normal traffic lights. **HC** r199 **RES** s8
Toucan crossing 	Toucan crossings, which work in a similar way to puffin crossings, allow cyclists to cross at the same time as pedestrians. **HC** r199 **RES** s8

Meeting the standards

You must be able to

help other road users to understand what you intend to do by signalling correctly

support the signals that you make with the position of your machine. For example, if you're turning right, position the motorcycle in good time and use the right-turn lane if there is one

control your reaction to other road users. Try not to get annoyed or frustrated

give other road users enough time and space.

You must know and understand

what can happen if you wrongly use the headlights or the horn as a signal

what lane discipline is and why it's important

that it's an offence to ride

- without due care and attention
- without reasonable consideration for other road users.

Notes

You can use this page to make your own notes or diagrams about the key points you need to remember.

Think about

- To which vehicles do you need to give priority?
- What would you do if someone was tailgating you?
- In what conditions should you keep a four-second distance between you and the vehicle in front?
- What problems might you cause if you're impatient and inconsiderate while riding?

Your notes

Things to discuss and practise with your trainer

These are just a few examples of what you could discuss and practise with your trainer. Read more about attitude to come up with your own ideas.

Discuss with your trainer

- the different crossings you may come across (puffin, toucan, etc) and who can use them
- which emergency vehicles you may see on the road (police, doctors, etc) and how to react to them
- how to behave when other road users don't obey the rules.

Practise with your trainer

- riding in an area with bus lanes, to
  - practise how to react when they're in operation
  - understand when motorcycles may or may not use them
- riding in heavy traffic, to get used to other vehicles that may be following you too closely
- riding in the countryside, or where you're likely to encounter horse riders.

You're riding towards a zebra crossing. Pedestrians are waiting to cross. What should you do?

☐ Give way to the elderly and infirm only

☒ Slow down and prepare to stop

☐ Use your headlights to signal them to cross

☐ Wave at them to cross the road

As you approach a zebra crossing, look out for people waiting to cross and be ready to stop. Some pedestrians may be a little slow to understand that it's safe to cross, so give them time. Be patient and don't rev your engine or surge forward before the crossing is clear.

You're following a large vehicle travelling at 40 mph. Where should you position your motorcycle?

☐ Close behind the vehicle, to make it easier to overtake

☐ To the left of the road, to make it easier to be seen

☐ Close to the vehicle, to keep out of the wind

☒ Well back, so that you can see past the vehicle

You need to be able to see well down the road and be ready for any hazards. Staying too close to the vehicle will reduce your view of the road ahead and the driver of the vehicle in front may not be able to see you either. Without a safe separation gap, you don't have the time and space you need to react to any hazards.

You're approaching two riders on horseback. What should you do?

☐ Continue at your normal speed

☐ Change down the gears quickly

☒ Slow down and be ready to stop

☐ Flash your headlights to warn them

Animals are easily frightened by moving motor vehicles. If you're approaching horses, keep your speed down and watch to see if the rider has any difficulty keeping control. Always be ready to stop if necessary. When it's safe to pass, give them plenty of room.

2.4

You're approaching a red light at a puffin crossing. Pedestrians are on the crossing. When will your red light change?

☐ When you start to edge forward onto the crossing

☑ When the pedestrians have reached a safe position

☐ When the pedestrians are clear of the front of your motorcycle

☐ When a driver from the opposite direction reaches the crossing

An electronic device will automatically detect when the pedestrians have reached a safe position. Don't move forward until the green light shows and you've checked that it's safe to proceed.

2.5

You're riding a motorcycle that has an engine of less than 50 cc. What should you do if you see a queue of traffic building up behind?

☐ Keep well out to stop vehicles overtaking dangerously

☐ Wave vehicles behind you to pass if you think they can overtake

☑ Pull in when you can to let faster vehicles behind you overtake

☐ Give a left signal when it's safe for vehicles to overtake you

Try not to hold up a queue of traffic. This might lead to other road users becoming impatient and attempting dangerous manoeuvres. If you're riding a slow-moving scooter or small motorcycle and a queue of traffic has built up behind you, look for a safe place to pull in so they can pass safely.

2.6

When you're riding a motorcycle, what should your normal road position allow?

☐ Other vehicles will be able to pass easily on your left

☐ You'll keep within half a metre (1 foot 8 inches) of the kerb

☐ Faster traffic will be able to overtake you easily

☐ Drivers at junctions ahead will be able to see you approaching

Aim to ride in the middle of your lane. Avoid riding in the gutter or in the centre of the road, where you might

- obstruct overtaking traffic
- put yourself in danger from oncoming traffic
- encourage other traffic to overtake you on the left.

Why are young motorcyclists more likely to be involved in crashes?

☐ Because they're too cautious at junctions

☐ Because they ride in the middle of lanes

☒ Because they're inexperienced

☐ Because they ride in groups

Overconfidence, lack of experience and poor judgement can cause a motorcyclist to make poor decisions, which can lead to a collision. It's just as important to make sure you have the right attitude and self-awareness as a rider as it is to develop skilful riding techniques.

At a pelican crossing, what must you do when the amber light is flashing?

☐ Stop and wait for the green light

☐ Stop and wait for the red light

☐ Give way to pedestrians waiting to cross

☒ Give way to pedestrians already on the crossing

Pelican crossings are signal-controlled crossings operated by pedestrians. Push-button controls change the signals. Pelican crossings have no red-and-amber stage before green; instead, they have a flashing amber light. This means you must give way to pedestrians who are already on the crossing. If the crossing is clear, however, you can continue.

Why should you never wave people across at pedestrian crossings?

☒ Another vehicle may be coming

☐ They may not be looking

☐ It's safer for you to carry on

☐ They may not be ready to cross

If people are waiting to use a pedestrian crossing, slow down and be prepared to stop. Don't wave them across the road, because another driver may not have seen them, may not have seen your signal, and may not be able to stop safely.

What does 'tailgating' mean?

☐ Using the rear door of a hatchback car

☐ Reversing into a parking space

☒ Following another vehicle too closely

☐ Driving with rear fog lights on

'Tailgating' is the term used when a driver or rider follows the vehicle in front too closely. It's dangerous because it restricts their view of the road ahead and leaves no safety margin if the vehicle in front needs to slow down or stop suddenly. Tailgating is often the underlying cause of rear-end collisions or multiple pile-ups.

2.11 · Mark one answer · RES s10, HC r222

Why is it unwise to follow this vehicle too closely?

Staying back will increase your view of the road ahead. This will help you to see any hazards that might occur and give you more time to react.

☐ Your brakes will overheat
☐ Your view ahead will be increased
☐ Your engine will overheat
☒ Your view ahead will be reduced

2.12 · Mark one answer · RES s8, 10, 11, HC r126

What's the minimum time gap you should leave when following a vehicle on a wet road?

Water will reduce your tyres' grip on the road. The safe separation gap of at least two seconds in dry conditions should be doubled, to at least four seconds, in wet weather.

☐ One second
☐ Two seconds
☐ Three seconds
☒ Four seconds

2.13 · Mark one answer · RES s8, HC r168

A long, heavily laden lorry is taking a long time to overtake you. What should you do?

A long lorry with a heavy load will need more time to pass you than a car, especially on an uphill stretch of road. Slow down and allow the lorry to pass.

☐ Speed up
☒ Slow down
☐ Hold your speed
☐ Change direction

2.14 · Mark one answer · RES s8

Which vehicle will use a blue flashing beacon?

Emergency vehicles use blue flashing lights. If you see or hear one, move out of its way as soon as it's safe and legal to do so.

☐ Motorway maintenance
☒ Bomb disposal
☐ Snow plough
☐ Breakdown recovery

2.15
Mark one answer
RES s8, HC r219

You're being followed by an ambulance showing flashing blue lights. What should you do?

☑ Pull over as soon as it's safe to do so

☐ Accelerate hard to get away from it

☐ Maintain your speed and course

☐ Brake harshly and stop well out into the road

Pull over in a place where the ambulance can pass safely. Check that there are no bollards or obstructions in the road that will prevent it from passing.

2.16
Mark one answer
RES s8, HC r219

What type of emergency vehicle is fitted with a green flashing beacon?

☐ Fire engine

☐ Road gritter

☐ Ambulance

☑ Doctor's car

A green flashing beacon on a vehicle means the driver or passenger is a doctor on an emergency call. Give way to them if it's safe to do so. Be aware that the vehicle may be travelling quickly or may stop in a hurry.

2.17
Mark one answer
RES s7, HC r300, KYTS p31

Who should obey diamond-shaped traffic signs?

☑ Tram drivers

☐ Bus drivers

☐ Lorry drivers

☐ Taxi drivers

These signs apply only to tram drivers, but you should know their meaning so that you're aware of the priorities and are able to anticipate the actions of the driver.

2.18

Mark one answer

RES s7, HC r306

On a road where trams operate, which of these vehicles will be most at risk from the tram rails?

☐ Cars

☑ Cycles

☐ Buses

☐ Lorries

The narrow wheels of a bicycle can become stuck in the tram rails, causing the cyclist to stop suddenly, wobble or even lose balance altogether. The tram lines are also slippery, which could cause a cyclist to slide or fall off.

2.19

Mark one answer

RES s5, HC r112

What should you use your horn for?

☑ To alert others to your presence

☐ To allow you right of way

☐ To greet other road users

☐ To signal your annoyance

Your horn mustn't be used between 11.30 pm and 7.00 am in a built-up area or when you're stationary, unless a moving vehicle poses a danger. Its function is to alert other road users to your presence.

2.20

Mark one answer

RES s8, HC r143

You're in a one-way street and want to turn right. There are two lanes. Where should you position your vehicle?

☐ In the right-hand lane

☐ In the left-hand lane

☐ In either lane, depending on the traffic

☐ Just left of the centre line

When you're in a one-way street and want to turn right, you should take up a position in the right-hand lane. This will allow other road users, not wishing to turn, to pass on the left. Indicate your intention and take up the correct position in good time.

2.21

Mark one answer

RES s8, 9, HC r179

You wish to turn right ahead. Why should you take up the correct position in good time?

☐ To allow other drivers to pull out in front of you

☐ To give a better view into the road that you're joining

☐ To help other road users know what you intend to do

☐ To allow drivers to pass you on the right

If you wish to turn right into a side road, take up your position in good time. Move to the centre of the road when it's safe to do so. This will allow vehicles to pass you on the left. Early planning will show other traffic what you intend to do.

2.22

Mark one answer

RES s8, HC r25, KYTS p124

At which type of crossing are cyclists allowed to ride across with pedestrians?

☑ Toucan

☐ Puffin

☐ Pelican

☐ Zebra

A toucan crossing is designed to allow pedestrians and cyclists to cross at the same time. Look out for cyclists approaching the crossing at speed.

2.23

Mark one answer

HC r168

You're driving at the legal speed limit. A vehicle comes up quickly behind you, flashing its headlights. What should you do?

☐ Accelerate to make a gap behind you

☐ Touch the brakes sharply to show your brake lights

☐ Maintain your speed to prevent the vehicle from overtaking

☑ Allow the vehicle to overtake

Don't enforce the speed limit by blocking another vehicle's progress. This will only lead to the other driver becoming more frustrated. Allow the other vehicle to pass when you can do so safely.

2.24

Mark one answer

RES s6, HC r110–111

When should you flash your headlights at other road users?

☐ When showing that you're giving way

☐ When showing that you're about to turn

☐ When telling them that you have right of way

☑ When letting them know that you're there

You should only flash your headlights to warn others of your presence. Don't use them to greet others, show impatience or give priority to other road users, because they could misunderstand your signal.

2.25

Mark one answer

RES s9, HC r146

You're approaching an unmarked crossroads. How should you deal with this type of junction?

☐ Accelerate and keep to the middle

☐ Slow down and keep to the right

☐ Accelerate and look to the left

☑ Slow down and look both ways

Be cautious, especially when your view is restricted by hedges, bushes, walls, large vehicles, etc. In the summer months, these junctions can become more difficult to deal with, because growing foliage may further obscure your view.

2.26
Mark one answer   RES s8, 10, 11, HC r126

The conditions are good and dry. When should you use the 'two-second rule'?

☐ Before restarting the engine after it has stalled

☑ When checking your gap from the vehicle in front

☐ Before using the 'Mirrors – Signal – Manoeuvre' routine

☐ When traffic lights change to green

In good conditions, the 'two-second rule' can be used to check the distance between your vehicle and the one in front. This technique works on roads carrying faster traffic. Choose a fixed object, such as a bridge, sign or tree. When the vehicle ahead passes this object, say to yourself 'Only a fool breaks the two-second rule.' If you reach the object before you finish saying this, you're too close.

2.27
Mark one answer   RES s8, HC r199

At a puffin crossing, which colour follows the green signal?

☑ Steady red

☐ Flashing amber

☐ Steady amber

☐ Flashing green

Puffin crossings have infra-red sensors that detect when pedestrians are crossing and hold the red traffic signal until the crossing is clear. The use of a sensor means there's no flashing amber phase as there is with a pelican crossing.

2.28
Mark one answer   RES s8, 10, 11, HC r126

You're in a line of traffic. The driver behind you is following very closely. What action should you take?

☐ Ignore the following driver and continue to travel within the speed limit

☐ Slow down, gradually increasing the gap between you and the vehicle in front

☐ Signal left and wave the following driver past

☐ Move over to a position just left of the centre line of the road

If the driver behind is following too closely, there's a danger they'll collide with the back of your vehicle if you stop suddenly. You can reduce this risk by slowing down and increasing the safety margin in front of you. This reduces the chance that you'll have to stop suddenly and allows you to spread your braking over a greater distance. This is an example of defensive driving.

Case study practice – 2
Attitude

You ride your motorcycle to a motorcycle show on a single carriageway road.

The road surface is damp from overnight rain.

You come up behind two horse riders. Soon, you pass them.

Near the showground, the traffic volume increases. There's a large vehicle in front, so you drop back.

You see a vehicle with a green flashing light in your mirrors, so you make room for it to pass.

2.1 What's the national speed limit for motorcycles on this road?
Mark **one** answer

☐ 40 mph
☐ 50 mph
☐ 60 mph
☐ 70 mph

HC r124

2.2 How should you ride on this road surface?
Mark **one** answer

☐ Carefully, while increasing the distance from any vehicle in front
☐ Faster, as this will help warm the tyres and dry the road surface
☐ Very slowly, to help prevent surface water spraying over others
☐ As close as possible to the vehicle in front, for added protection

RES s8 **HC** r126

2.3 What's the safest way to pass the two riders?

Mark **one** answer

- ☐ Quickly, while flashing headlights
- ☐ Slowly, while sounding the horn
- ☐ Quickly, leaving a large gap
- ☐ Slowly, leaving plenty of room

RES s10 **HC** r214–215

2.4 Why did you drop back?

Mark **one** answer

- ☐ To avoid any buffeting from the wind
- ☐ To allow space for other road users to pull in
- ☐ To avoid any mud splashing up from the tyres
- ☐ To allow you to see past the large vehicle

RES s10 **HC** r164

2.5 What did you see in your mirrors?

Mark **one** answer

- ☐ A fire engine being driven to a fire
- ☐ A doctor driving to an emergency
- ☐ A police officer driving to a disturbance
- ☐ A traffic officer attending an incident

RES s8 **HC** r219

Section three

Safety and your motorcycle

In this section, you'll learn about

- ❯ carrying out basic maintenance on your motorcycle
- ❯ what to do if your motorcycle has a fault
- ❯ carrying passengers and loads safely
- ❯ being seen by, and making sure you can see, other road users
- ❯ making your motorcycle secure
- ❯ parking safely
- ❯ being aware of the environment
- ❯ avoiding congestion.

Safety and your motorcycle

Look after your motorcycle and it will look after you, not only by being less likely to break down, but also by being more economical and lasting longer. Remember that an efficient engine is kinder to the environment.

> Looking after your motorcycle

Regular maintenance should ensure that your motorcycle is safe and fit to be on the road. It will also help to make sure that your motorcycle uses fuel as efficiently as possible and keep its exhaust emissions to a minimum.

Check the following items on a regular basis.

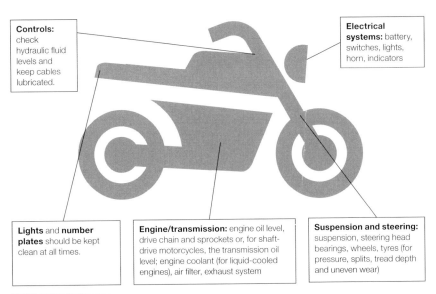

Controls: check hydraulic fluid levels and keep cables lubricated.

Electrical systems: battery, switches, lights, horn, indicators

Lights and **number plates** should be kept clean at all times.

Engine/transmission: engine oil level, drive chain and sprockets or, for shaft-drive motorcycles, the transmission oil level; engine coolant (for liquid-cooled engines), air filter, exhaust system

Suspension and steering: suspension, steering head bearings, wheels, tyres (for pressure, splits, tread depth and uneven wear)

HC p128 RES s6, 15

The drive chain and sprockets: a loose drive chain and worn sprockets can cause the chain to jump off the rear sprocket and lock the rear wheel. When adjusting the chain tension, check the wheel alignment too as this can increase tyre wear and cause instability when cornering.

Tyre pressures: check them when the tyres are cold. Increase the pressure when you're carrying passengers or loads, or if riding at high speeds. Under-inflation can affect stopping and steering, as well as increase fuel consumption. Check your motorcycle handbook for correct pressures.

Tyre tread: the depth must be more than 1 mm to be legal. When replacing the tyres, replace the tubes as well if necessary. Check the wheel alignment after refitting the rear wheel. Ride carefully on your new tyres until the shiny surface wears off.

HC p129 RES s15

Use this handy guide to give your motorcycle a health check.

❯ **http://think.direct.gov.uk/assets/pdf/dg_195267.pdf**

Also remember to check

- brake fluid levels regularly: low levels can affect braking efficiency
- oil and coolant levels and tyre pressures before a long journey
- battery fluid levels; if necessary, top up with distilled water to just above the cell plates.

HC p128 RES s6, 15

> Dealing with faults

A basic understanding of how your motorcycle works will help you recognise when there's a problem with it. It's important that your motorcycle is checked regularly by a qualified mechanic, especially the brakes.

Warning lights on the instrument panel tell you about the performance of the engine and warn you of any faults.

- Check your motorcycle handbook to make sure that you know what all the warning lights mean.
- Don't ignore a warning: it could affect your safety.

HC p128 **RES** s5, 15

Motorcycles fitted with anti-lock braking systems (ABS) will have a warning light on the instrument panel, which should go out at a speed of 5–10 mph. If this doesn't happen, have the ABS checked by a qualified mechanic.

Remember to check oil seals for leakage. Leaks of damping oil from shock absorbers or front forks can

- make your shock absorbers stop working and make your motorcycle difficult to control
- get onto the brakes and increase your stopping distance
- get onto your tyres, causing loss of grip and increased risk of skidding.

Don't overfill your motorcycle's engine with oil as this could cause damage to engine seals and oil leaks.

Visit a garage as soon as possible if

- the motorcycle vibrates – the wheels may need **wheel balancing**
- the motorcycle becomes difficult to control – the steering head bearings may be worn or need adjustment
- indicators flash too fast – they should flash between one and two times a second
- you notice uneven tyre wear – this can indicate faults with the brakes, suspension or wheel alignment.

RES s6, 15

Definition

wheel balancing
making sure that the wheels and tyres are adjusted to minimise any vibrations in the ride

If this happens while you're riding ...	here's what to do
The oil pressure light comes on.	Stop as quickly as possible and investigate.
A tyre bursts.	Slow gently to a stop, holding the handlebars firmly.
You forget to switch the choke off.	Turn it off as soon as you realise. Leaving it on can cause increased pollution and engine wear, and it wastes fuel.

HC p128 RES s6, 15

❯ Carrying passengers and loads

Once you've passed your practical tests, you can carry a passenger if your motorcycle is designed to do so. You're responsible for ensuring that any passenger you carry is

- sitting properly
- facing forward
- on a proper seat with appropriate footrests
- wearing an approved safety helmet, which is correctly fastened.

Make sure that you secure any load or luggage so it doesn't fall off or affect your control of the motorcycle.

 r83, 85 **RES** s14

❯ Seeing and being seen

Many road traffic incidents are caused by one road user not seeing another. Motorcyclists are particularly vulnerable in this way, because they take up less space than cars and are more easily hidden by other vehicles.

Visibility

Before you start riding, adjust the mirrors so that you can see as clearly as possible all around. Convex mirrors give a wider view but can make vehicles look further away than they are.

If you're riding in conditions where visibility is seriously reduced, you **MUST** use dipped headlights. It's important for other road users to see you. If there's thick fog, use your fog lights (if fitted) but remember to switch them off again when visibility improves.

Hazard warning lights are fitted so that you can warn road users of a hazard ahead, such as

- when you've broken down
- queuing traffic on a dual carriageway or motorway.

Don't use them as an excuse to park illegally, even for a short time.

HC r116, 226, 274, 277–278 **RES** s5, 11

Clothing

You can make it easier for other road users to see you by wearing a light or brightly coloured helmet, brightly coloured clothing and a high-visibility or reflective jacket or vest. Reflective clothing is especially important at night.

Always wear proper protective clothing and footwear when riding. It can protect you in all types of weather and in the event of an incident. Having a fairing fitted to your motorcycle can protect your hands, legs and feet from bad weather and cold winds.

HC r83–88 **RES** s4

Find out more about protective gear for motorcyclists in this guide.

❯ **http://think.direct.gov.uk/ assets/pdf/dg_195215.pdf**

 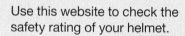

Use this website to check the safety rating of your helmet.

❯ **www.gov.uk**

Helmet visors and goggles should be

- kept clean: check the manufacturer's guidelines for recommended cleaning materials
- undamaged: replace scratched visors or goggles as soon as possible.

If your visor or goggles become fogged up during a ride, stop as soon as possible to clear them.

HC r83–88 **RES** s4

Never use a second-hand helmet. Even if the helmet has no obvious damage, it could have damage that can't be seen. This could make it unreliable in a road traffic incident, so it's best not to take the risk.

RES s4

> Security

It's impossible to make a motorcycle completely secure. However, the harder you make it for a potential thief to steal it, the less likely you are to be targeted.

Make it as difficult as you can for a thief to steal your motorcycle.

Use a steering lock.

Use an extra locking device, eg a high-tension steel cable or chain with high-quality padlock, a U-lock or a disc lock.

Lock it to an immovable object or another motorcycle.

At night, park in a well-lit area.

HC p131 **RES** s8

To make it more difficult for an opportunist thief, you can

- fit an anti-theft alarm or immobiliser
- have the Vehicle Identification Number (VIN) security-marked onto the motorcycle.

RES s8

You **MUST NOT** leave your vehicle unattended with the engine running.

HC r123

Always switch off the engine and secure your motorcycle before leaving it. Use the steering lock and, if possible, chain the motorcycle to an immovable object for extra security.

Consider joining a Vehicle Watch scheme if there's one in your area. Contact the crime prevention officer at your local police station to find out more.

 Use this link to find out more about thefts from vehicles.

❯ **crimestoppers-uk.org/keeping-safe/vehicles**

❯ Parking safely

Where you park your motorcycle can affect the safety of other road users. Avoid parking where your motorcycle would block access or visibility for others, such as

- in front of a property entrance
- at or near a bus stop
- near the brow of a hill, where the limited view of the road ahead makes it difficult to see whether it's safe to pass the obstruction
- at a dropped kerb, as this is a place for wheelchair and mobility scooter users to get onto the road or pavement.

HC r243

You **MUST NOT** stop or park on the zigzag lines at a pedestrian crossing. This would block the view of pedestrians and other road users, and endanger people trying to use the crossing.

HC r239–250, 291 **RES** s8

If you have to park on a hill or sloped area, make sure your motorcycle can't roll downhill by

- leaving it in a low gear
- blocking a wheel or wedging it against the kerb.

When leaving your motorcycle on a two-way road at night, park in the direction of the traffic. If the speed limit is more than 30 mph (46 km/h), switch on your parking lights.

❯ Being aware of the environment

Motorcycle engines burn petrol, which is a fossil fuel. Burning fossil fuel causes air pollution and damages the environment, while using up natural resources that can't be replaced.

You can help the environment by riding in an ecosafe way. You'll help to

- improve road safety
- reduce exhaust emissions
- reduce your fuel consumption, which will save you money.

RES s17

Ecosafe riding

Follow these guidelines to make your riding ecosafe.

Reduce your speed. Vehicles travelling at 70 mph (112 km/h) use up to 30% more fuel than those travelling at 50 mph (80 km/h).

Plan well ahead so that you can ride smoothly. Avoiding rapid acceleration and heavy braking can cut your fuel bill by up to 15%.

Follow these guidelines to make your riding ecosafe.

Have your motorcycle regularly serviced and tuned properly.

Make sure your tyres are correctly inflated.

RES s17

Avoid

- carrying unnecessary loads
- over-revving the engine in lower gears
- leaving the engine running unnecessarily – if your motorcycle is stationary and likely to remain so for some time, switch off the engine.

HC r123 RES s17

Try not to use your motorcycle to make lots of short journeys: consider walking or cycling instead. Using public transport or sharing a vehicle can reduce the volume of traffic and vehicle emissions.

RES s17

Keeping your motorcycle in good condition

Having your motorcycle serviced regularly will give better fuel economy and its exhaust emissions will be reduced. If your motorcycle is over three years old (over four years old in Northern Ireland), it will have to pass an emissions test as part of the MOT test.

If you service your own motorcycle, dispose of old engine oil and batteries responsibly. Take them to a local-authority site or a garage. Don't pour oil down the drain.

Make sure your filler cap is securely fastened. If it's loose, it could spill fuel, which wastes both fuel and money. Spilt fuel makes the road slippery for other road users.

HC p130 **RES** s15

If you notice a strong smell of petrol, check where it's coming from as soon as possible. Use the engine cut-out switch in an emergency.

RES s17

Noise pollution

Don't make excessive noise with your motorcycle. In built-up areas, you **MUST NOT** use your horn between 11.30 pm and 7.00 am, unless another vehicle poses a danger.

HC r112 **RES** s5

> Avoiding congestion

Sometimes it's impossible to avoid road congestion, but if you can it will make riding less stressful for you.

Always try to

- plan your route before starting out
- avoid riding at times when roads will be busy, if possible
- allow plenty of time for your journey, especially if you have an appointment to keep or a connection to make.

RES s18

Plan your route by

- looking at a map
- using satellite navigation equipment
- checking for roadworks or major events with a motoring organisation
- using a route planner on the internet.

In some towns and cities, you may see red lines on the side of the road, which indicate 'Red Routes'. They help the traffic flow by restricting stopping on these routes.
HC p115 **RES** s7

If you're travelling on a new or unfamiliar route, it's a good idea to print out or write down the directions, and also to plan an alternative route in case your original route is blocked.

If you can avoid travelling at busy times, you'll

- be less likely to be delayed
- help to ease congestion for those who have to travel at these times.

In some areas, you may have to pay a congestion charge to use congested road space. In London, those exempt from paying include

- disabled people who hold a Blue Badge
- drivers of electrically powered or alternative fuel vehicles
- riders of two-wheeled vehicles (and sidecars).

RES s18

Find out more about congestion charging in London using this website.

➤ **tfl.gov.uk/roadusers/ congestioncharging**

Meeting the standards

You must be able to

check that all lights and reflectors are

- legal
- clean
- in good working order

make sure that your tyres

- are at the right pressure
- have enough tread depth

get to know the machine if it's the first time you've ridden it

carry out pre-start checks.

You must know and understand

that these must be kept clean at all times

- lights
- indicators
- reflectors
- number plates

how to check that tyres

- are correctly fitted
- are correctly inflated
- have enough tread depth
- are legal to use.

> Notes

You can use this page to make your own notes or diagrams about the key points you need to remember.

Think about

- What maintenance does your motorcycle need each week, month and year?
- What should you do if a warning light appears on your instrument panel while you're riding?
- Which security features does your motorcycle have? How could you improve your machine's security?
- Are there more efficient alternative forms of transport available for your journey?
- How can you find out about local traffic congestion? (For example, local radio stations, websites and mobile phone apps.)

Your notes

Things to discuss and practise with your trainer

These are just a few examples of what you could discuss and practise with your trainer. Read more about safety and your motorcycle to come up with your own ideas.

Discuss with your trainer

- the importance of the state of your tyres, eg on safety, fuel consumption, vehicle handling, etc. Also, discuss how often you should check your tyres
- how you can ride in an ecosafe way, eg use of gears, controlling your speed, etc
- what you think is suitable clothing for riding in different weather conditions.

Practise with your trainer

- riding through built-up areas to get used to different methods of traffic calming
- identifying the warning lights on your instrument panel
- planning your journey. Do this with a new lesson route and see how you can avoid busy times and places.

3.1
Mark one answer RES s15

What could happen if you ride your motorcycle when it has a very loose drive chain?

☐ The front wheel could wobble

☐ The ignition could cut out

☐ The brakes could fail

☒ The rear wheel could lock

Drive chains are subject to wear and need frequent adjustment to maintain the correct tension. Allowing the drive chain to run dry will greatly increase the rate of wear, so it's important to keep it lubricated. If the chain becomes worn or slack, it can jump off the sprocket and lock the rear wheel.

3.2
Mark one answer RES s15

What's the most important reason why you should keep your motorcycle regularly maintained?

☐ To accelerate faster than other traffic

☐ So the motorcycle can carry panniers

☒ To keep the machine roadworthy

☐ So the motorcycle can carry a passenger

Whenever you use any motorcycle on the road, it must be in a roadworthy condition. Regular maintenance should identify any faults at an early stage and help prevent more serious problems.

3.3
Mark one answer RES s15

How should you ride a motorcycle when new tyres have just been fitted?

☒ Carefully, until the shiny surface is worn off

☐ By braking hard, especially into bends

☐ Normally, but with higher tyre pressures

☐ By riding at faster-than-normal speeds

New tyres have a shiny finish, which needs to wear off before the tyre will give the best grip. Take extra care if the road surface is wet or slippery.

3.4
Mark one answer RES s4, HC r86

What will be the effect of wearing brightly coloured clothing while you're riding?

☐ You'll dazzle other road users

☒ You'll be seen more easily by other road users

☐ You'll distract other road users

☐ You'll be able to ride on unlit roads at night with sidelights

For your own safety, you need other road users to see you easily. Wearing brightly coloured or fluorescent clothing will help you to achieve this during daylight. At night, wearing clothing that includes reflective material is the best way of helping others to see you.

3.5
Mark one answer   RES s4

What should you do when you're riding a motorcycle in very hot weather?

☐ Ride with your visor fully open

☑ Continue to wear protective clothing

☐ Wear trainers instead of boots

☐ Slacken your helmet strap

Always wear your protective clothing, whatever the weather. In very hot weather it's tempting to ride in light summer clothes, but it isn't worth the risk. If you fall from your motorcycle, you'll have no protection from the hard road surface.

3.6
Mark one answer   RES s4, HC r86

Why should you wear fluorescent clothing when riding in daylight?

☐ It reduces wind resistance

☐ It prevents injury if you come off the machine

☑ It helps other road users to see you

☐ It keeps you cool in hot weather

Motorcycles are smaller and therefore harder to see than most other vehicles on the road. You need to make yourself as visible as possible to other road users. Fluorescent and reflective clothing will help achieve this. You must be visible from all sides.

3.7
Mark one answer   RES s4, HC r87

Why should riders wear reflective clothing?

☐ To protect them from the cold

☐ To protect them from direct sunlight

☐ To be seen better in daylight

☑ To be seen better at night

Fluorescent clothing will help others to see you during the day. At night, however, you should wear clothing that reflects the light. This allows other road users to see you more easily in their headlights. Ask your local motorcycle dealer about fluorescent and reflective clothing.

3.8
Mark one answer   RES s4

Which fairing would give you the best weather protection?

☐ Handlebar

☐ Sports

☐ Touring

☐ Windscreen

Fairings give protection to the hands, legs and feet. They also make riding more comfortable by keeping you out of the wind.

3.9
Mark one answer

RES s4, HC r84

What should you do if your visor becomes badly scratched?

☐ Polish it with a fine abrasive

☑ Replace it

☐ Wash it in soapy water

☐ Clean it with petrol

Your visor protects your eyes from wind, rain, insects and road dirt. It's important to keep it clean and in good repair. A badly scratched visor can obscure your view and cause dazzle from the lights of oncoming vehicles.

3.10
Mark one answer

RES s15, HC p129

What's the legal minimum depth of tread for motorcycle tyres?

☑ 1 mm

☐ 1.6 mm

☐ 2.5 mm

☐ 4 mm

The law says that the entire original tread must be visible, with a depth of at least 1 mm in a continuous band across at least three-quarters of the breadth of the tread. However, your tyres are your only contact with the road, so it's recommended that you replace them before they get to this level.

3.11
Mark one answer

RES s4, HC r86

What can you wear to make it easier for other road users to see you?

☐ Black leathers

☐ Tinted visor

☑ White helmet

☐ Grey helmet

Many incidents and collisions involving motorcyclists occur because other road users don't see them. Be aware that you're vulnerable and make yourself as visible as possible by wearing fluorescent clothing and a light or brightly coloured helmet.

3.12
Mark one answer

RES s5

What should you do if the oil-pressure warning light comes on while you're riding?

☐ Go to a dealer for an oil change

☐ Go to the nearest garage to ask their advice

☐ Ride slowly for a few miles to see if the light goes out

☑ Stop as soon as possible and try to find the cause

If the oil-pressure warning light comes on when the engine is running, pull over as soon as you can, stop the engine and investigate the cause; if you don't, you risk serious engine damage.

3.13 — Mark one answer — RES s15

What must you check on both the front and rear motorcycle tyres?

- ☐ That they're the same tread pattern
- ☑ That they're correctly inflated
- ☐ That they're the same size
- ☐ That they're the same make

Your safety and that of others depends on the condition of your tyres. Before every trip, make sure they

- are correctly inflated
- have at least the minimum legal depth of tread
- have no cuts or bulges.

Do these checks as part of a routine before every journey.

3.14 — Mark one answer — RES s15

What could happen if you ride your motorcycle with a slack or worn drive chain?

- ☐ The engine could misfire
- ☐ The tyres could wear more quickly
- ☐ The engine could produce more emissions
- ☑ The rear wheel could lock

Check your drive chain regularly; adjust and lubricate it if necessary. It needs to be adjusted until the 'free play' is as it says in the vehicle handbook. If the chain is too loose, it can jump off its sprocket and lock your rear wheel while you're riding.

3.15 — Mark one answer — RES s15

When riding your motorcycle, a tyre bursts. What should you do?

- ☑ Slow gently to a stop
- ☐ Brake firmly to a stop
- ☐ Change to a high gear
- ☐ Lower the side stand

If a tyre bursts, close the throttle smoothly and slow gently to a stop, holding the handlebars firmly to help you keep a straight course.

3.16 — Mark one answer — RES s15, 17

What will be the effect of having your motorcycle engine properly maintained?

- ☐ It will use much more fuel
- ☑ It will have lower exhaust emissions
- ☐ It will increase your insurance premiums
- ☐ It will reduce your journey times

A badly maintained engine will emit more exhaust fumes than one that's correctly serviced. This is damaging to the environment. The engine will also use more fuel.

3.17
Mark one answer | **RES s4**

What should you clean visors and goggles with?

- ☐ Petrol
- ☐ White spirit
- ☐ Anti-freeze
- ☑ Soapy water

It's very important to keep your visor or goggles clean. Clean them using warm soapy water. Don't use solvents or petrol.

3.18
Mark one answer | **RES s4**

You're riding on a quiet road. Your visor fogs up. What should you do?

- ☐ Continue at a reduced speed
- ☑ Stop as soon as possible and wipe it
- ☐ Build up speed to increase the air flow
- ☐ Close the helmet air vents

In cold and wet weather, your visor may fog up. If this happens when you're riding, choose somewhere safe to stop, and wipe it clean with a damp cloth. Special anti-fog products are available at motorcycle dealers.

3.19
Mark one answer | **RES s4**

You're riding in hot weather. What's the safest type of footwear?

- ☐ Sandals
- ☐ Trainers
- ☐ Shoes
- ☑ Boots

It's important to wear good boots when you ride a motorcycle. Boots protect your feet and shins from knocks, and give some protection in a crash. They also help keep you warm and dry in cold or wet weather.

3.20
Mark one answer | **RES s4, HC r83**

Which method of fastening your helmet is unsafe?

- ☐ Double D-ring fastening
- ☑ Velcro tab
- ☐ Quick-release fastening
- ☐ Bar and buckle

Some helmet straps have a Velcro tab in addition to the main fastening, which is intended to secure the strap so that it doesn't flap in the wind. It shouldn't be used on its own to fasten the helmet.

3.21
Mark one answer RES s17

Your motorcycle has a catalytic converter. What does this reduce?

☐ Exhaust noise

☐ Fuel consumption

☑ Exhaust emissions

☐ Engine noise

Catalytic converters reduce the toxic and polluting gases given out by the engine. Never use leaded or lead-replacement petrol in a motorcycle with a catalytic converter; even one tankful can permanently damage the system.

3.22
Mark one answer RES s15

What should you check after refitting your rear wheel?

☐ Your steering damper

☐ Your side stand

☑ Your wheel alignment

☐ Your suspension preload

After refitting the rear wheel or adjusting the drive chain, you should check your wheel alignment. Incorrect alignment will result in excessive tyre wear and poor roadholding.

3.23
Mark one answer RES s15

You're checking your direction indicators. How many times per second must they flash?

☑ Between 1 and 2 times

☐ Between 3 and 4 times

☐ Between 5 and 6 times

☐ Between 7 and 8 times

You should check that all your lights work properly before every journey. If you aren't sure whether your signals can be seen, you can use arm signals as well to make your intentions clear; avoid this if you're riding at speed because it can upset your stability.

3.24
Mark one answer RES s15

What should you check after adjusting the final drive chain?

☑ The rear wheel alignment

☐ The suspension adjustment

☐ The rear shock absorber

☐ The front suspension forks

Always check the rear wheel alignment after adjusting the final drive chain. Marks on the chain adjuster may be provided to make this easy. Incorrect alignment can cause instability and increased tyre wear.

3.25

Mark one answer

RES s15

Your steering feels wobbly. Which of these is a likely cause?

- ☐ Tyre pressure is too high
- ☐ Incorrectly adjusted brakes
- ☑ Worn steering-head bearings
- ☐ A broken clutch cable

Worn bearings in the steering head can make your motorcycle very difficult to control. They should be checked for wear or correct adjustment and replaced if necessary.

3.26

Mark one answer

RES s15

You have a faulty oil seal on a shock absorber. Why is this a serious problem?

- ☐ It will cause excessive chain wear
- ☑ The motorcycle will be difficult to control
- ☐ Your motorcycle will be harder to ride uphill
- ☐ Your motorcycle won't accelerate so quickly

As well as making your motorcycle difficult to control, the leaking oil could find its way onto your tyres and brakes. This could result in a loss of control, putting you and other road users in danger.

3.27

Mark one answer

RES s15

Oil is leaking from your forks. Why shouldn't you ride a motorcycle in this condition?

- ☑ Your suspension will be ineffective
- ☐ Your steering is likely to seize up
- ☐ The forks will quickly begin to rust
- ☐ The motorcycle will become too noisy

If an oil seal on your forks or shock absorbers fails, fork oil will leak out, making the suspension ineffective and the motorcycle difficult to control. It can also be very dangerous if the oil gets onto brakes or tyres. Replace faulty oil seals without delay.

3.28

Mark one answer

RES s15

You've adjusted your drive chain. If this isn't done properly, what problem could it cause?

- ☐ Inaccurate speedometer reading
- ☐ Loss of braking power
- ☑ Incorrect rear wheel alignment
- ☐ Excessive fuel consumption

After carrying out drive-chain adjustment, you should always check the rear wheel alignment. Many motorcycles have alignment guides stamped onto the frame to help you do this correctly.

3.29
Mark one answer

RES s15, HC p129

There's a cut in the sidewall of one of your tyres. What should you do about this?

☐ Replace the tyre before riding the motorcycle

☐ Check regularly to see if it gets any worse

☐ Repair the cut before riding the motorcycle

☐ Reduce the tyre pressure before you ride

A cut in the sidewall can be very dangerous. The tyre is in danger of blowing out if you ride the motorcycle in this condition.

3.30
Mark one answer

RES s15

You need to put air into your tyres. How would you find out the correct pressure to use?

☐ It will be shown on the tyre wall

☐ It will be stamped on the wheel

☐ By checking the vehicle handbook

☐ By checking the registration document

Tyre pressures should be checked regularly. Look in your vehicle handbook for the correct pressures to use.

3.31
Mark one answer

RES s15

What can you do to prevent a cable-operated clutch from becoming stiff?

☐ Keep the cable tight

☐ Keep the cable dry

☐ Keep the cable slack

☑ Keep the cable oiled

Keeping the clutch cable oiled will help it to move smoothly through its outer casing. This will extend the life of the cable and help prevent the clutch's operation from becoming stiff.

3.32
Mark one answer

RES s15

What can incorrect wheel alignment cause?

☐ A serious loss of power

☐ Reduced braking performance

☑ Increased tyre wear

☐ Reduced ground clearance

If a motorcycle's wheels are incorrectly aligned, tyres may wear unevenly and the motorcycle can become unstable, especially when cornering.

3.33   Mark one answer   RES s4

Why should you wear specialist motorcycle clothing when riding?

☐ Because the law requires you to do so

☐ Because it looks better than ordinary clothing

☐ Because it gives the best protection from the weather

☐ Because it will reduce your insurance premium

If you become cold and wet when riding, this can have a serious effect on your concentration and control of your motorcycle. Proper riding gear can help shield you from the weather, as well as giving protection in the event of a crash.

3.34   Mark one answer   RES s8

What should you do when leaving your motorcycle parked?

☐ Remove the battery lead

☐ Pull it onto the kerb

☐ Use the steering lock

☐ Leave the parking lights on

You should always use the steering lock when leaving your motorcycle. Also consider using additional locking devices, such as a U-lock, disc lock or chain. If possible, fasten the motorcycle to an immovable post or another machine.

3.35   Mark one answer   RES s8

You're parking your motorcycle. How can you reduce the chances of it being stolen?

☐ Park in a space marked for motorcycles only

☐ Chain it to an immovable object

☐ Switch off the engine cut-out switch

☐ Leave it on its side stand

Theft of motorcycles is a very common crime. If you can, secure your vehicle to a lamppost or other such object, to help reduce the chances of it being stolen.

3.36   Mark one answer   RES s8

You're parking your motorcycle and sidecar on a hill. What's the best way to stop it rolling away?

☐ Leave it in neutral

☐ Put the rear wheel on the pavement

☐ Leave it in a low gear

☐ Park very close to another vehicle

To make sure a sidecar outfit doesn't roll away after you've parked it, you should leave it in a low gear and wedge it against the kerb or place a block behind the wheel.

3.37
Mark one answer   RES s5

When would you use the engine cut-out switch?

☐ To reduce speed in an emergency

☐ To prevent the motorcycle being stolen

☐ To stop the engine normally

☐ To stop the engine in an emergency

If you're involved in a collision, using the engine cut-out switch will help to reduce the risk of fire. When stopping the engine normally, use the ignition switch.

3.38
Mark one answer   RES s7, HC r153

What should you do when you ride along a road where there are road humps?

☐ Maintain a reduced speed throughout

☐ Accelerate quickly between each one

☐ Always keep to the maximum legal speed

☐ Ride slowly at school times only

The humps are there to reduce the speed of the traffic. Don't accelerate harshly between them, as you'll then have to brake sharply to negotiate the next hump. Harsh braking and acceleration uses more fuel, as well as causing wear and tear to your vehicle.

3.39
Mark one answer   RES s15

When should you especially check the engine oil level?

☐ Before a long journey

☐ When the engine is hot

☐ Early in the morning

☐ Every 6000 miles

As well as the oil, you'll need to check other items. These include fuel, water and tyres.

3.40
Mark one answer   RES s17

You service your own motorcycle. How should you get rid of the old engine oil?

☐ Take it to a local-authority site

☐ Pour it down a drain

☐ Tip it into a hole in the ground

☐ Put it into your dustbin

Never pour the oil down any drain. The oil is highly polluting and could harm wildlife. Put it in a container and dispose of it properly at an authorised site.

3.41
Mark one answer — RES s17

What safeguard could you take against fire risk to your motorcycle?

☐ Keep water levels above maximum

☐ Check out any strong smell of petrol

☐ Avoid riding with a full tank of petrol

☐ Use unleaded petrol

The fuel in your motorcycle can be a dangerous fire hazard. Don't use a naked flame if you can smell fuel, and don't smoke when refuelling.

3.42
Mark one answer — RES s4, HC r86

What would make you more visible in daylight?

☐ Wearing a black helmet

☐ Wearing a brightly coloured helmet

☐ Switching off your headlights

☐ Wearing a dark jacket

Wearing bright or fluorescent clothes will help other road users to see you. Wearing a light or brightly coloured helmet can also make you more visible.

3.43
Mark one answer — RES s4, HC r83

When is it illegal to ride with a helmet on?

☐ When the helmet isn't fastened correctly

☐ When the helmet is more than four years old

☐ When you've borrowed someone else's helmet

☐ When the helmet doesn't have chin protection

A helmet that's incorrectly fastened or not fastened at all is likely to come off in a crash and will provide little or no protection. By law, you must wear a helmet when riding on the road, and it must be correctly fastened. (Members of the Sikh religion who wear a turban are exempt.)

3.44
Mark one answer — RES s15

When should you increase the tyre pressures on your motorcycle?

☐ When riding in hot weather

☐ After a long journey

☐ When carrying a heavy load

☐ When riding in wet weather

The vehicle handbook will explain when it's recommended that you increase tyre pressures – for example, when you're carrying extra weight from a passenger or a heavy load.

3.45 Mark one answer RES s15, HC p128

Which of these items must be kept clean?

☐ Number plate

☐ Wheels

☐ Engine

☐ Fairing

Maintenance is a vital part of road safety. Lights, indicators, reflectors and number plates must be kept clean and clear.

3.46 Mark one answer RES s5

For what purpose should you use the engine cut-out switch on your motorcycle?

☐ To save wear and tear on the battery

☐ To stop the engine for a short time

☐ To stop the engine in an emergency

☐ To save wear and tear on the ignition

Only use the engine cut-out switch in an emergency. When stopping the engine normally, use the ignition switch. This will remind you to take your keys with you when parking. It could also prevent starting problems if you forget you've left the cut-out switch in the 'off' position.

3.47 Mark one answer RES s15

What should you check after you've adjusted the tension on your drive chain?

☐ Rear wheel alignment

☐ Tyre pressures

☐ Valve clearances

☐ Sidelights

Drive chains wear and need frequent adjustment and lubrication. If the drive chain is worn or slack, it can jump off the sprocket and lock the rear wheel. When you've adjusted the chain tension, you need to check the rear wheel alignment. Marks by the chain adjusters may be provided to make this easier.

A friend offers you a second-hand safety helmet for you to use. Why may this be a bad idea?

A second-hand helmet may look in good condition but it could have received damage that isn't visible externally. A damaged helmet could be unreliable in a crash. Don't take the risk.

☐ It may be damaged

☐ You'll be breaking the law

☐ You'll affect your insurance cover

☐ It may be a full-face type

You're riding a motorcycle with an engine larger than 50 cc. What would make a tyre illegal?

☐ Tread less than 1.6 mm deep

☐ Tread less than 2 mm deep

☐ A large bulge in the sidewall

☐ A stone wedged in the tread

When checking tyres, make sure there are no bulges or cuts in the sidewalls. Keeping your tyres correctly inflated and in good condition is a vital part of maintaining your motorcycle.

How should you maintain cable-operated brakes?

☐ By removing all free play at the lever or pedal

☐ By checking them at normal operating temperature

☐ By always fitting new ones for the MOT

☐ By lubricating and adjusting them regularly

Cables will stretch with use and need checking and adjusting regularly. They also need lubricating to prevent friction and wear of the cables and pivots. Don't over-adjust brake cables or the brakes will bind, causing increased fuel consumption, risk of skidding and risk of the brakes overheating.

3.51
Mark one answer
RES s15

What benefit will you see if you have your motorcycle serviced regularly?

☐ Lower insurance premiums

☐ A refund on your vehicle tax

☐ Increased exhaust emissions

☐ Better fuel economy

Your motorcycle will run much better and its fuel consumption will be lower if you have it serviced regularly. Check at what intervals you should have your motorcycle serviced – this can vary by model or manufacturer. Keep the service record up to date.

3.52
Mark one answer
RES s15

What could a loose drive chain cause?

☐ A locked rear wheel

☐ Wobbly wheels

☐ A braking fault

☐ Headlight misalignment

A motorcycle chain will stretch as it wears. It may need frequent checking and adjustment to keep the tension correct. In extreme cases, a loose chain can jump off the sprocket and become wedged in the rear wheel. This could cause serious loss of control and result in a crash.

3.53
Mark one answer
RES s12, HC r226

Your motorcycle isn't fitted with daytime running lights. When must you use dipped headlights during the day?

☐ On country roads

☐ In poor visibility

☐ On narrow streets

☐ When parking

It's important that other road users can see you clearly at all times. It will help other road users to see you if you use dipped headlights during the day. You must use dipped headlights during the day if visibility is seriously reduced; that is, when you can't see for more than 100 metres (328 feet).

3.54
Mark one answer
RES s14

When should you consider increasing your tyre pressures?

☐ When riding on a wet road

☐ When carrying a pillion passenger

☐ When travelling on an uneven surface

☐ When riding on twisty roads

Sometimes, manufacturers advise you to increase your tyre pressures for high-speed riding and when carrying extra weight, such as a pillion passenger. This information can be found in the vehicle handbook.

3.55

You have too much oil in your engine. What could this cause?

☐ Low oil pressure
☐ Engine overheating
☐ Chain wear
☐ Oil leaks

Too much oil in the engine will create excess crankcase pressure. This could damage engine seals and cause oil leaks. Any excess oil should be drained off.

3.56

You're leaving your motorcycle unattended on a road. When may you leave the engine running?

☐ When parking for less than five minutes
☐ If the battery is flat
☐ When in a 20 mph zone
☐ Not on any occasion

When you leave your motorcycle parked and unattended on a road, switch off the engine, use the steering lock and remove the ignition key. Also take any tank bags, panniers or loose luggage with you, set the alarm if the motorcycle has one, and use an additional lock and chain, or cable lock.

3.57

You're involved in a crash. What should you do to reduce the risk of fire?

☐ Keep the engine running
☐ Open the choke
☐ Turn the fuel tap to reserve
☐ Use the engine cut-out switch

The engine cut-out switch is used to stop the engine in an emergency. In the event of a crash, this may help to reduce any fire risk.

3.58

What should you do when riding at night?

☐ Give arm signals
☐ Wear reflective clothing
☐ Wear a tinted visor
☐ Ride in the centre of the road

At night, you should wear clothing with reflective material, to help other road users to see you. If your jacket doesn't have reflective patches, you could wear garments that do, such as

• a hi-visibility vest or tabard
• a reflective belt.

Also use your headlights on dipped or main beam, as appropriate.

3.59
Mark one answer RES s15, HC p129

What's badly affected if the tyres are under-inflated?

☐ Braking

☐ Indicating

☐ Changing gear

☐ Parking

Your tyres are your only contact with the road. To prevent problems with braking and steering, keep your tyres free from defects; they must have sufficient tread depth and be correctly inflated. Correct tyre pressures help reduce the risk of skidding and provide a safer and more comfortable drive or ride.

3.60
Mark one answer RES s5, HC r112

When mustn't you sound your vehicle's horn?

☐ Between 10.00 pm and 6.00 am in a built-up area

☐ At any time in a built-up area

☑ Between 11.30 pm and 7.00 am in a built-up area

☐ Between 11.30 pm and 6.00 am on any road

Every effort must be made to prevent excessive noise, especially in built-up areas at night. Don't rev your engine or sound the horn unnecessarily. It's illegal to sound your horn in a built-up area between 11.30 pm and 7.00 am, except when another road user poses a danger.

3.61
Mark one answer RES s8

What makes the vehicle in the picture 'environmentally friendly'?

Trams are powered by electricity and therefore don't emit exhaust fumes. They ease traffic congestion by offering drivers an alternative to using their car, particularly in busy cities and towns.

☐ It's powered by gravity

☐ It's powered by diesel

☑ It's powered by electricity

☐ It's powered by unleaded petrol

3.62
Mark one answer   RES s18, HC p115

Why have 'red routes' been introduced in major cities?

- ☐ To raise the speed limits
- ☑ To help the traffic flow
- ☐ To provide better parking
- ☐ To allow lorries to load more freely

Inconsiderate parking can obstruct the flow of traffic and so make traffic congestion worse. Red routes are designed to prevent this by enforcing strict parking restrictions. Driving slowly in traffic increases fuel consumption and causes a build-up of exhaust fumes.

3.63
Mark one answer   RES s7, HC r153

What's the purpose of road humps, chicanes and narrowings?

- ☐ To separate lanes of traffic
- ☐ To increase traffic speed
- ☐ To allow pedestrians to cross
- ☐ To reduce traffic speed

Traffic-calming measures help to keep vehicle speeds low in congested areas where there are pedestrians and children. A pedestrian is much more likely to survive a collision with a vehicle travelling at 20 mph than they are with a vehicle travelling at 40 mph.

3.64
Mark one answer   RES s15, HC p129

It's essential that tyre pressures are checked regularly. When should this be done?

- ☐ After any lengthy journey
- ☐ After travelling at high speed
- ☐ When tyres are hot
- ☑ When tyres are cold

Check the tyre pressures when the tyres are cold. This will give you a more accurate reading. The heat generated on a long journey will raise the pressure inside the tyre.

3.65
Mark one answer   RES s15, 17

When will your vehicle use more fuel?

- ☐ When its tyres are under-inflated
- ☐ When its tyres are of different makes
- ☐ When its tyres are over-inflated
- ☐ When its tyres are new

Check your tyre pressures frequently – normally once a week. If they're lower than those recommended by the manufacturer, there will be more 'rolling resistance'. The engine will have to work harder to overcome this, leading to increased fuel consumption.

3.66
Mark one answer

RES s17

How should you dispose of a used vehicle battery?

☐ Bury it in your garden

☐ Put it in the dustbin

☐ Take it to a local-authority site

☐ Leave it on waste land

Batteries contain acid, which is hazardous, and they must be disposed of safely. This means taking them to an appropriate disposal site.

3.67
Mark one answer

RES s17, HC r123

What's most likely to cause high fuel consumption?

☐ Poor steering control

☐ Accelerating around bends

☐ Staying in high gears

☑ Harsh braking and accelerating

Accelerating and braking gently and smoothly will help to save fuel and reduce wear on your vehicle. This makes it better for the environment too.

3.68
Mark one answer

RES s15

The fluid level in your battery is low. What should you top it up with?

☐ Battery acid

☐ Distilled water

☐ Engine oil

☐ Engine coolant

Some modern batteries are maintenance-free. Check your vehicle handbook and, if necessary, make sure that the plates in each battery cell are covered with fluid.

3.69
Mark one answer

RES s13

You're parked on the road at night. Where must you use parking lights?

☐ Where there are continuous white lines in the middle of the road

☐ Where the speed limit exceeds 30 mph

☐ Where you're facing oncoming traffic

☐ Where you're near a bus stop

When parking at night, park in the direction of the traffic. This will enable other road users to see the reflectors on the rear of your vehicle. Use your parking lights if the speed limit is over 30 mph.

Section three Questions

3.70

Mark one answer

RES s17

How can you reduce the environmental harm caused by your motor vehicle?

☐ Only use it for short journeys

☐ Don't service it

☐ Drive faster than normal

☐ Keep engine revs low

Engines that burn fossil fuels produce exhaust emissions that are harmful to health. The harder you make the engine work, the more emissions it will produce. Engines also use more fuel and produce higher levels of emissions when they're cold. Anything you can do to reduce your use of fossil fuels will help the environment.

3.71

Mark one answer

RES s15, HC p129

What can cause excessive or uneven tyre wear?

☐ A faulty gearbox

☒ A faulty braking system

☐ A faulty electrical system

☐ A faulty exhaust system

If you see that parts of the tread on your tyres are wearing before others, it may indicate a brake, steering or suspension fault. Regular servicing will help to detect faults at an early stage and this will avoid the risk of minor faults becoming serious or even dangerous.

3.72

Mark one answer

RES s15

You need to top up your battery. What level should you fill it to?

☐ The top of the battery

☐ Halfway up the battery

☐ Just below the cell plates

☒ Just above the cell plates

Top up the battery with distilled water and make sure each cell plate is covered.

3.73

Mark one answer

RES s18

Before starting a journey, it's wise to plan your route. How can you do this?

☐ Look at a map

☐ Contact your local garage

☐ Look in your vehicle handbook

☐ Check your vehicle registration document

Planning your journey before you set out can help to make it much easier and more pleasant, and may help to ease traffic congestion. Look at a map to help you do this. You may need maps of different scales, depending on where and how far you're going. Printing or writing out the route can also help.

3.74

Mark one answer   RES s18

How can you plan your route before starting a long journey?

☐ Check your vehicle handbook

☐ Ask your local garage

☐ Use a route planner on the internet

☐ Consult a travel agent

Various route planners are available on the internet. Most of them give you several options, allowing you to choose between the most direct route and quieter roads. They may also identify rest and fuel stops. Print off the directions and take them with you.

3.75

Mark one answer   RES s18

Planning your route before setting out can be helpful. How can you do this?

☐ Look in a motoring magazine

☐ Only visit places you know

☐ Try to travel at busy times

☐ Print or write down the route

Print or write down your route before setting out. Some places aren't well signed, so including both place names and road numbers in your directions may help you avoid problems en route. Try to get an idea of how far you're going before you leave. You can also recheck the next stage at each rest stop.

3.76

Mark one answer   RES s18

Why is it a good idea to plan your journey to avoid busy times?

☐ You'll have an easier journey

☐ You'll have a more stressful journey

☐ Your journey time will be longer

☐ It will cause more traffic congestion

No-one likes to spend time in traffic queues. Try to avoid busy times related to school or work travel.

3.77

Mark one answer   RES s18

You avoid busy times when travelling. How will this affect your journey?

☐ You're more likely to be held up

☐ Your journey time will be longer

☐ You'll travel a much shorter distance

☐ You're less likely to be delayed

If possible, avoid the early morning, late afternoon and early evening 'rush hour'. Doing this should allow you to travel in a more relaxed frame of mind, concentrate solely on what you're doing and arrive at your destination feeling less stressed.

It can be helpful to plan your route before starting a journey. Why should you also plan an alternative route?

☑ Your original route may be blocked

☐ Your maps may have different scales

☐ You may find you have to pay a congestion charge

☐ You may get held up by a tractor

It can be frustrating and worrying to find your planned route is blocked by roadworks or diversions. If you've planned an alternative, you'll feel less stressed and more able to concentrate fully on your driving or riding. If your original route is mostly on motorways, it's a good idea to plan an alternative using non-motorway roads. Always carry a map with you just in case you need to refer to it.

You're making an appointment and will have to travel a long distance. How should you plan for the journey?

☑ Allow plenty of time for the trip

☐ Plan to travel at busy times

☐ Avoid roads with the national speed limit

☐ Prevent other drivers from overtaking

Always allow plenty of time for your journey in case of unforeseen problems. Anything can happen; for example, punctures, breakdowns, road closures, diversions and delays. You'll feel less stressed and less inclined to take risks if you aren't 'pushed for time'.

3.80

Mark one answer

RES s17

What can rapid acceleration and heavy braking lead to?

☐ Reduced pollution

☐ Increased fuel consumption

☐ Reduced exhaust emissions

☐ Increased road safety

Using the controls smoothly can reduce fuel consumption by about 15%, as well as reducing wear and tear on your vehicle. Plan ahead and anticipate changes of speed well in advance. This will reduce the need to accelerate rapidly or brake sharply.

3.81

Mark one answer

HC p130

Which of these, if allowed to get low, could cause you to crash?

☐ Anti-freeze level

☐ Brake fluid level

☐ Battery water level

☐ Radiator coolant level

You should carry out frequent checks on all fluid levels but particularly brake fluid. As the brake pads or shoes wear down, the brake fluid level will drop. If it drops below the minimum mark on the fluid reservoir, air could enter the hydraulic system and lead to a loss of braking efficiency or even complete brake failure.

Case study practice – 3 Safety and your motorcycle

You're riding your motorcycle to work. It's winter and the weather is dry, but cold.

You're wearing leather motorcycle clothing, boots, gloves, a fluorescent safety vest with reflective panels and a brightly coloured helmet.

At the service station, you buy fuel. You clean both handlebar mirrors, which have longer stems.

You also make your weekly check of tyre pressures and tread depths. The rear tyre is worn down to the legal limit.

3.1 What could affect your concentration on your ride to work?
Mark **one** answer

- ☐ Getting cold
- ☐ Getting wet
- ☐ Getting hot
- ☐ Getting blown off course

RES s12

3.2 How does your helmet's colour help?
Mark **one** answer

☐ It matches your motorcycle

☐ It won't show the dirt

☐ It makes you easier to see

☐ It helps you to blend in

RES s4 **HC** r86

3.3 How can being dressed in this way help you while you're riding?
Mark **one** answer

☐ It helps to keep you cool

☐ It helps to lower your insurance premiums

☐ It helps your friends to recognise you

☐ It helps to improve your safety

RES s4 **HC** r86

3.4 Why might you have this adaptation to your mirrors?
Mark **one** answer

☐ Because they look very cool and fashionable

☐ To give you an unobstructed view behind

☐ So that other vehicles will allow you more room

☐ To help balance and control the motorcycle

RES s5

3.5 What depth is the tread on your rear tyre?
Mark **one** answer

☐ 1 mm across three-quarters of the tread breadth and all around

☐ 2 mm across the entire tread breadth and all around

☐ 2 mm across three-quarters of the tread breadth and all around

☐ 1 mm across the entire tread breadth and all around

RES s15 **HC** p129

> Section four
Safety margins

In this section, you'll learn about

- keeping yourself and others safe by staying within safety margins
- stopping, thinking and braking distances
- risks caused by different weather conditions and road surfaces
- the risk of skidding
- contraflow systems.

Safety margins

It's essential that you always keep in mind your safety, and that of your passenger and other road users, as you're riding.

You can reduce your chances of being involved in an incident on the road by knowing the safety margins and what can happen if you don't ride within them. Never take risks.

Keep control of your motorcycle by using the correct procedures. For instance, when you're travelling on a long downhill stretch of road, control your speed by selecting a lower gear and using your brakes carefully. Excessive braking on hills can cause your brakes to overheat and become less effective.

HC r160 **RES** s6, 8

Don't 'coast' – this means travelling in neutral or with the clutch disengaged – as this can reduce your control over the machine.

HC r122

> Stopping distance

Leave enough room between your motorcycle and the vehicle in front so that you can pull up safely if it slows down or stops suddenly.

Your overall stopping distance is the distance your motorcycle travels from the moment you realise that you must brake to the moment your motorcycle stops.

HC r126 **RES** s8

Thinking distance		**Braking distance**		**Stopping distance**
(distance travelled in the time it takes to react to a situation)	**+**	(distance travelled from when you start to use the brakes to when your motorcycle completely stops)	**=**	

➤ Typical stopping distances

Look at the typical stopping, thinking and braking distances given in *The Official Highway Code*. Remember that these are based on vehicles travelling

- with good tyres and brakes
- on a dry road
- in good conditions.

HC r126 **RES** s8

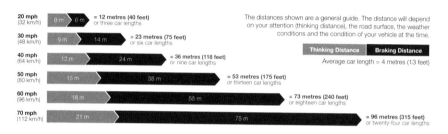

20 mph (32 km/h) — 6 m + 6 m = **12 metres (40 feet)** or three car lengths

30 mph (48 km/h) — 9 m + 14 m = **23 metres (75 feet)** or six car lengths

40 mph (64 km/h) — 12 m + 24 m = **36 metres (118 feet)** or nine car lengths

50 mph (80 km/h) — 15 m + 38 m = **53 metres (175 feet)** or thirteen car lengths

60 mph (96 km/h) — 18 m + 55 m = **73 metres (240 feet)** or eighteen car lengths

70 mph (112 km/h) — 21 m + 75 m = **96 metres (315 feet)** or twenty-four car lengths

The distances shown are a general guide. The distance will depend on your attention (thinking distance), the road surface, the weather conditions and the condition of your vehicle at the time.

Thinking Distance	Braking Distance

Average car length = 4 metres (13 feet)

To help you learn and understand more about stopping distances, try the interactive exercise at this link.

➤ **safedrivingforlife.info/stopping-distances-game**

Don't just learn the stopping distance figures: you need to be able to judge the distance when you're riding.

HC r126 **RES** s12

In good conditions, leave a two-second gap between your motorcycle and the vehicle in front. Use a fixed point, like a road sign, to measure the time gap between your motorcycle and the vehicle in front. You can measure two seconds by saying the sentence 'Only a fool breaks the two-second rule.'

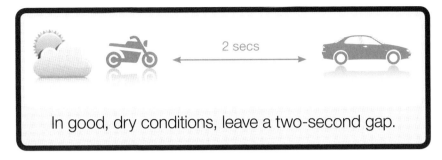

In good, dry conditions, leave a two-second gap.

In other conditions, you need to increase this distance.

In wet weather, leave a four-second gap.

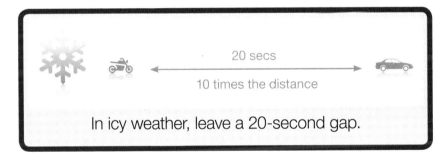

In icy weather, leave a 20-second gap.

Keeping a safe distance from the vehicle in front will help to lower your risk of having a collision. If someone overtakes you and pulls into the gap in front, drop back to keep a safe distance from them.

HC r126 **RES** s12

Remember, your overall stopping distance may be longer when carrying a passenger.

RES s14

❯ Weather conditions

Weather conditions have a major effect on your safety margins. If there's bad weather, such as snow, ice or thick fog, think about whether you really need to make your journey. Never underestimate the dangers and always wear suitable clothing.

`HC` r228–231 `RES` s4

 Read more about protective clothing at this website.

❯ **www.gov.uk**

Weather	Actions to take
Heavy rain/wet road  	When there's heavy rainfall, water can collect on the road surface and may cause aquaplaning. This is where the tyres lift off the road surface and skate on a film of water. If this happens • ease off the throttle smoothly • don't brake or try to change direction until you can feel the tyres gripping again. `HC` r121, 227 `RES` s12 Use a low gear when riding through a ford or flood water, and test your brakes afterwards. If necessary, dry them out by applying the brakes lightly as you go along. `HC` r121 `RES` s12 If it rains after a long dry spell, the road surface can be unusually slippery and requires extra care. `HC` r237

Weather	Actions to take

Hot and/or bright

Hot weather can also be dangerous. The road surface can become soft. This could affect your braking and steering.

Bright sunlight can dazzle. Other drivers might not be able to see your indicators flashing. Give an arm signal if you think it will be helpful.

HC r237 **RES** s12

Foggy

Fog reduces your visibility. Remember to

- think about whether you could use a different form of transport or delay your journey until conditions improve
- allow more time for your journey
- slow down, because you can't see as far ahead as usual
- increase the gap between your motorcycle and the vehicle in front
- keep your visor or goggles clear
- beware of other road users not using their headlights
- use dipped headlights, even in daylight.

If visibility falls below 100 metres (328 feet), use fog lights if you've got them. You **MUST** switch them off when the fog lifts.

HC r234–236 **RES** s12

Windy

High winds can blow you off course, especially on an open stretch of road. The wind can affect all road users but those worst affected include

- high-sided vehicles
- other motorcyclists
- vehicles towing trailers or caravans
- cyclists.

Take care and allow extra room if you pass these road users, as they may be blown off course by a sudden gust of wind.

HC r232–233 **RES** 12

Weather	Actions to take
Freezing 	Freezing conditions can make roads very slippery, which will make your motorcycle harder to control.
	Before starting a journey, think about
	• whether your journey is necessary
	• whether you could use a different form of transport.
	If you must travel, clear ice and snow from your lights, mirrors and number plate.
	RES 12
	When riding
	• try and keep to main roads
	• keep your speed down
	• brake gently and in plenty of time.
	HC r234–236 **RES** s12

 Take extra care when there are side winds from your left. These can blow you off course and into the path of oncoming vehicles.

At night

When riding at night

- wear reflective clothing
- use dipped headlights (you can also use these in the daytime to become more visible to others)
- don't use tinted glasses, lenses or visors.

RES s13

❯ Skidding

Skidding is when the tyres lose grip on the road, and it's caused by the rider. Road surface and tyre conditions can increase the risk of skidding, but skids are the result of how the rider controls acceleration, braking, speed and steering.

There's a greater risk of skidding in wet or icy conditions. To reduce the risk of skidding in slippery conditions, ride

- at a low speed
- in the highest gear you can use effectively.

Skidding can be caused by

- heavy or uncoordinated braking, which can lock one or both wheels
- too much acceleration, causing rear wheel spin
- steering harshly – making a sudden change of direction
- travelling too fast and leaning over too far when cornering, which may cause tyres to lose grip.

If you accelerate too harshly and start to skid

- ease off the throttle to regain control
- steer in the direction of the skid; for example, if the back of the motorcycle skids to the right, steer to the right.

If the skid is caused by braking, release the brakes to allow the wheels to turn again, then apply the brakes again as firmly as you can in the riding conditions.

HC r119, 231 **RES** s8, 12

To reduce the risk of skidding, look at the road ahead for clues such as road signs and markings, and hazards like potholes, debris, drain covers, oil patches or loose gravel. You can then plan your riding so that you can

- slow down gradually before you reach a hazard, such as a bend
- avoid sudden steering movements.

HC r119, 231 **RES** s6, 8, 12

Anti-lock braking systems

An anti-lock braking system (ABS) will help to prevent wheel lock caused by excessive braking, such as in an emergency. The sensor will keep the wheel at the point of lock-up for as long as the rider continues to brake hard enough to activate the system, or until the motorcycle stops. Refer to your motorcycle handbook for details of the manufacturer's recommended method of use.

HC r120 **RES** s5

ABS doesn't necessarily reduce your stopping distance, but you can continue to steer while braking because the wheels are prevented from locking. It may not work as well if there's

- surface water, such as when there's been heavy rainfall
- a loose road surface, such as gravel.

Contraflow systems

 contraflow system
where one or more lanes have a direction of traffic against that of the rest of the carriageway

When you enter a **contraflow system**, you should

- reduce your speed in good time
- choose a suitable lane in good time: look for signs advising you to use a particular lane if you want to take an exit that will be coming up soon
- keep a safe distance behind the vehicle in front.

HC r290 **RES** s11

Meeting the standards

You must be able to

keep a safe distance from the vehicle in front

use the throttle and brakes correctly to

- regulate your speed
- bring the machine to a stop safely

always use a safe, systematic approach to keep you and other road users safe.
For example, **observation, signal, manoeuvre, position, speed, look.**

You must know and understand

the importance of keeping a safe separation distance in all weather and traffic conditions

about skidding

- why a skid may occur
- how to avoid skids
- how to correct them if they do occur

the distance that a machine needs to stop

- from different speeds
- in different road conditions
- in different weather conditions

how traffic and weather conditions may affect other road users and what to do.
For example, their visibility may be reduced.

> Notes

You can use this page to make your own notes or diagrams about the key points you need to remember.

Think about

- What are typical stopping distances and how do wet or icy roads affect them?
- What extra considerations or precautions might you need to take if the weather is
  - snowy or icy
  - wet
  - foggy
  - hot
  - bright and dazzling
  - windy?
- How can you reduce the risk of skidding and what should you do if your motorcycle starts to skid?
- How does the manufacturer recommend using ABS on your motorcycle?
- Picture yourself entering a contraflow system. What actions can you take to reduce risk?

Your notes

Things to discuss and practise with your trainer

These are just a few examples of what you could discuss and practise with your trainer. Read more about safety margins to come up with your own ideas.

Discuss with your trainer
- how you should ride when you see various road markings, eg bus-stop markings
- what lights you may use in foggy conditions
- stopping distances on dry, wet and icy roads.

Practise with your trainer
- riding in different weather conditions to practise vehicle handling, eg high winds, heavy rain
- leaving a two-second gap between yourself and the vehicle in front on dry roads.

Mark one answer

When will your overall stopping distance be longer?

☐ When you're riding at night
☐ When you're riding in fog
☐ When you're riding with a passenger
☐ When you're riding up a hill

When you're carrying a passenger on a motorcycle, the overall weight will be much more than when you're riding alone. This additional weight will make it harder for you to stop quickly in an emergency, so you'll need to increase the distance between your motorcycle and the vehicle in front.

Mark one answer

What's the safest way to stop on a wet road?

☐ Change gear without braking
☐ Use the back brake only
☐ Use the front brake only
☐ Use both brakes

Motorcyclists need to take extra care when stopping on wet road surfaces. Plan well ahead so that you're able to brake in good time. For maximum stability, you should use both brakes, and brake when your motorcycle is upright and travelling in a straight line.

Mark one answer

You're riding in heavy rain. Your rear wheel skids as you accelerate. What must you do to regain control?

☐ Change down to a lower gear
☐ Ease off the throttle
☐ Brake to reduce speed
☐ Put your feet down

If you feel your back wheel beginning to skid as you accelerate, ease off the throttle. This will give your rear tyre the chance to grip the road and stop the skid.

Mark one answer

Before starting a journey in the snow, what should you do?

☐ Consider whether your journey is essential
☐ Try to avoid taking a passenger
☐ Plan a route avoiding towns
☐ Have a hot drink and a meal

Don't ride in snowy or icy conditions unless your journey is essential. If you must go out, try to keep to main roads, which are more likely to be treated and clear.

4.5

Why should you ride with dipped headlights on in the daytime?

- ☑ They help other road users to see you
- ☐ They mean that you can ride faster
- ☐ Other vehicles will get out of the way
- ☐ So that they're already on when it gets dark

Make yourself as visible as possible, from the side as well as from the front and rear. Having your headlights on, even in good daylight, can help make you more conspicuous.

4.6

When are motorcyclists allowed to use high-intensity rear fog lights?

- ☐ When a pillion passenger is being carried
- ☐ When they ride a large touring machine
- ☐ When visibility is 100 metres (328 feet) or less
- ☐ When they're riding on the road for the first time

If your motorcycle is fitted with high-intensity rear fog lights, you must only use them when visibility is seriously reduced. That's when you can see no further than 100 metres (328 feet). This rule about high-intensity rear fog lights applies to all motor vehicles.

4.7

When must you use your headlights?

- ☐ When riding in a group
- ☑ When visibility is poor
- ☐ When carrying a passenger
- ☐ When parked on an unlit road

Your headlights help you to see in the dark, and help other road users to see you. Use your headlights whenever visibility is poor. Using them at other times may also help other road users to see you. On many motorcycles, the headlights are switched on automatically when you start the engine. Most European countries require headlights to be used at all times.

4.8

You're riding in town at night. The roads are wet after rain. How will the reflections from wet surfaces affect you?

- ☐ They'll make it easier to stop
- ☐ They'll make it harder to accelerate
- ☐ They'll make it easier to see unlit objects
- ☐ They'll make it harder to see unlit objects

After rain, the reflections from wet surfaces will make it hard to see unlit objects. Make sure that your visor or goggles are clean, so your vision is as clear as possible. Pedestrians will be difficult to see, especially if they're wearing dark clothing.

4.9
Mark one answer　　　**RES s12, HC r121**

You've just ridden through a flood. What should you test when you're clear of the water?

☐ The starter motor

☐ The headlights

☐ The steering

☑ The brakes

Water can make your brakes less effective. If they've been affected, ride slowly while gently applying them until normal braking is restored.

4.10
Mark one answer　　　**RES s12**

How should you ride through flood water?

☐ Quickly, in a high gear

☐ Slowly, in a high gear

☐ Quickly, in a low gear

☑ Slowly, in a low gear

If you have to ride through a flood, ride slowly in a low gear. Keep the engine running fast enough to keep water out of the exhaust. You may need to slip the clutch to do this.

4.11
Mark one answer　　　**RES s13, HC r94**

How should you ride at night on a busy main road?

☐ With main-beam headlights on at all times

☐ Wearing non-reflective dark clothing

☑ Using dipped-beam headlights

☐ Wearing tinted glasses or a tinted visor

If there's other traffic on the road at night, use your headlights on dipped beam. Only switch to main beam when you won't dazzle other road users. At night, don't wear tinted glasses or contact lenses, or use a tinted visor, because these make it more difficult to see the road ahead.

4.12
Mark one answer　　　**RES s12, HC r226, 235**

What should you do to help stay safe when you're riding in fog?

☐ Keep close to the vehicle in front

☐ Keep the vehicle in front in view

☐ Keep close to the centre of the road

☑ Keep your visor or goggles clear

You must use your dipped headlights when visibility is seriously reduced. In fog, a film of mist can form over the outside of your visor or goggles. This can further reduce your ability to see. Be aware of this hazard and keep your visor or goggles clear; anti-mist sprays can help.

Mark one answer RES s8

You're riding in heavy rain. Why should you try to avoid this marked area?

Painted lines and road markings can be very slippery, especially for motorcyclists. Try to avoid them if you can do so safely.

☐ It's illegal to ride over bus stops

☑ The painted lines may be slippery

☐ Cyclists may be using the bus stop

☐ Only emergency vehicles may drive over bus stops

4.14 Mark one answer RES s4, HC r87

What should you do when riding at night?

☑ Wear reflective clothing

☐ Wear a tinted visor

☐ Ride in the middle of the road

☐ Always give arm signals

You need to make yourself as visible as possible – from the front and back, and also from the side. Don't just rely on your headlight and tail light. Wear clothing with reflective material, as this stands out in other vehicles' headlights.

4.15 Mark one answer RES s4

When riding in extremely cold conditions, what can you do to keep warm?

☐ Stay close to the vehicles in front

☑ Wear suitable clothing

☐ Lie flat on the tank

☐ Put one hand on the exhaust pipe

Motorcyclists are exposed to the elements and can become very cold when riding in wintry conditions. It's important to keep warm or your concentration could be affected. The only way to stay warm is to wear suitable clothing. If you do find yourself getting cold, then stop at a suitable place to warm up.

Mark one answer

What can you do to be seen more easily when you're riding at night?

☑ Wear reflective clothing

☐ Wear waterproof clothing

☐ Keep your motorcycle clean

☐ Stay well out to the right

It's vital to make yourself as visible as you can. Use the correct lights on your motorcycle. Wear reflective clothing and a light or brightly coloured helmet. Fluorescent clothing is effective in daytime but won't show up as well at night. Most high-visibility clothing will have a combination of fluorescent and reflective materials.

Mark one answer

When will your overall stopping distance increase?

☑ When it's raining

☐ When it's sunny

☐ When it's dark

☐ When it's windy

Extra care should be taken in wet weather. Wet roads will affect the time it takes you to stop: your stopping distance could be as much as doubled.

Mark one answer

Which road surface is most likely to reduce the stability of your motorcycle?

☐ Tarmac

☐ Shellgrip

☐ Concrete

☑ Loose gravel

Some road surfaces can affect the stability of a motorcycle far more than they affect other vehicles. Look out for loose or slippery road surfaces and be aware of any traffic around you. You may need to take avoiding action and change direction quickly.

4.19　Mark one answer　RES s8, HC r167

You're riding past queuing traffic. Why should you be more cautious when approaching this road marking?

When riding past queuing traffic, look out for 'keep clear' road markings, which will indicate a side road or entrance on the left. Vehicles may emerge or turn between gaps in the traffic.

- ☐ Lorries will be unloading here
- ☐ Schoolchildren will be crossing here
- ☐ Pedestrians will be standing in the road
- ☑ Traffic could be turning here

4.20　Mark one answer　RES s8

What can cause your tyres to lose their grip on the road surface and skid?

- ☐ Giving hand signals
- ☐ Riding one-handed
- ☐ Looking over your shoulder
- ☑ Heavy braking

You can cause your motorcycle to skid by heavy braking, as well as excessive acceleration, swerving or changing direction too sharply, and leaning over too far.

4.21　Mark one answer　RES s12, HC r227

When riding in heavy rain, a film of water can build up between your tyres and the road. This is known as aquaplaning. What should you do to keep control when aquaplaning occurs?

- ☐ Use your rear brakes gently
- ☐ Steer to the crown of the road
- ☑ Ease off the throttle smoothly
- ☐ Change up to a higher gear

If your motorcycle starts to aquaplane, ease off the throttle smoothly. Don't brake or turn the steering until tyre grip has been restored.

4.22

Mark one answer

RES s12, HC r121

After riding through deep water, you notice your scooter brakes aren't working properly. What would be the best way to dry them out?

- ☑ Ride slowly, braking lightly
- ☐ Ride quickly, braking harshly
- ☐ Stop and dry them with a cloth
- ☐ Stop and wait for a few minutes

You can help to dry out brakes by riding slowly and applying light pressure to the brake pedal/lever. Don't ride at normal speeds until they're working normally again.

4.23

Mark one answer

RES s12, HC r226, 235

What should you do if you have to ride in foggy weather?

- ☐ Stay close to the centre of the road
- ☐ Switch on only your sidelights
- ☑ Switch on your dipped headlights
- ☐ Ride in the gutter so you can see the kerb

Only travel in fog if your journey is absolutely necessary. Fog is often patchy and visibility can reduce suddenly, without warning, so use your dipped headlights to help others to see you in these difficult conditions.

4.24

Mark one answer

RES s8, HC r126

'Only a fool breaks the two-second rule.' What does this refer to?

- ☐ The time recommended when using the choke
- ☑ The time gap when following another vehicle in good conditions
- ☐ The time you should allow to restart a stalled engine
- ☐ The time you should keep your foot down at a junction

It's very important that you always leave a safe gap between your motorcycle and any vehicle you're following. In good conditions, you need to leave at least one metre for every mile per hour of your speed, or a two-second time interval.

4.25

Mark one answer

RES s9

What should a motorcyclist avoid at a mini-roundabout?

- ☐ Turning right
- ☐ Using signals
- ☐ Taking 'lifesavers'
- ☑ The painted area

Avoid riding over the painted area of a mini-roundabout, as this can become very slippery – especially when wet. At any given moment, only a small part of a motorcycle tyre makes contact with the road, so any reduction in grip can seriously affect stability.

4.26 — Mark one answer — RES s11

You're riding on an exposed stretch of motorway and there's a strong side wind. When should you take extra care?

☐ As you approach a service area
☐ When you overtake a large vehicle
☐ When there's slow queuing traffic
☐ As you approach an exit slip road

Beware of side winds when riding on exposed stretches of road. Take extra care when overtaking large vehicles. As you pass them, you may emerge from their shelter into a gust of wind that can suddenly blow you off course. Bear in mind that strong winds can affect the stability of other road users too.

4.27 — Mark one answer — RES s8

Why should you try to avoid riding over this marked area?

☐ It's illegal to ride over bus stops
☐ It will alter your machine's centre of gravity
☐ Pedestrians may be waiting at the bus stop
☒ A bus may have left patches of oil

Try to anticipate slippery road surfaces. Watch out for oil patches at places where vehicles stop for some time, such as bus stops, lay-bys and busy junctions.

4.28 — Mark one answer — RES s8, HC r126

Your overall stopping distance comprises thinking distance and braking distance. You're on a good, dry road surface, with good brakes and tyres. What's the typical braking distance at 50 mph?

☐ 14 metres (46 feet)
☐ 24 metres (79 feet)
☒ 38 metres (125 feet)
☐ 55 metres (180 feet)

Various factors – such as weather and road conditions, vehicle condition and loading – affect how long it takes you to stop. You also need to add reaction time to this. The overall stopping distance at 50 mph includes a thinking distance of 15 metres (the reaction time before braking starts) plus your braking distance of 38 metres, giving a typical overall stopping distance of 53 metres (175 feet) in good conditions.

By how much can stopping distances increase in icy conditions?

☐ Two times

☐ Three times

☐ Five times

☑ Ten times

Tyre grip is greatly reduced in icy conditions. For this reason, you need to allow up to ten times the stopping distance you would allow on dry roads.

In windy conditions, which activity requires extra care?

☐ Using the brakes

☐ Moving off on a hill

☐ Turning into a narrow road

☑ Passing pedal cyclists

Always give cyclists plenty of room when overtaking them. You need to give them even more room when it's windy. A sudden gust could easily blow them off course and into your path.

When approaching a right-hand bend, you should keep well to the left. Why is this?

Doing this will give you an earlier view around the bend and enable you to see any hazards sooner. It also reduces the risk of collision with an oncoming vehicle that may have drifted over the centre line while taking the bend.

☑ To improve your view of the road

☐ To overcome the effect of the road's slope

☐ To let faster traffic from behind overtake

☐ To be positioned safely if you skid

4.32   **Mark one answer**   **RES s12, HC r121**

You've just gone through deep water. What should you do to make sure your brakes are working properly?

☐ Accelerate and keep to a high speed for a short time

☑ Go slowly while gently applying the brakes

☐ Avoid using the brakes at all for a few miles

☐ Stop for at least an hour to allow them time to dry

Water on the brakes will act as a lubricant, causing them to work less efficiently. Using the brakes lightly as you go along will quickly dry them out.

4.33   **Mark one answer**   **RES s12, HC r237**

In very hot weather the road surface can become soft. What will this affect?

☐ The suspension

☐ The exhaust emissions

☐ The fuel consumption

☑ The tyre grip

If the road surface becomes very hot, it can soften. Tyres are unable to grip a soft surface as well as they can a firm dry one. Take care when cornering and braking.

4.34   **Mark one answer**   **RES s12, HC r232**

Where are you most likely to be affected by side winds?

☐ On a narrow country lane

☑ On an open stretch of road

☐ On a busy stretch of road

☐ On a long, straight road

In windy conditions, care must be taken on exposed roads. A strong gust of wind can blow you off course. Watch out for other road users who are particularly likely to be affected, such as cyclists, motorcyclists, high-sided lorries and vehicles towing trailers.

4.35   **Mark one answer**   **HC r126**

In good conditions, what's the typical stopping distance at 70 mph?

☐ 53 metres (175 feet)

☐ 60 metres (197 feet)

☐ 73 metres (240 feet)

☑ 96 metres (315 feet)

Note that this is the typical stopping distance. It will take at least this distance to think, brake and stop in good conditions. In poor conditions, it will take much longer.

4.36

What's the shortest overall stopping distance on a dry road at 60 mph?

☐ 53 metres (175 feet)

☐ 58 metres (190 feet)

☑ 73 metres (240 feet)

☐ 96 metres (315 feet)

This distance is the equivalent of 18 car lengths. Try pacing out 73 metres and then look back. It's probably further than you think.

4.37

You're following a vehicle at a safe distance on a wet road. Another driver overtakes you and pulls into the gap you've left. What should you do?

☐ Flash your headlights as a warning

☐ Try to overtake safely as soon as you can

☑ Drop back to regain a safe distance

☐ Stay close to the other vehicle until it moves on

Wet weather will affect the time it takes for you to stop and can affect your control. Your speed should allow you to stop safely and in good time. If another vehicle pulls into the gap you've left, ease back until you've regained your stopping distance.

4.38

You're travelling at 50 mph on a good, dry road. What's your typical overall stopping distance?

☐ 36 metres (118 feet)

☑ 53 metres (175 feet)

☐ 75 metres (245 feet)

☐ 96 metres (315 feet)

Even in good conditions, it will usually take you further than you think to stop. Don't just learn the figures; make sure you understand how far the distance is.

4.39

You're on a good, dry road surface. Your brakes and tyres are good. What's the typical overall stopping distance at 40 mph?

☐ 23 metres (75 feet)

☑ 36 metres (118 feet)

☐ 53 metres (175 feet)

☐ 96 metres (315 feet)

Stopping distances are affected by a number of variables. These include the type, model and condition of your vehicle, the road and weather conditions, and your reaction time. Look well ahead for hazards and leave enough space between you and the vehicle in front. This should allow you to pull up safely if you have to, without braking sharply.

4.40 — Mark one answer — HC r126

Overall stopping distance is made up of thinking distance and braking distance. You're on a good, dry road surface, with good brakes and tyres. What's the typical braking distance from 50 mph?

- ☐ 14 metres (46 feet)
- ☐ 24 metres (80 feet)
- ☑ 38 metres (125 feet)
- ☐ 55 metres (180 feet)

Be aware that this is just the braking distance. You need to add the thinking distance to this to give the overall stopping distance. At 50 mph, the typical thinking distance will be 15 metres (50 feet), plus a braking distance of 38 metres (125 feet), giving an overall stopping distance of 53 metres (175 feet). The stopping distance could be greater than this, depending on your attention and response to any hazards. These figures are a general guide.

4.41 — Mark one answer — RES s8, HC r126

In heavy motorway traffic, the vehicle behind you is following too closely. How can you lower the risk of a collision?

On busy roads, traffic may still travel at high speeds despite being close together. Don't follow the vehicle in front too closely. If a driver behind seems to be 'pushing' you, gradually increase your distance from the vehicle in front by slowing down gently. This will give you more space in front if you have to brake, and will reduce the risk of a collision involving several vehicles.

- ☑ Increase your distance from the vehicle in front
- ☐ Brake sharply
- ☐ Switch on your hazard warning lights
- ☐ Move onto the hard shoulder and stop

Mark one answer

You're following other vehicles in fog. You have your lights on. What else can you do to reduce the chances of being in a collision?

☐ Keep close to the vehicle in front

☐ Use your main beam instead of dipped headlights

☐ Keep up with the faster vehicles

☑ Reduce your speed and increase the gap in front

When it's foggy, use dipped headlights. This will help you see and be seen by other road users. If visibility is seriously reduced, consider using front and rear fog lights if you have them. Keep to a sensible speed and don't follow the vehicle in front too closely. If the road is wet and slippery, you'll need to allow twice the normal stopping distance.

Mark one answer

You're using a contraflow system. What should you do?

☑ Choose an appropriate lane in good time

☐ Switch lanes at any time to make progress

☐ Increase speed to pass through quickly

☐ Follow other motorists closely to avoid long queues

In a contraflow system, you'll be travelling close to oncoming traffic and sometimes in narrow lanes. You should get into the correct lane in good time, obey any temporary speed-limit signs and keep a safe separation distance from the vehicle ahead.

Case study practice – 4 Safety margins

You're taking a pillion passenger to collect their new motorcycle. The weather is fine, with a strong side wind.

There's a cyclist in front and the road surface is cracked, with areas of loose and crumbled tarmac.

Further on, the traffic is heavier.

On reaching your destination, you turn right into the dealer's forecourt.

4.1 What might you need to adjust before the journey?

Mark **one** answer

☐ Tyre pressures and headlight aim
☐ Front forks and handlebar height
☐ Pillion seating and wheel alignment
☐ Passenger footrests and chain tension

RES s14

4.2 How would the weather conditions affect you?

Mark **one** answer

☐ It would be difficult to keep to the speed limits
☐ It would cause the motorcycle to use more fuel
☐ It would be difficult to hold a steady course
☐ It would reduce the overall stopping distance

RES s12 **HC** r232

4.3 How would the road surface affect the cyclist?
Mark **one** answer

☐ They would ride along the middle of the road
☐ They would get off and walk along the road
☐ They would try to avoid cracks and holes
☐ They would be able to ride faster

RES s10 **HC** r213

4.4 How would you need to ride on this road surface?
Mark **one** answer

☐ More slowly
☐ Using main-beam headlights
☐ More quickly
☐ In the highest gear possible

RES s8 **HC** r213

4.5 What should you do just before turning into the dealership?
Mark **one** answer

☐ Check over your right shoulder for overtaking vehicles
☐ Give a slowing-down arm signal
☐ Check over your left shoulder for overtaking vehicles
☐ Ask your passenger to give a right-turn arm signal

RES s3 **HC** r180

> Section five
Hazard awareness

In this section, you'll learn about

- > static hazards, eg parked cars, junctions, roundabouts
- > moving hazards, eg pedestrians, cyclists, drivers
- > road and weather conditions
- > physical conditions that make someone unfit to ride.

Hazard awareness

When you start your compulsory basic training (CBT) to learn to ride, you'll be concentrating on the basic controls of your motorcycle. As your skills improve, so will your ability to recognise hazards on the road.

A hazard is a situation that may require you, as a rider, to respond by taking action, such as braking or steering.

Hazards can be …

static, such as parked cars, junctions or roundabouts

moving, such as pedestrians, cyclists or drivers

road and weather conditions

you, if you aren't alert and fit to ride

The 'Perfect day' video shows what riding would be like in an ideal world.

▶ **youtube.com/thinkuk**

❯ Static hazards

There are many types of static hazard, including

- bends
- junctions
- roundabouts
- parked vehicles and obstructions in the road
- roadworks
- road surfaces
- different types of crossings
- traffic lights.

HC r153 **RES** s8, 9, 10

All of these may require you to respond in some way, so

- be aware that they're there
- slow down and be ready to stop if necessary.

At level crossings with traffic light signals, you **MUST** stop before the barrier when the red lights are flashing, even if the barrier isn't yet down.

HC r293

Road signs

Road signs and markings are there to give you clues about possible hazards, so it's vital that you learn their meanings. You can find them in *The Official Highway Code* (book, eBook, interactive CD-ROM, app and online) and *Know Your Traffic Signs* (book, eBook and online).

Watch out for signs and markings so that you can slow down in good time and are prepared for any action you may need to take. For example, if you see a sign for a bend, ask yourself 'What if there's a pedestrian or an obstruction just around the bend – could I stop in time? Could I do it safely?'

HC p106–116 **RES** s7 **KYTS** p10–71, 77–93

Parked vehicles

In busy areas, parked cars can cause a hazard – especially if they're parked illegally, for example on the zigzag lines by a pedestrian crossing.

Watch out for

- children running out from between vehicles
- vehicle doors opening
- vehicles moving away.

Would you be able to stop, or safely avoid them, in time?

HC r205–206 **RES** s8, 10

Junctions

Your view is often reduced at junctions, especially in built-up areas (for example, in towns). Take extra care and pull forward slowly until you can see down the road. You may also be able to see reflections of traffic in the windows of buildings, such as shops.

Be careful not to block a junction; leave it clear so that other vehicles can enter and emerge.

Where lanes are closed, be ready for vehicles cutting in front of you and keep a safe distance from the vehicle in front.

HC r151 **RES** s10

At a traffic-light-controlled junction where the lights aren't working, treat it as an unmarked junction and be prepared to stop. There may be police officers controlling traffic in these circumstances – make sure that you know and understand their signals.

HC r105, 176, p105 **RES** s10

Motorways and dual carriageways

If you're riding on a motorway or dual carriageway and see a hazard or obstruction ahead, you may use your hazard warning lights briefly to warn the traffic behind.

Slow-moving or stationary vehicles with a large arrow displayed on the back show where you need to change lanes when approaching roadworks.

Breakdowns

If your motorcycle breaks down and is causing an obstruction, switch on your hazard warning lights to warn other road users.

HC r116 **RES** s9, 11

 Find out more about what to do if you break down on a motorway at this link.

❯ survivegroup.org/pages/safety-information/stopping-on-the-hard-shoulder

❯ Moving hazards

Moving hazards tend to be hazards caused by other types of road user.

Road user	What to do
Pedestrians 	If you see pedestrians in the road, be patient and wait for them to finish crossing. On country roads there may be no pavement, so look out for pedestrians in the road. They may be walking towards you on your side of the road. **HC** r205–206 **RES** s8, 10
Cyclists 	Be aware of cyclists and give them plenty of room. They may wobble or swerve to avoid drains or potholes. At junctions or traffic lights, give cyclists time to turn or pull away. When travelling in slow traffic, before you turn left, check for cyclists filtering through the traffic on your left. **HC** r211–213 **RES** s10

Road user	What to do
Horse riders 	Horses can be unpredictable and easily spooked. Reduce your speed and give them plenty of room when overtaking. **HC** r215 **RES** s10
Drivers of large vehicles  	If you see a bus at a bus stop, remember that • people may get off and then cross the road • the bus may be about to move off. **HC** r223 **RES** s10 School buses might stop at places other than bus stops. At some bridges, high vehicles may need to use the centre of the road to be able to pass underneath. **HC** r221 **RES** s10 Large goods vehicles over 13 metres long have red and yellow markings at the back of the vehicle. **HC** p117
Drivers of vehicles carrying hazardous loads  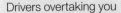	Some vehicles have information signs on the back, to show that they contain a hazardous load. Learn what the signs mean. **HC** p117
Drivers overtaking you 	Watch out for vehicles, especially other motorcyclists, overtaking and cutting in front of you. If you need to, drop back to keep a safe distance from the vehicle in front. When turning right, don't forget the 'lifesaver' look to your right to check for vehicles overtaking you before you make the turn. **HC** r211–213 **RES** s10

Road user	What to do
Disabled people using powered vehicles 	Reduce your speed and be careful. These small vehicles are extremely vulnerable on the road because • they're difficult to see • they travel slowly.
Older drivers 	Older drivers may not react very quickly, so be patient with them. **HC** r216 **RES** s10

A vehicle driving too closely behind you can be dangerous and intimidating. Move over and let the vehicle through if you can. If there's no room and the driver behind seems to be 'pushing' you, increase your distance from the vehicle in front. This will make an incident involving several vehicles less likely.

RES s10

If it looks like the road user in front has forgotten to cancel their right indicator, be careful. Stay behind and don't overtake – they may be unsure of the position of a junction and turn suddenly.

HC r104

Find out about the hazard perception test on DVSA's YouTube channel.

➤ **youtube.com/dvsagovuk**

If you have a provisional licence, you **MUST NOT**

- ride on public roads until you've successfully completed compulsory basic training (CBT)
- carry a pillion passenger
- tow a trailer
- ride on a motorway.

Until you've passed your practical riding tests, you can only ride unaccompanied on a motorcycle displaying red L plates, with an engine capacity less than 125 cc. To ride a larger machine displaying red L plates you must be

- at least 19 years old
- accompanied by a direct access scheme (DAS) trainer who's in radio contact with you
- wearing fluorescent safety clothing.

HC r253, p118–120

❯ Road and weather conditions

Different types of weather – rain, ice, fog and even bright sunlight – can create extra hazards by making it harder to see the road or affecting your control of the vehicle. Change the way you ride to suit the weather conditions, and be aware of the added dangers.

Find out more about winter riding at this link.

❯ **bikesafe.co.uk/advice-centre/ winter-riding**

In these conditions ...	remember to do this
Rain	Double your distance from the vehicle in front to four seconds.
Ice	Slow down and increase your separation distance: allow up to 10 times the gap you'd leave in the dry.
Fog	Slow down and use dipped headlights.
Bright sunlight	Be aware that sunlight can dazzle you or other drivers.

HC r227 **RES** s12

Remember that if you're wet and cold, you could lose concentration and it may take you longer to react to a hazard. Always wear proper protective clothing and footwear when riding.

Yourself

Don't allow yourself to become a hazard on the road. You need to be alert and concentrate on your riding at all times.

Awareness

Make sure you use your mirrors so that you're aware of what's going on around you at all times. These may be convex (curved outwards slightly) to give a wider field of vision.

HC r161

Tiredness

Don't ride if you're tired. Plan your journey so that you have enough rest and refreshment breaks. Try to stop at least once every two hours.

If you feel tired

- pull over at a safe and legal place to rest
- on a motorway, leave at the next exit or services.

HC r91 **RES** s1, 11

See the GEM Motoring Assist website for more information about riding and tiredness.

❯ **motoringassist.com/fatigue**

Distractions

Your concentration can be affected by

- using a hands-free phone headset
- listening to loud music
- looking at navigation equipment
- how you're feeling.

It's important to avoid being distracted by these things while you're riding.

- Turn off your mobile phone or switch it to voicemail.
- Before looking at navigation equipment or using your phone, find somewhere safe and legal to stop.
- Keep music at a reasonable volume.
- If you're upset or angry, take time to calm down before you begin riding.

When you're riding for long distances at speed, noise can make you feel tired and can damage your hearing. It's a good idea to wear ear plugs to protect your hearing when you ride.

HC r148–150 **RES** s1, 11

Alcohol

Never ride if you've been drinking alcohol: it's not worth taking the chance. If you ride to a social event, don't drink alcoholic drinks. If you've had a drink, find another way to get home, such as public transport, taxi, walking or getting a lift.

HC r95

Did you know?

Alcohol can

- reduce your concentration, coordination and control
- give you a false sense of confidence
- reduce your judgement of speed
- slow down your reactions.

See the Think! road safety information on drink-driving.

❯ **http://think.direct.gov.uk/drink-driving.html**

See the Think! road safety information on drug driving.

❯ **http://drugdrive.direct.gov.uk**

Medicines and drugs

You must be fit to ride. Some medicines can make you sleepy: check the label or ask your doctor or pharmacist if it's safe for you to ride your motorcycle after taking any medication that may affect your riding.

HC r90, 95–96 **RES** s1

Using illegal drugs is highly dangerous and the effects of some can last up to 72 hours. Never take them before riding.

If you've been convicted of riding while unfit through drink or drugs, the cost of your insurance will rise considerably. Riding while under the influence of drink or drugs may even invalidate your insurance.

RES s1

Eyesight

Your eyesight **MUST** be of the required legal standard; if you need glasses or contact lenses to bring your eyesight up to this standard, you **MUST** wear them every time you ride. Tinted glasses, visors and goggles can restrict your vision, so you mustn't wear them for riding at night.

You **MUST** tell the licensing authority if you suffer from any medical condition that may affect your ability to ride a motorcycle.

HC r90, 92–94 **RES** s1

Find out about the eyesight rules for riding at this website.

❯ **www.gov.uk**

Meeting the standards

You must be able to

use visual clues to prepare you for possible hazards; for example, reflections in shop windows

judge which possible hazards are most likely to affect you, so that you can plan what to do

respond to hazards safely.

You must know and understand

methods that you can use to scan around you, both close and into the distance

which kinds of hazard you may find on different roads; for example

- tractors on country roads
- deer on forest roads
- children crossing near schools.

> Notes

You can use this page to make your own notes or diagrams about the key points you need to remember.

Think about

- What are some examples of static hazards and why are they potentially dangerous?
- What kinds of moving hazards do you need to look out for when riding?
- What types of weather conditions can be hazardous and what can you do to reduce the risks?
- Think of the physical conditions that can make you unfit to ride. Have you experienced any? How did it affect you?

Your notes

Things to discuss and practise with your trainer

These are just a few examples of what you could discuss and practise with your trainer. Read more about hazard awareness to come up with your own ideas.

Discuss with your trainer

- the effects that alcohol and drugs can have on your riding
- how your riding is affected by tiredness and what you can do to help stay alert
- how to deal with other people's bad driving and riding behaviour.

Practise with your trainer

- riding through a busy town centre and identifying all the potential hazards, eg wobbling cyclists, pedestrians, vans pulling out of junctions, etc. Discuss these after your lesson
- riding
  - up to blind junctions
  - along roads where many vehicles are parked
- identifying road markings.

5.1 **Mark one answer** RES s4

What's likely to happen if you get cold and wet when riding a motorcycle?

- ☑ Your concentration will be impaired
- ☐ Your riding will improve
- ☐ Your visor will freeze up
- ☐ Your reactions will be quicker

When riding, make sure you wear suitable clothing for the conditions. Getting cold and wet will make you uncomfortable. This can cause you to lose concentration and considerably slow down your reaction time. Stop in a safe place to have a hot drink and warm up before this happens.

5.2 **Mark one answer** RES s6, HC p103

You're riding up to a zebra crossing. You intend to stop for waiting pedestrians. How could you let them know you're stopping?

- ☐ By signalling with your left arm
- ☐ By waving them across
- ☐ By flashing your headlights
- ☑ By signalling with your right arm

Giving the correct arm signal would indicate to approaching vehicles, as well as pedestrians, that you're stopping at the pedestrian crossing.

5.3 **Mark one answer** RES s4, HC r92

You're about to ride home but you can't find the glasses you need to wear. What should you do?

- ☐ Ride home slowly, keeping to quiet roads
- ☐ Borrow a friend's glasses and use those
- ☐ Ride home at night, so that the lights will help you
- ☑ Find a way of getting home without riding

If you need glasses to bring your eyesight up to the legal standard for driving or riding, you must wear them whenever you ride. Don't be tempted to ride if you've lost or forgotten your glasses; you'll endanger yourself and other road users, and you'll be breaking the law.

5.4 **Mark one answer** RES s1, HC r95

Which of these is an effect of drinking alcohol?

- ☐ Faster reactions
- ☐ Colour blindness
- ☐ Poor judgement
- ☐ Increased concentration

Even a small amount of alcohol will impair a person's judgement. It can increase confidence to a point where a person's behaviour may become 'out of character'. Someone who normally behaves sensibly may take risks and could endanger themselves and others. Don't drink and ride, or accept a lift from anyone who's been drinking.

5.5
Mark one answer   RES s4, HC r92

You find that you need glasses to read vehicle number plates at the required distance. When must you wear them?

☐ Only in bad weather conditions

☑ At all times when riding

☐ Only when you think it's necessary

☐ Only in bad light or at night time

Have your eyesight tested before you start your practical training. Then have checks periodically throughout your riding life, as your vision may change.

5.6
Mark one answer   RES s1, HC r95

How are you likely to be affected by drinking alcohol?

☐ You'll be more cautious and perceptive

☐ The speed of your reactions will increase

☑ Your judgement of speed will be worse

☐ Your awareness of danger will improve

Never drink if you're going to drive or ride. Your judgement can be seriously affected, even if you aren't over the drink-drive limit. Don't take risks; it isn't worth it.

5.7
Mark one answer   RES s4, HC r94

Which type of glasses shouldn't be worn when riding at night?

☐ Half-moon

☐ Round

☐ Bifocal

☑ Tinted

If you're riding at night or in poor visibility, tinted lenses or a tinted visor will reduce the amount of available light reaching your eyes, making you less able to see clearly.

5.8
Mark one answer   HC r116

In which of these circumstances may you use hazard warning lights?

☑ When riding on a motorway, to warn traffic behind of a hazard ahead

☐ When you're double parked on a two-way road

☐ When your direction indicators aren't working

☐ When riding in town, to warn oncoming traffic that you intend to stop

Hazard warning lights are an important safety feature. Use them when riding on a motorway to warn following traffic of danger ahead. You should also use them if your motorcycle has broken down and is causing an obstruction.

5.9
Mark one answer

RES s1, HC r84

Why should you wear ear plugs when riding a motorcycle?

- ☑ To help prevent hearing damage
- ☐ To make you less aware of traffic
- ☐ To help keep you warm
- ☐ To make your helmet fit better

The use of ear plugs is recommended to protect your hearing from being damaged by the noise of air turbulence around your helmet. Staying within the national speed limit, a rider may experience noise levels in excess of 100 decibels.

5.10
Mark one answer

HC r95

You're going to a social event and alcohol will be available. You'll be riding your motorcycle shortly afterwards. What's the safest thing to do?

- ☐ Stay just below the legal limit
- ☐ Have soft drinks and alcohol in turn
- ☐ Don't go beyond the legal limit
- ☑ Stick to non-alcoholic drinks

Drinking even the smallest amount of alcohol can affect your judgement and reactions. The safest and best option is to avoid any alcohol at all when riding or driving.

5.11
Mark one answer

HC p128

You're convicted of riding after drinking too much alcohol. How could this affect your insurance?

- ☑ Your insurance may become invalid
- ☐ The amount of excess you pay will be reduced
- ☐ You'll only be able to get third-party cover
- ☐ Cover will only be given for riding smaller motorcycles

Riding while under the influence of drink or drugs can invalidate your insurance. It also endangers yourself and others. The risk isn't worth taking.

5.12
Mark one answer

RES s8

Why should you check over your shoulder before turning right into a side road?

- ☐ To make sure the side road is clear
- ☐ To check for emerging traffic
- ☐ To check for overtaking vehicles
- ☐ To confirm your intention to turn

Take a check over your shoulder before committing yourself to a manoeuvre. This is especially important when turning right, as other road users may not have seen your signal or may not understand your intentions.

5.13
Mark one answer
RES s1, HC r96

You aren't sure whether your cough medicine will affect your ability to ride safely. What should you do?

- ☑ Ask your doctor
- ☐ Don't take the medicine
- ☐ Ride if you feel all right
- ☐ Ask a friend or relative for advice

If you're taking medicine or drugs prescribed by your doctor, check to make sure they won't make you drowsy. If you forget to ask when you're at the surgery, check with your pharmacist.

5.14
Mark one answer
HC r116

When should you use hazard warning lights?

- ☐ When you're double-parked on a two-way road
- ☐ When your direction indicators aren't working
- ☐ When warning oncoming traffic that you intend to stop
- ☑ When your motorcycle has broken down and is causing an obstruction

Hazard warning lights are an important safety feature and should be used if you've broken down and are causing an obstruction. Don't use them as an excuse to park illegally, even for a short time. You may also use them on motorways to warn following traffic of danger ahead.

5.15
Mark one answer
RES s12

It's a very hot day. What would you expect to find?

- ☐ Mud on the road
- ☑ A soft road surface
- ☐ Roadworks ahead
- ☐ Banks of fog

In very hot weather, the road surface can become soft and may melt. Take care when braking and cornering on soft tarmac, as this can lead to reduced grip and cause skidding.

5.16
Mark one answer
HC p117

Where would you expect to see these markers?

These markers must be fitted to vehicles over 13 metres long, large goods vehicles, and rubbish skips placed in the road. They're reflective to make them easier to see in the dark.

- ☐ On a motorway sign
- ☐ On a railway bridge
- ☑ On a large goods vehicle
- ☐ On a diversion sign

What's the main hazard shown in this picture?

Look at the picture carefully and try to imagine you're there. The cyclist in this picture appears to be trying to cross the road. You must be able to deal with the unexpected, especially when you're approaching a hazardous junction. Look well ahead to give yourself time to deal with any hazards.

☐ Vehicles turning right

☐ Vehicles doing U-turns

☑ The cyclist crossing the road

☐ Parked cars around the corner

Which road user has caused a hazard?

The car arrowed A is parked within the area marked by zigzag lines at the pedestrian crossing. Parking here is illegal. It also

• blocks the view for pedestrians wishing to cross the road

• restricts the view of the crossing for approaching traffic.

☑ The parked car (arrowed A)

☐ The pedestrian waiting to cross (arrowed B)

☐ The moving car (arrowed C)

☐ The car turning (arrowed D)

5.19
Mark one answer

RES s8, HC r195

What should the driver of the car approaching the crossing do?

Look well ahead to see whether any hazards are developing. This will give you more time to deal with them in the correct way. The man in the picture is clearly intending to cross the road. You should be travelling at a speed that allows you to check your mirror, slow down and stop in good time. You shouldn't have to brake harshly.

☐ Continue at the same speed

☐ Sound the horn

☐ Drive through quickly

☐ Slow down and get ready to stop

5.20
Mark one answer

RES s8, 10, HC r205–206

What should the driver of the grey car (arrowed) be especially aware of?

When passing parked cars, there's a risk that a driver or passenger may not check before opening the door into the road. A defensive driver will drive slowly and be looking for people who may be about to get out of their car.

☐ The uneven road surface

☐ Traffic following behind

☐ Doors opening on parked cars

☐ Empty parking spaces

5.21
Mark one answer

RES s7, HC p109, KYTS p11

You see this sign ahead. What should you expect?

This sign indicates that the road will bend sharply to the left. Slow down in plenty of time and select the correct gear before you start to turn. Braking hard and late, while also sharply changing direction, is likely to cause a skid.

☐ The road will go steeply uphill

☐ The road will go steeply downhill

☑ The road will bend sharply to the left

☐ The road will bend sharply to the right

Mark one answer

You're approaching this cyclist. What should you do?

Keep well back and give the cyclist time and room to turn safely. Don't intimidate them by getting too close or trying to squeeze past.

☐ Overtake before the cyclist gets to the junction

☐ Flash your headlights at the cyclist

☑ Slow down and allow the cyclist to turn

☐ Overtake the cyclist on the left-hand side

Mark one answer

Why must you take extra care when turning right at this junction?

You may have to pull forward slowly until you can see up and down the road. Be aware that the traffic approaching the junction can't see you either. If you don't know that it's clear, don't go.

☐ The road surface is poor

☐ The footpaths are narrow

☐ The road markings are faint

☑ The view is restricted

5.24   Mark one answer   RES s7, KYTS p24

Which type of vehicle should you be ready to give way to as you approach this bridge?

A double-deck bus or high-sided lorry will have to take a position in the centre of the road to clear the bridge. There's normally a sign to show this. Look well ahead, past the bridge and be ready to stop and give way to large oncoming vehicles.

- [ ] Bicycles
- [✓] Buses
- [ ] Motorcycles
- [ ] Cars

5.25   Mark one answer   RES s7, KYTS p24

What type of vehicle could you expect to meet in the middle of the road?

The highest point of the bridge is in the centre, so a large vehicle might have to move to the centre of the road to have enough room to pass under the bridge.

- [✓] Lorry
- [ ] Bicycle
- [ ] Car
- [ ] Motorcycle

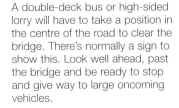

Section five Questions

5.26
Mark one answer — RES s7, HC r171

What must you do at this junction?

The 'stop' sign has been put here because the view into the main road is poor. You must stop because it won't be possible to take proper observation while you're moving.

- ☑ Stop behind the line, then edge forward to see clearly
- ☐ Stop beyond the line, at a point where you can see clearly
- ☐ Stop only if there's traffic on the main road
- ☐ Stop only if you're turning right

5.27
Mark one answer — RES s1, HC r147

A driver pulls out of a side road in front of you, causing you to brake hard. What should you do?

- ☑ Ignore the error and stay calm
- ☐ Flash your lights to show your annoyance
- ☐ Sound your horn to show your annoyance
- ☐ Overtake as soon as possible

Be tolerant if a vehicle emerges and you have to brake quickly. Anyone can make a mistake, so don't react aggressively. Be alert where there are side roads and be especially careful where there are parked vehicles, because these can make it difficult for emerging drivers to see you.

5.28
Mark one answer — RES s1, HC r216

How would age affect an elderly person's driving ability?

- ☐ They won't be able to obtain car insurance
- ☐ They'll need glasses to read road signs
- ☑ They'll take longer to react to hazards
- ☐ They won't signal at junctions

Be tolerant of older drivers. They may take longer to react to a hazard and they may be hesitant in some situations – for example, at a junction.

5.29
Mark one answer RES s7, HC r105, 208

You've just passed these warning lights. What hazard would you expect to see next?

These lights warn that children may be crossing the road to a nearby school. Slow down so that you're ready to stop if necessary.

- ☐ A level crossing with no barrier
- ☐ An ambulance station
- ☑ A school crossing patrol
- ☐ An opening bridge

5.30
Mark one answer RES s1, 11, HC r91

You're planning a long journey. Do you need to plan rest stops?

- ☐ Yes, you should plan to stop every half an hour
- ☑ Yes, regular stops help concentration
- ☐ No, you'll be less tired if you get there as soon as possible
- ☐ No, only fuel stops will be needed

Try to plan your journey so that you can take rest stops. It's recommended that you take a break of at least 15 minutes after every two hours of driving or riding. This should help to maintain your concentration.

5.31
Mark one answer RES s7, HC r291–299

The red lights are flashing. What should you do when approaching this level crossing?

At level crossings, the red lights flash before and while the barrier is down. At most crossings, an amber light will precede the red lights. You must stop behind the white line unless you've already crossed it when the amber light comes on. Never zigzag around half-barriers.

- ☐ Go through quickly
- ☐ Go through carefully
- ☑ Stop before the barrier
- ☐ Switch on hazard warning lights

You're approaching a crossroads. The traffic lights have failed. What should you do?

☐ Brake and stop only for large vehicles

☐ Brake sharply to a stop before looking

☐ Be prepared to brake sharply to a stop

☑ Be prepared to stop for any traffic

When approaching a junction where the traffic lights have failed, you should proceed with caution. Treat the situation as an unmarked junction and be prepared to stop.

What should the driver of the red car (arrowed) do?

☐ Wave towards the pedestrians who are waiting to cross

☑ Wait for the pedestrian in the road to cross

☐ Quickly drive behind the pedestrian in the road

☐ Tell the pedestrian in the road she shouldn't have crossed

Some people might take a long time to cross the road. They may be older or have a disability. Be patient and don't hurry them by showing your impatience. If pedestrians are standing at the side of the road, don't signal or wave them to cross. Other road users might not have seen your signal and this could lead the pedestrians into a hazardous situation.

You're following a slower-moving vehicle on a narrow country road. There's a junction just ahead on the right. What should you do?

☐ Overtake after checking your mirrors and signalling

☑ Only consider overtaking when you're past the junction

☐ Accelerate quickly to pass before the junction

☐ Slow down and prepare to overtake on the left

You should never overtake as you approach a junction. If a vehicle emerged from the junction while you were overtaking, a dangerous situation could develop very quickly.

5.35

What should you do as you approach this overhead bridge?

Oncoming large vehicles may need to move to the middle of the road to pass safely under the bridge. There won't be enough room for you to continue, so you should be ready to stop and wait.

☐ Move out to the centre of the road before going through

☐ Find another route; this one is only for high vehicles

☑ Be prepared to give way to large vehicles in the middle of the road

☐ Move across to the right-hand side before going through

5.36

Why are mirrors often slightly curved (convex)?

☑ They give a wider field of vision

☐ They totally cover blind spots

☐ They make it easier to judge the speed of following traffic

☐ They make following traffic look bigger

Although a convex mirror gives a wide view of the scene behind, you should be aware that it won't show you everything behind or to the side of your vehicle. Before you move off, you'll need to look over your shoulder to check for anything not visible in the mirrors.

A slow-moving lorry showing this sign is travelling in the middle lane of a three-lane motorway. How should you pass it?

This sign is found on slow-moving or stationary works vehicles. If you wish to overtake, do so on the left, as indicated. Be aware that there might be workmen in the area.

- ☐ Cautiously approach the lorry, then pass on either side
- ☐ Don't pass the lorry and leave the motorway at the next exit
- ☐ Use the right-hand lane and pass the lorry normally
- ☑ Approach with care and pass on the left of the lorry

You think the driver of the vehicle in front has forgotten to cancel their right indicator. What should you do?

Be cautious and don't attempt to overtake. The driver may be unsure of the location of a junction and may turn suddenly.

- ☐ Flash your lights to alert the driver
- ☐ Sound your horn before overtaking
- ☐ Overtake on the left if there's room
- ☑ Stay behind and don't overtake

What's the main hazard the driver of the red car (arrowed) should be aware of?

If you can do so safely, give way to buses signalling to move off at bus stops. Try to anticipate the actions of other road users around you. The driver of the red car should be prepared for the bus pulling out. As you approach a bus stop, look to see how many passengers are waiting to board. If the last one has just got on, the bus is likely to move off.

- ☐ Glare from the sun may affect the driver's vision
- ☐ The black car may stop suddenly
- ☑ The bus may move out into the road
- ☐ Oncoming vehicles will assume the driver is turning right

What type of vehicle displays this yellow sign?

Buses which carry children to and from school may stop at places other than scheduled bus stops. Be aware that they might pull over at any time to allow children to get on or off. This will normally be when traffic is heavy during rush hour.

- ☐ A broken-down vehicle
- ☑ A school bus
- ☐ An ice-cream van
- ☐ A private ambulance

Mark one answer

What hazard should you be aware of when travelling along this street?

On roads where there are many parked vehicles, you might not be able to see children between parked cars and they may run out into the road without looking.

- ☐ Glare from the sun
- ☐ Lack of road markings
- ☑ Children running out between vehicles
- ☐ Large goods vehicles

Mark one answer

What's the main hazard you should be aware of when following this cyclist?

When following a cyclist, be aware that they have to deal with the hazards around them. They may wobble or swerve to avoid a pothole in the road or see a potential hazard and change direction suddenly. Don't follow them too closely or rev your engine impatiently.

- ☐ The cyclist may move to the left and dismount
- ☑ The cyclist may swerve into the road
- ☐ The contents of the cyclist's carrier may fall onto the road
- ☐ The cyclist may wish to turn right at the end of the road

5.43 — Mark one answer — RES s1, HC r147

A driver's behaviour has upset you. What can you do to safely get over this incident?

☐ Stop and take a break
☐ Shout abusive language
☐ Gesture to them with your hand
☐ Follow them, flashing your headlights

If you feel yourself becoming tense or upset, stop in a safe place and take a break. Tiredness can make things worse and may cause a different reaction to upsetting situations.

5.44 — Mark one answer — RES s7, HC r153

How should you drive in areas with traffic-calming measures?

☑ At a reduced speed
☐ At the speed limit
☐ In the centre of the road
☐ With headlights on dipped beam

Traffic-calming measures such as road humps, chicanes and narrowings are intended to slow drivers down to protect vulnerable road users. Don't speed up until you reach the end of the traffic-calmed zone.

5.45 — Mark one answer — RES s7, HC r291–299, p108–109

When approaching this hazard, why should you slow down?

You should be slowing down and selecting the correct gear in case you have to stop at the level crossing. Look for the signals and be prepared to stop if necessary.

☑ Because of the level crossing
☐ Because it's hard to see to the right
☐ Because of approaching traffic
☐ Because of animals crossing

5.46 — Mark one answer — RES s7, HC p116, KYTS p70–71

Why are place names painted on the road surface?

☐ To restrict the flow of traffic
☐ To warn you of oncoming traffic
☑ To enable you to change lanes early
☐ To prevent you changing lanes

The names of towns and cities may be painted on the road at busy junctions and complex road systems. Their purpose is to let you move into the correct lane in good time, allowing traffic to flow more freely.

5.47
Mark one answer HC r135

Some two-way roads are divided into three lanes. Why are these particularly dangerous?

- ☑ Traffic in both directions can use the middle lane to overtake
- ☐ Traffic can travel faster in poor weather conditions
- ☐ Traffic can overtake on the left
- ☐ Traffic uses the middle lane for emergencies only

If you intend to overtake, you must consider that approaching traffic could be planning the same manoeuvre. When you've considered the situation and decided it's safe, indicate your intentions early. This will show the approaching traffic that you intend to pull out.

5.48
Mark one answer RES s10, HC r220

You're on a dual carriageway. Ahead, you see a vehicle with an amber flashing light. What could this be?

- ☐ An ambulance
- ☐ A fire engine
- ☐ A doctor on call
- ☑ A disabled person's vehicle

An amber flashing light on a vehicle indicates that it's slow-moving. Battery-powered vehicles used by disabled people are limited to 8 mph. It isn't advisable for them to be used on dual carriageways where the speed limit exceeds 50 mph. If they are, then an amber flashing light must be used.

5.49
Mark one answer HC p104

What does this signal from a police officer mean to oncoming traffic?

Police officers may need to direct traffic; for example, at a junction where the traffic lights have broken down. Check your copy of The Highway Code for the signals that they use.

- ☐ Go ahead
- ☑ Stop
- ☐ Turn left
- ☐ Turn right

5.50

Mark one answer

RES s10, HC r223

Why should you be cautious when going past this stationary bus?

A stationary bus at a bus stop can hide pedestrians who might try to cross the road just in front of it. Drive at a speed that will enable you to respond safely if you have to.

- [ ] There is traffic approaching in the distance
- [ ] The driver may open the door
- [x] People may cross the road in front of it
- [ ] The road surface will be slippery

5.51

Mark one answer

RES s8, HC r162–167

Where shouldn't you overtake?

- [ ] On a single carriageway
- [ ] On a one-way street
- [x] Approaching a junction
- [ ] Travelling up a long hill

You should overtake only when it's really necessary and you can see it's clear ahead. Look out for road signs and markings that show it's illegal or would be unsafe to overtake; for example, approaching junctions or bends. In many cases, overtaking is unlikely to significantly improve your journey time.

5.52

Mark one answer

HC r95

What's an effect of drinking alcohol?

- [x] Poor judgement of speed
- [ ] A loss of confidence
- [ ] Faster reactions
- [ ] Greater awareness of danger

Alcohol will severely reduce your ability to drive or ride safely and there are serious consequences if you're caught over the drink-drive limit. It's known that alcohol can

- affect your judgement
- cause overconfidence
- reduce coordination and control.

Case study practice – 5 Hazard awareness

> Your rear-view mirrors are convex and give a wide-angle field of view.
>
> You're travelling to a local pub to see some friends, and you stay for several hours.
>
> At the end of the evening, you ride home. The weather has changed and it's raining steadily.
>
> There's a skip parked on the road ahead, showing a flashing beacon and vertical markings.

5.1 How would the reflections in your mirrors differ from those in a normal mirror?

Mark **one** answer

- ☐ They would be larger
- ☐ They would be brighter
- ☐ They would be smaller
- ☐ They would be dimmer

RES s5

5.2 What's the safest thing to do while you're with your friends?

Mark **one** answer

- ☐ Drink pints of shandy
- ☐ Alternate soft drinks with alcoholic drinks
- ☐ Drink shorts with lots of water
- ☐ Drink soft drinks the whole time

RES s1 **HC** r95

5.3 How would the conditions affect visibility during your journey home?

Mark **one** answer

☐ By making you less visible to others
☐ By making it easier for you to see others
☐ By making the street lights seem brighter
☐ By making it easier for others to see you

RES s10 HC r126

5.4 On the ride home, how large a time gap should you leave between your motorcycle and any vehicle you're following?

Mark **one** answer

☐ Two seconds
☐ Three seconds
☐ Four seconds
☐ Five seconds

RES s11 HC r227

5.5 What colour is the flashing beacon?

Mark **one** answer

☐ Amber
☐ Blue
☐ Green
☐ White

HC p117

Section six

Vulnerable road users

In this section, you'll learn about

> who is particularly vulnerable on the road

> how to help keep other road users safe.

Vulnerable road users

As a motorcyclist, you'll share the road with many other road users. Some of these are more vulnerable than you, because of their

- inexperience or lack of judgement
- size
- speed
- unpredictable behaviour.

Among the most vulnerable road users are

- pedestrians – especially children and older people
- cyclists
- other motorcyclists
- horse riders.

Remember to treat all road users with courtesy and consideration. It's particularly important to be patient when there are children, older or disabled people using the road.

The most vulnerable drivers and riders are those who are still learning, inexperienced or older. Keep calm and make allowances for them.

❯ Pedestrians

People walking on or beside the road – pedestrians – are vulnerable because they move more slowly than other road users and have no protection if they're involved in a collision. Everybody is a pedestrian at some time, but not every pedestrian has the understanding of how to use roads safely.

Pedestrians normally use a pavement or footpath. Take extra care if they have to walk in the road – for example, when the pavement is closed for repairs or on country roads where there's no pavement. Always check for road signs that indicate people may be walking in the road.

HC r206 **RES** s10 **KYTS** p13

177

On country roads, it's usually safest for pedestrians to walk on the right-hand side of the road, so that they're facing oncoming traffic and can see the vehicles approaching.

HC r2

A large group of people, such as those on an organised walk, may walk on the left-hand side. At night, the person at the front of the group should show a white light while the person at the back of the group should show a bright red light to help approaching drivers to see them.

HC r5

Watch out for pedestrians already crossing when you're turning into a side road. They have priority, so allow them to finish crossing.

HC r170 **RES** s9

When you see a bus stopped on the other side of the road, watch out for pedestrians who may come from behind the bus and cross the road, or dash across the road from your left to catch the bus.

HC r223 **RES** s10

Pedestrian crossings

Pedestrian crossings allow people to cross the road safely: be ready to slow down and stop as you approach them. Make sure you know how different types of crossing work. See section 2, Attitude, for more details.

Remember that you should never park on or near a pedestrian crossing; for example, on the zigzag lines either side of a zebra crossing.

HC r195–199 **RES** s8

Look for tell-tale signs that someone is going to cross the road between parked cars, such as

• seeing their feet when looking between the wheels of the parked cars
• a ball bouncing out into the road
• a bicycle wheel sticking out between cars.

Slow down and be prepared to stop.

HC r205 **RES** s10

Children

Children are particularly vulnerable as road users because they can be unpredictable. They're less likely than other pedestrians to look before stepping into the road.

 See this link for information on teaching road safety to children.

❯ **http://think.direct.gov.uk/ education/early-years-and- primary/**

Ride carefully near schools.

 There may be flashing amber lights under a school warning sign, to show that children are likely to be crossing the road on their way to or from school. Slow down until you're clear of the area.

 Be prepared for a school crossing patrol to stop the traffic by stepping out into the road with a stop sign. You **MUST** obey the stop signal given by a school crossing patrol.

 Don't wait or park on yellow zigzag lines outside a school. A clear view of the crossing area outside the school is needed by

- drivers and riders on the road
- pedestrians on the pavement.

HC r208–210, 238 **RES** s7, 10 **KYTS** p56

Buses and coaches carrying schoolchildren show a special sign in the back. This tells you that they may stop often, and not just at normal bus stops.

HC r209, p117 **RES** s10

▶ Older and disabled pedestrians

If you see older people about to cross the road ahead, be careful as they may have misjudged your speed.

If they're crossing, be patient and allow them to cross in their own time: they may need extra time to cross the road.

HC r207 **RES** s10

A pedestrian with hearing difficulties may have a dog with a distinctive yellow or burgundy coat.

Take extra care as they may not be aware of vehicles approaching.

A person carrying a white stick with a red band is both deaf and blind. They may also have a guide dog with a red and white checked harness.

HC r207 **RES** s10

⊙ Cyclists

Cyclists should normally follow the same rules of the road as drivers, but they're slower and more vulnerable than other vehicles.

Find out about cycling safely at this link.

⊙ **bikeability.org.uk**

Cycle routes

In some areas there may be special cycle or shared cycle and pedestrian routes, which are marked by signs.

KYTS p35–36

At traffic lights, advanced stop lines are sometimes marked on the road so that cyclists can stop in front of other traffic. When the lights are red or about to become red, you should stop at the first white line.

HC r178

Overtaking cyclists

If you're overtaking a cyclist, give them as much room as you would a car. They may swerve

- to avoid an uneven road surface
- if a gust of wind blows them off course.

HC r211–213 RES s8, 10

A cyclist travelling at a low speed, or glancing over their shoulder to check for traffic, may be planning to turn right. Stay behind and give them plenty of room.

Never overtake a slow-moving vehicle just before you turn left. Hold back and wait until it has passed the junction before you turn.

Cyclists at junctions

When you're emerging from a junction, look carefully for cyclists. They're not as easy to see as larger vehicles. Also look out for cyclists emerging from junctions.

HC r77, 187 **RES** s9

Be aware of cyclists at a roundabout. They travel at lower speeds and are more vulnerable than other road users, and may decide to stay in the left-hand lane whichever direction they're planning to take. Hold back and allow plenty of room.

❯ Other motorcyclists

As you'll know, motorcyclists can be hard to see because their vehicles are smaller than cars. They're usually fast-moving too, so they can be very vulnerable in a collision.

Remember to leave enough room while overtaking another motorcycle; the rider may swerve to avoid an uneven surface or be affected by a gust of wind. Look carefully for motorcyclists at junctions too, as they may be easily hidden by other vehicles, **street furniture** or other roadside features, such as trees.

street furniture
objects and pieces of equipment on roads and pavements; for example, street lights and signs, bus stops, benches, bollards, etc

Before you turn right, always check for other traffic, especially motorcyclists, who may be overtaking. Always use the 'lifesaver' look before making your manoeuvre.

`HC` r180

See the Think! road safety information about riding safely near motorcyclists.

> **http://think.direct.gov.uk/ motorcycles.html**

When you're moving in queues of traffic, be aware that other motorcyclists may also

- filter between lanes
- cut in just in front of you
- pass very close to you.

Keep checking your mirrors for motorcycles approaching from behind and give them space if possible.

If there's a slow-moving motorcyclist ahead and you're not sure what the rider is going to do, stay behind them in case they change direction suddenly.

`HC` r180 `RES` s9

If a motorcyclist is injured in an incident, get medical assistance. Don't remove their helmet unless it's essential.

`HC` r283 `RES` s16

If you have a collision, you **MUST** stop. By law, you **MUST** stop at the scene of the incident if damage or injury is caused to any other person, vehicle, animal or property.

HC r286 RES s16

> Animals

Horses and other animals can behave in unpredictable ways on the road because they get frightened by the noise and speed of vehicles. Always ride carefully if there are animals on the road.

- Stay well back.
- Don't rev your engine or sound your horn near horses as this may startle them.
- Go very slowly and be ready to stop.

When it's safe to overtake

- ride past slowly
- leave plenty of room.

HC r214–215 RES s10

Take extra care when approaching a roundabout. Horse riders, like cyclists, may keep to the left, even if they're signalling right. Stay well back.

HC r187, 215 RES s9

See the Think! road safety advice about horses on the road.

> **http://think.direct.gov.uk/horses.html**

 Drivers

Drivers, especially those who are inexperienced or older, may not react as quickly as you to what's happening on the road. Learner drivers and riders may make mistakes, such as stalling at a junction. Be patient and be ready to slow down or stop if necessary.

HC r216–217 **RES** s1

 A flashing amber beacon on the top of a vehicle means it's a slow-moving vehicle. A powered wheelchair or mobility scooter used by a disabled person **MUST** have a flashing amber light when travelling on a dual carriageway with a speed limit that exceeds 50 mph.

HC r220

If you find another vehicle is following you too closely in fast-moving traffic, slow down gradually to increase your distance from the vehicle in front. This gives you more room to slow down or stop if necessary, and so reduces the risk of the vehicle behind crashing into you because the driver hasn't left enough room to stop safely.

Learner riders and drivers, and newly qualified riders and drivers

Statistics show that 17- to 25-year-olds are the most likely to be involved in a road traffic incident. Over-confidence, lack of experience and poor judgement are the main causes of incidents for young and new drivers and riders.

Newly qualified riders can decrease their risk of being involved in road traffic incidents by taking further training; for example, under the enhanced rider scheme.
HC p134 **RES** s11

Find out more about the enhanced rider scheme at this website.

❯ **www.gov.uk**

Meeting the standards

You must be able to

look out for the effect of starting your engine near vulnerable road users. Passing cyclists or pedestrians may be affected

look for vulnerable road users at junctions, roundabouts and crossings. For example

- cyclists
- other motorcyclists
- horse riders.

You must know and understand

when other road users are vulnerable and how to allow for them

the rules that apply to vulnerable road users, like cyclists, and the position that they may select on the road as a result

how vulnerable road users may act on the road. For example

- cyclists may wobble
- children may run out
- older people may take longer to cross the road.

> Notes

You can use this page to make your own notes or diagrams about the key points you need to remember.

Think about

- Which types of pedestrian crossing might you see, and what are the differences between them?
- When might you need to watch out for children near the road?
- Which disability might a person have if they're walking with a dog that has a red and white checked harness?
- What might a cyclist be about to do if they're checking over their shoulder?
- What mustn't you do when riding near horses or other animals on the road?

Your notes

Things to discuss and practise with your trainer

These are just a few examples of what you could discuss and practise with your trainer. Read more about vulnerable road users to come up with your own ideas.

Discuss with your trainer

- which sticks are used by people with different disabilities, eg a white stick with a red band
- what you think a cyclist's experience of riding through traffic may be? How can you make them feel safer?
- where pedestrians may have to walk in the road and what you should look out for.

Practise with your trainer

- riding near schools at times when students and parents are likely to be arriving or leaving
- riding up to different types of crossing to practise how to respond to their users and any lights
- identifying the signs warning you of vulnerable road users, eg a red triangle with a picture of a bicycle. Discuss these after your lesson.

6.1
Mark one answer   RES s10, HC r222

Why should you keep a large gap between your motorcycle and a lorry in front?

☐ So you don't breathe in the lorry's exhaust fumes

☐ So wind from the lorry won't slow you down

☐ So drivers behind can see you

☑ So your view ahead isn't obstructed

If you follow a large vehicle too closely, your view beyond it will be restricted. Drop back. This will help you to see more of the road ahead. It will also help the driver of the large vehicle to see you in their mirrors and will give you a safe separation distance if the lorry needs to stop suddenly.

6.2
Mark one answer   RES s10, HC r214

You're riding on a country lane. What should you do if you come across cattle on the road?

☐ Ride up close behind them

☐ Rev your engine

☑ Give them plenty of room

☐ Sound your horn

Try not to startle the animals. They can be easily frightened by noise or by traffic passing too closely. Slow down, give them plenty of room and be prepared to stop if necessary. Obey any directions given by people in charge of the animals.

6.3
Mark one answer   RES s10

A learner driver begins to emerge into your path from a side road on the left. What should you do?

☑ Be ready to slow down and stop

☐ Let them emerge, then ride close behind

☐ Turn into the side road

☐ Brake hard, then wave them out

You should always be looking for vehicles emerging from side roads as you approach them. If you see another vehicle begin to emerge into your path, be ready to slow down or stop if necessary.

6.4
Mark one answer   RES s10, HC r204, 217

The vehicle ahead is being driven by a learner. What should you do?

☑ Keep calm and be patient

☐ Ride close behind

☐ Put your headlights on main beam

☐ Sound your horn and overtake

Learner drivers might take longer to react to traffic situations, so be patient and give them time. Don't unnerve them by riding close behind or showing signs of impatience.

6.5
Mark one answer
RES s8, HC r126

You're riding in fast-flowing traffic. The vehicle behind is following too closely. What should you do?

☑ Slow down gradually to increase the gap in front of you

☐ Slow down as quickly as possible by braking

☐ Accelerate to get away from the vehicle behind you

☐ Apply the brakes sharply to warn the driver behind

By increasing the separation distance between you and the vehicle in front, you have a greater safety margin. If the vehicle in front of you brakes suddenly to avoid a hazard, you'll have time to reduce speed gradually. This will reduce the risk of the close-following vehicle running into you.

6.6
Mark one answer
RES s8, HC r195

You're riding towards a zebra crossing. Waiting to cross is a person in a wheelchair. What should you do?

☐ Continue on your way

☐ Wave to the person to cross

☐ Wave to the person to wait

☑ Be prepared to stop

As you would with any pedestrian, you should prepare to stop. Don't wave the person across, as other traffic may not slow down.

6.7
Mark one answer
RES s12, HC r233

Why should you allow extra room when overtaking another motorcyclist on a windy day?

☐ The rider may turn off suddenly to get out of the wind

☑ The rider may be blown across in front of you

☐ The rider may stop suddenly

☐ The rider may be travelling faster than normal

On a windy day, be aware that the blustery conditions might blow you or other motorcyclists out of position. Think about this before deciding to overtake.

6.8
Mark one answer RES s8, HC r198

You've stopped at a pelican crossing, where a disabled person is crossing very slowly in front of you. What should you do when the lights change to green?

- ☑ Allow the person to finish crossing
- ☐ Edge forward slowly
- ☐ Ride behind the person
- ☐ Sound your horn

At a pelican crossing, the green light means you may proceed as long as the crossing is clear. If someone hasn't finished crossing, be patient and wait until the road is clear.

6.9
Mark one answer RES s9, HC r170

Where should you take particular care to look out for other motorcyclists and cyclists?

- ☐ On dual carriageways
- ☑ At junctions
- ☐ At zebra crossings
- ☐ On one-way streets

Other motorcyclists and cyclists may be difficult to see on the road, particularly at junctions. If your view is blocked by other traffic, you may not be able to see them approaching.

6.10
Mark one answer RES s8

Why is it vital for a rider to make a lifesaver check before turning right?

- ☑ To check for any overtaking traffic
- ☐ To confirm that they're about to turn
- ☐ To make sure the side road is clear
- ☐ To check that the rear indicator is flashing

The lifesaver glance makes you aware of what's happening behind and alongside you before you alter your course. This glance must be timed so that you still have time to react if it isn't safe to carry out your manoeuvre.

6.11
Mark one answer   RES s10, HC r214

You're about to overtake a group of horse riders. What's most likely to scare the horses?

☐ Your dipped headlights
☐ Giving arm signals
☐ Riding slowly
☑ Revving your engine

When passing horses, allow them plenty of space and slow down. Animals can be frightened by sudden or loud noises, so don't sound your horn or rev your engine.

6.12
Mark one answer   RES s1

Young and new motorcyclists are involved in more incidents than other motorcyclists. Why is this?

☐ They use borrowed equipment
☑ They lack experience and judgement
☐ They ride in bad weather conditions
☐ They don't maintain their motorcycles

Young and inexperienced motorcyclists are far more likely to be involved in incidents than more experienced riders. The reasons for this include natural exuberance, showing off, competitive behaviour and overconfidence. Don't overestimate your abilities and never ride too fast for the conditions.

6.13
Mark one answer   RES s1

What would make a young motorcyclist especially vulnerable?

☐ Wearing newer gear than experienced riders
☐ Having faster reactions than older riders
☑ Overestimating their own ability
☐ Getting cheap insurance

Young and inexperienced motorcyclists often have more confidence than ability. It takes time to gain experience and become a good rider. Make sure you have the right attitude and put safety first.

The road outside this school is marked with yellow zigzag lines. What do these lines mean?

Parking here will block the view of the road, endangering the lives of children crossing the road on their way to and from school.

☐ You may park on the lines when dropping off schoolchildren

☐ You may park on the lines when picking up schoolchildren

☑ You must not wait or park your motorcycle here

☐ You must stay with your motorcycle if you park here

Which sign means that there may be people walking along the road?

☐   ☐

☐   ☑

Always check the road signs. Triangular signs are warning signs: they inform you about hazards ahead and help you to anticipate any problems. There are a number of different signs showing pedestrians. Learn the meaning of each one.

6.16 | Mark one answer | RES s9, HC r170

You're turning left at a junction where pedestrians have started to cross. What should you do?

When you're turning into a side road, pedestrians who are crossing have priority. You should wait to allow them to finish crossing safely. Be patient if they're slow or unsteady. Don't try to rush them by sounding your horn, flashing your lights, revving your engine or giving any other inappropriate signal.

- ☐ Go around them, leaving plenty of room
- ☐ Stop and wave at them to cross
- ☐ Sound your horn and proceed
- ☑ Give way to them

6.17 | Mark one answer | RES s9, HC r170

You're turning left into a side road. What hazard should you be especially aware of?

- ☐ One-way street
- ☑ Pedestrians
- ☐ Traffic congestion
- ☐ Parked vehicles

Make sure that you've reduced your speed and are in the correct gear for the turn. Look into the road before you turn and always give way to any pedestrians who are crossing.

6.18 | Mark one answer | RES s9, HC r211

You intend to turn right into a side road. Why should you check for motorcyclists just before turning?

- ☐ They may be overtaking on your left
- ☐ They may be following you closely
- ☐ They may be emerging from the side road
- ☑ They may be overtaking on your right

Never attempt to change direction to the right without first checking your right-hand mirror and blind spot. A motorcyclist might not have seen your signal and could be hidden by other traffic. This observation should become a matter of routine.

6.19 | Mark one answer | RES s8, HC r25

Why is a toucan crossing different from other crossings?

- ☐ Moped riders can use it
- ☐ It's controlled by a traffic warden
- ☐ It's controlled by two flashing lights
- ☐ Cyclists can use it

Toucan crossings are shared by pedestrians and cyclists, who are permitted to cycle across. They're shown the green light together. The signals are push-button-operated and there's no flashing amber phase.

How will a school crossing patrol signal you to stop?

☐ By pointing to children on the opposite pavement

☐ By displaying a red light

☑ By displaying a 'stop' sign

☐ By giving you an arm signal

If a school crossing patrol steps out into the road with a 'stop' sign, you must stop. Don't wave anyone across the road and don't get impatient or rev your engine.

Where would you see this sign?

Vehicles that are used to carry children to and from school will be travelling at busy times of the day. If you're following a vehicle with this sign, be prepared for it to make frequent stops. It might pick up or set down passengers in places other than normal bus stops.

☐ In the window of a car taking children to school

☐ At the side of the road

☐ At playground areas

☑ On the rear of a school bus or coach

What does this sign mean?

This sign shows a shared route for pedestrians and cyclists: when it ends, the cyclists will be rejoining the main road.

☐ No route for pedestrians and cyclists

☐ A route for pedestrians only

☐ A route for cyclists only

☑ A route for pedestrians and cyclists

6.23   Mark one answer   RES s10, HC r207

You see a pedestrian carrying a white stick with a red band. What does this tell you?

☐ They have limited mobility

☐ They're deaf

☐ They're blind

☑ They're deaf and blind

When someone is deaf as well as blind, they may carry a white stick with a red reflective band. They may not be aware that you're approaching and they may not be able to hear anything; so, for example, your horn would be ineffective as a warning to them.

6.24   Mark one answer   RES s10, HC r207

What action would you take when elderly people are crossing the road?

Be aware that older people might take a long time to cross the road. They might also be hard of hearing and not hear you approaching. Don't hurry older people across the road by getting too close to them or revving your engine.

☐ Wave them across so they know that you've seen them

☑ Be patient and allow them to cross in their own time

☐ Rev the engine to let them know that you're waiting

☐ Tap the horn in case they're hard of hearing

6.25   Mark one answer   RES s10, HC r207

What should you do when you see two elderly pedestrians about to cross the road ahead?

Older people may have impaired hearing, vision, concentration and judgement. They may also walk slowly and so could take a long time to cross the road.

☐ Expect them to wait for you to pass

☐ Speed up to get past them quickly

☐ Stop and wave them across the road

☑ Be careful; they may misjudge your speed

6.26
Mark one answer
RES s9, HC r187

You're coming up to a roundabout. A cyclist is signalling to turn right. What should you do?

☐ Overtake on the right
☐ Give a warning with your horn
☐ Signal the cyclist to move across
☑ Give the cyclist plenty of room

If you're following a cyclist who's signalling to turn right at a roundabout, leave plenty of room. Give them space and time to get into the correct lane.

6.27
Mark one answer
RES s8, HC r163

Which of these should you allow extra room when overtaking?

☐ Lorry
☐ Tractor
☑ Bicycle
☐ Road-sweeping vehicle

Don't pass cyclists too closely, as they may

- need to veer around a pothole or other obstacle
- be buffeted by side wind
- be made unsteady by your vehicle.

Always leave as much room as you would for a car, and don't cut in front of them.

6.28
Mark one answer
RES s10, HC r211

Why should you look particularly for motorcyclists and cyclists at junctions?

☐ They may want to turn into the side road
☐ They may slow down to let you turn
☑ They're harder to see
☐ They might not see you turn

Cyclists and motorcyclists are smaller than other vehicles and so are more difficult to see. They can easily be hidden from your view by cars parked near a junction.

6.29
Mark one answer
RES s10, HC r211

You're waiting to come out of a side road. Why should you look carefully for motorcycles?

☐ Motorcycles are usually faster than cars
☐ Police patrols often use motorcycles
☑ Motorcycles can easily be hidden behind obstructions
☐ Motorcycles have right of way

If you're waiting to emerge from a side road, look carefully for motorcycles: they can be difficult to see. Be especially careful if there are parked vehicles or other obstructions restricting your view.

6.30 — Mark one answer — RES s4, HC r86

In daylight, an approaching motorcyclist is using dipped headlights. Why?

- ☑ So that the rider can be seen more easily
- ☐ To stop the battery overcharging
- ☐ To improve the rider's vision
- ☐ The rider is inviting you to proceed

A motorcycle can be lost from sight behind another vehicle. The use of the headlights helps to make it more conspicuous and therefore more easily seen.

6.31 — Mark one answer — RES s4, HC r86

Why should motorcyclists wear bright clothing?

- ☐ They must do so by law
- ☐ It helps keep them cool in summer
- ☐ The colours are popular
- ☑ Drivers often do not see them

Motorcycles and scooters are generally smaller than other vehicles and can be difficult to see. Wearing bright clothing makes it easier for other road users to see a motorcyclist approaching, especially at junctions.

6.32 — Mark one answer — RES s8, HC r211–213

You're unsure what a slow-moving motorcyclist ahead of you is going to do. What should you do?

- ☐ Pass on the left
- ☐ Pass on the right
- ☑ Stay behind
- ☐ Move closer

When a motorcyclist is travelling slowly, it's likely that they're looking for a turning or entrance. Be patient and stay behind them in case they stop or change direction suddenly.

6.33 — Mark one answer — RES s8, HC r212

Why will a motorcyclist look round over their right shoulder just before turning right?

- ☐ To listen for following traffic
- ☐ Motorcycles don't have mirrors
- ☐ It helps them balance as they turn
- ☑ To check for traffic in their blind area

When you see a motorcyclist take a glance over their shoulder, they're probably about to change direction. Recognising a clue like this helps you to anticipate their next action. This can improve road safety for you and others.

6.34

RES s10, HC r207, 211

Which is the most vulnerable road user at road junctions?

- [ ] Car driver
- [ ] Tractor driver
- [ ] Lorry driver
- [x] Motorcyclist

Pedestrians and riders on two wheels can be harder to see than other road users. Make sure you look for them, especially at junctions. Effective observation, coupled with appropriate action, can save lives.

6.35

Mark one answer

RES s9, HC r187, 215

You're approaching a roundabout. There are horses just ahead of you. What should you do?

- [ ] Sound your horn as a warning
- [ ] Treat them like any other vehicle
- [x] Give them plenty of room
- [ ] Accelerate past as quickly as possible

Horse riders often keep to the outside of the roundabout even if they're turning right. Give them plenty of room and remember that they may have to cross lanes of traffic.

6.36

Mark one answer

RES s8, HC r207

As you approach a pelican crossing, the lights change to green. What should you do if elderly people are halfway across?

- [ ] Wave them to cross as quickly as they can
- [ ] Rev your engine to make them hurry
- [ ] Flash your lights in case they haven't noticed you
- [x] Wait patiently because they'll probably take longer to cross

If the lights turn to green, wait for any pedestrians to clear the crossing. Allow them to finish crossing the road in their own time, and don't try to hurry them by revving your engine.

6.37

Mark one answer

RES s7, 8, 10, HC r208

There are flashing amber lights under a school warning sign. What action should you take?

- [x] Reduce speed until you're clear of the area
- [ ] Keep up your speed and sound the horn
- [ ] Increase your speed to clear the area quickly
- [ ] Wait at the lights until they change to green

The flashing amber lights are switched on to warn you that children may be crossing near a school. Slow down and take extra care, as you may have to stop.

6.38 Mark one answer RES s7, HC r208, 238, KYTS p56

Why must these road markings be kept clear?

☐ To allow schoolchildren to be dropped off

☐ To allow teachers to park

☐ To allow schoolchildren to be picked up

☑ To allow a clear view of the crossing area

The markings are there to show that the area must be kept clear. This is to allow an unrestricted view for

• approaching drivers and riders

• children wanting to cross the road.

6.39 Mark one answer HC p117

Where would you see this sign?

☐ Near a school crossing

☐ At a playground entrance

☑ On a school bus

☐ At a 'pedestrians only' area

Watch out for children crossing the road from the other side of the bus.

6.40 Mark one answer RES s9, HC r77, 187

You're following two cyclists. They approach a roundabout in the left-hand lane. In which direction should you expect the cyclists to go?

☐ Left

☐ Right

☑ Any direction

☐ Straight ahead

Cyclists approaching a roundabout in the left-hand lane may be turning right but may not have been able to get into the correct lane due to heavy traffic. They may also feel safer keeping to the left all the way around the roundabout. Be aware of them and give them plenty of room.

You're travelling behind a moped. What should you do when you want to turn left just ahead?

☐ Overtake the moped before the junction

☐ Pull alongside the moped and stay level until just before the junction

☐ Sound your horn as a warning and pull in front of the moped

☑ Stay behind until the moped has passed the junction

Passing the moped and turning into the junction could mean that you cut across the front of the rider. This might force them to slow down, stop or even lose control. Stay behind the moped until it has passed the junction and then you can turn without affecting the rider.

You see a horse rider as you approach a roundabout. What should you do if they're signalling right but keeping well to the left?

Allow the horse rider to enter and exit the roundabout in their own time. They may feel safer keeping to the left all the way around the roundabout. Don't get up close behind or alongside them, because that would probably upset the horse and create a dangerous situation.

☐ Proceed as normal

☐ Keep close to them

☐ Cut in front of them

☑ Stay well back

How would you react to drivers who appear to be inexperienced?

☐ Sound your horn to warn them of your presence

☑ Be patient and prepare for them to react more slowly

☐ Flash your headlights to indicate that it's safe for them to proceed

☐ Overtake them as soon as possible

Learners might not have confidence when they first start to drive. Allow them plenty of room and don't react adversely to their hesitation. We all learn from experience, but new drivers will have had less practice in dealing with all the situations that might occur.

6.44
Mark one answer
RES s1, HC r217

What should you do when you're following a learner driver who stalls at a junction?

☑ Be patient, as you expect them to make mistakes

☐ Stay very close behind and flash your headlights

☐ Start to rev your engine if they take too long to restart

☐ Immediately steer around them and drive on

Learning to drive is a process of practice and experience. Try to understand this and tolerate those who make mistakes while they're learning.

6.45
Mark one answer
RES s10, HC r5, 154

You're on a country road. What should you expect to see coming towards you on your side of the road?

☐ Motorcycles

☐ Bicycles

☑ Pedestrians

☐ Horse riders

On a quiet country road, always be aware that there may be a hazard just around the next bend, such as a slow-moving vehicle or pedestrians. Pedestrians are advised to walk on the right-hand side of the road if there's no pavement, so they may be walking towards you on your side of the road.

6.46
Mark one answer
RES s1, HC r216

What should you do when following a car driven by an elderly driver?

☐ Expect the driver to drive badly

☐ Flash your lights and overtake

☑ Be aware that their reactions may be slower than yours

☐ Stay very close behind but be careful

You must show consideration to other road users. The reactions of older drivers may be slower and they might need more time to deal with a situation. Be tolerant and don't lose patience or show annoyance.

You're following a cyclist. What should you do when you wish to turn left just ahead?

Make allowances for cyclists, and give them plenty of room. Don't overtake and then immediately turn left. Be patient and turn behind them when they've passed the junction.

- ☐ Overtake the cyclist before you reach the junction
- ☐ Pull alongside the cyclist and stay level until after the junction
- ☑ Hold back until the cyclist has passed the junction
- ☐ Go around the cyclist on the junction

A horse rider is in the left-hand lane approaching a roundabout. Where should you expect the rider to go?

- ☑ In any direction
- ☐ To the right
- ☐ To the left
- ☐ Straight ahead

Horses and their riders move more slowly than other road users. They might not have time to cut across heavy traffic to take up a position in the right-hand lane. For this reason, a horse and rider may approach a roundabout in the left-hand lane even though they're turning right.

Powered vehicles used by disabled people are small and hard to see. How do they give early warning when on a dual carriageway?

- ☐ They'll have a flashing red light
- ☐ They'll have a flashing green light
- ☐ They'll have a flashing blue light
- ☑ They'll have a flashing amber light

Powered vehicles used by disabled people are small, low, hard to see and travel very slowly. On a dual carriageway, a flashing amber light will warn other road users.

6.50

Mark one answer

RES s8, HC r182, 212

Where should you never overtake a cyclist?

☑ Just before you turn left

☐ On a left-hand bend

☐ On a one-way street

☐ On a dual carriageway

If you want to turn left and there's a cyclist in front of you, hold back. Wait until the cyclist has passed the junction and then turn left behind them. Don't try to intimidate them by driving too closely.

6.51

Mark one answer

HC r225

What does a flashing amber beacon mean when it's on a moving vehicle?

☑ The vehicle is slow moving

☐ The vehicle has broken down

☐ The vehicle is a doctor's car

☐ The vehicle belongs to a school crossing patrol

Different coloured beacons warn of different types of vehicle needing special attention. Blue beacons are used on emergency vehicles that need priority. Green beacons are found on doctors' cars. Amber beacons generally denote slower moving vehicles, which are often large. These vehicles are usually involved in road maintenance or local amenities and make frequent stops.

6.52

Mark one answer

HC p107, KYTS p35

What does this sign mean?

☐ Contraflow cycle lane

☑ With-flow cycle lane

☐ Cycles and buses only

☐ No cycles or buses

Usually, a picture of a cycle will also be painted on the road, and sometimes the lane will have a different coloured surface. Leave these areas clear for cyclists and don't pass too closely when you overtake.

You notice horse riders in front. What should you do first?

Be particularly careful when approaching horse riders – slow down and be prepared to stop. Always pass wide and slowly, and look out for signals given by the riders. Horses are unpredictable: always treat them as potential hazards and take great care when passing them.

☐ Pull out to the middle of the road

☑ Slow down and be ready to stop

☐ Accelerate around them

☐ Signal right

What's the purpose of these road markings?

These markings are found on the road outside schools. Don't stop or park on them, even to set down or pick up children. The markings are there to ensure that drivers, riders, children and other pedestrians have a clear view of the road in all directions.

☑ To ensure children have a clear view from the crossing area

☐ To enable teachers to have clear access to the school

☐ To ensure delivery vehicles have easy access to the school

☐ To enable parents to pick up or drop off children safely

The left-hand pavement is closed due to street repairs. What should you do?

☑ Watch out for pedestrians walking in the road

☐ Use your right-hand mirror more often

☐ Speed up to get past the roadworks more quickly

☐ Position close to the left-hand kerb

Where street repairs have closed off pavements, proceed carefully and slowly, as pedestrians might have to walk in the road.

6.56

Mark one answer

RES s10, HC r213

What should you do when you're following a motorcyclist along a road that has a poor surface?

- ☐ Drive closely so they can see you in their mirrors
- ☐ Overtake immediately to avoid delays
- ☑ Allow extra room in case they swerve to avoid potholes
- ☐ Allow the same room as normal to avoid wasting road space

To avoid being unbalanced, a motorcyclist might swerve to avoid potholes and bumps in the road. Be prepared for this and allow them extra space.

6.57

Mark one answer

HC p109, KYTS p36

What does this sign tell you?

- ☐ No cycling
- ☑ Cycle route ahead
- ☐ Cycle parking only
- ☐ End of cycle route

With people's concern today for the environment, cycle routes are being extended in our towns and cities.

Respect the presence of cyclists on the road and give them plenty of room if you need to pass.

6.58

Mark one answer

RES s9, HC r77, 187

You're approaching this roundabout and see the cyclist signal right. Why is the cyclist keeping to the left?

- ☐ It's a quicker route for the cyclist
- ☐ The cyclist is going to turn left instead
- ☐ The cyclist thinks The Highway Code doesn't apply to bicycles
- ☑ The cyclist is slower and more vulnerable

Cycling in today's heavy traffic can be hazardous. Some cyclists may not feel happy about crossing the path of traffic to take up a position in an outside lane. Be aware of this and understand that, although they're in the left-hand lane, the cyclist might be turning right.

Section six Questions

6.59
Mark one answer

RES s8, HC r195–199

What should you do when approaching this crossing?

- ☑ Prepare to slow down and stop
- ☐ Stop and wave the pedestrians across
- ☐ Speed up and pass by quickly
- ☐ Continue unless the pedestrians step out

Be courteous and prepare to stop. Don't wave people across, because this could be dangerous if another vehicle is approaching the crossing.

6.60
Mark one answer

RES s10, HC r207

You see a pedestrian with a dog wearing a yellow or burgundy coat. What does this indicate?

- ☐ The pedestrian is elderly
- ☐ The pedestrian is a dog trainer
- ☐ The pedestrian is colour-blind
- ☑ The pedestrian is deaf

Dogs trained to help deaf people have a yellow or burgundy coat. If you see one, you should take extra care, as the pedestrian may not be aware of vehicles approaching.

6.61
Mark one answer

RES s8, HC r25

Who may use toucan crossings?

- ☐ Motorcyclists and cyclists
- ☐ Motorcyclists and pedestrians
- ☐ Only cyclists
- ☑ Cyclists and pedestrians

There are some crossings where cycle routes lead cyclists to cross at the same place as pedestrians. These are called toucan crossings. Always look out for cyclists, as they're likely to be approaching faster than pedestrians.

6.62
Mark one answer

HC r178

Some junctions controlled by traffic lights have a marked area between two stop lines. What's this for?

- ☐ To allow taxis to position in front of other traffic
- ☐ To allow people with disabilities to cross the road
- ☐ To allow cyclists and pedestrians to cross the road together
- ☑ To allow cyclists to position in front of other traffic

These are known as advanced stop lines. When the lights are red (or about to become red), you should stop at the first white line. However, if you've crossed that line as the lights change, you must stop at the second line even if it means you're in the area reserved for cyclists.

6.63
Mark one answer

RES s8, HC r211–213

When you're overtaking a cyclist, you should leave as much room as you would give to a car. What's the main reason for this?

- ☐ The cyclist might speed up
- ☐ The cyclist might get off their bike
- ☑ The cyclist might swerve
- ☐ The cyclist might have to make a left turn

Before overtaking, assess the situation. Look well ahead to see whether the cyclist will need to change direction. Be especially aware of a cyclist approaching parked vehicles, as they'll need to alter course. Don't pass too closely or cut in sharply.

6.64
Mark one answer

RES s10, HC r214

What should you do when passing sheep on a road?

- ☐ Briefly sound your horn
- ☑ Go very slowly
- ☐ Pass quickly but quietly
- ☐ Herd them to the side of the road

Slow down and be ready to stop if you see animals in the road ahead. Animals are easily frightened by noise and vehicles passing too close to them. Stop if signalled to do so by the person in charge.

6.65
Mark one answer

HC r5

At night, you see a pedestrian wearing reflective clothing and carrying a bright red light. What does this mean?

- ☐ You're approaching roadworks
- ☑ You're approaching an organised walk
- ☐ You're approaching a slow-moving vehicle
- ☐ You're approaching a traffic danger spot

The people on the walk should be keeping to the left, but don't assume this. Pass carefully, making sure you have time to do so safely. Be aware that the pedestrians have their backs to you and may not know that you're there.

6.66
Mark one answer

HC p134

You've just passed your test. How can you reduce your risk of being involved in a collision?

- ☐ By always staying close to the vehicle in front
- ☐ By never going over 40 mph
- ☐ By staying in the left-hand lane on all roads
- ☑ By taking further training

New drivers and riders are often involved in a collision or incident early in their driving career. Due to a lack of experience, they may not react to hazards appropriately. Approved training courses are offered by driver and rider training schools for people who have passed their test but want extra training.

Case study practice – 6 Vulnerable road users

You live in a village and you're riding your motorcycle into town. As you leave the village, sheep are being herded across the road ahead.

Once in town, traffic is heavy. At a pelican crossing, amber lights are flashing and people are still crossing.

Later, you need to turn left into a side road where pedestrians are just beginning to cross.

Further along on your side of the road, there's a stationary refuse collection vehicle.

6.1 How should you behave as you leave the village?
Mark **one** answer

☐ Stop the motorcycle and wait until the animals have crossed
☐ Get off the motorcycle and wheel it past the animals
☐ Move slowly forward and ride through the herd
☐ Rev the engine to hurry the animals across

RES s10 **HC** r214

6.2 At the pelican crossing, what should you do?
Mark **one** answer

☐ Stop, but keep revving the engine to hurry the pedestrians up
☐ Stop and give way to the pedestrians crossing
☐ Keep moving slowly forward while the lights are flashing
☐ Keep going and ride slowly past the pedestrians

HC r196

6.3 What should you do at the left turn?

Mark **one** answer

☐ Get off and wheel the motorcycle on the pavement

☐ Indicate, then ride slowly round the pedestrians

☐ Flash your headlights and use the horn before turning

☐ Give way to the pedestrians crossing

RES s9 **HC** r170

6.4 What should you expect by the stationary vehicle?

Mark **one** answer

☐ Binmen

☐ Builders

☐ Cyclists

☐ Children

HC r225

6.5 What colour beacon does the vehicle at the end of your journey have?

Mark **one** answer

☐ Amber

☐ Red

☐ Blue

☐ Green

HC r225

Section seven

Other types of vehicle

In this section, you'll learn about

- different types of vehicles
- safety when riding towards or following other types of vehicle.

Other types of vehicle

When you're riding towards or following another type of vehicle, such as a bus or a lorry, you need to be aware of that vehicle's capabilities and how they differ from those of your motorcycle.

❯ Other motorcycles

Windy weather has a big effect on motorcyclists. Other motorcyclists can be blown into your path, so

- if you're overtaking another motorcyclist, allow extra room
- if a motorcyclist in front of you is overtaking a high-sided vehicle, keep well back, as they could be blown off course
- be particularly aware of other motorcyclists where there are side-wind warning signs.

HC r232–233, p109 **RES** s12

Side winds are likely to affect

- cyclists
- motorcyclists
- drivers towing caravans or trailers
- drivers of high-sided vehicles

more than car drivers. If you're following or overtaking, be aware that these vehicles might be blown off course, and give them extra room.

RES s12

Metal drain covers can become very slippery in wet weather and are particularly hazardous for two-wheeled vehicles. Take care to avoid uneven or slippery surfaces and watch out for other motorcyclists having to do so.

HC r213 **RES** s10

> Large vehicles

Large vehicles can make it difficult for you to see the road ahead. Keep well back if you're following a large vehicle, especially if you're planning to overtake. If another vehicle fills the gap you've left, drop back further. This will improve your view of the road ahead.

HC r164, 222 **RES** s8

Overtaking a large vehicle is risky because it takes more time to overtake than a car.

Keep well back until you can see that the road ahead is clear. This also helps the driver of the large vehicle to see you in their mirrors.

Never begin to overtake unless you're sure that you can complete the manoeuvre safely.

HC r164 **RES** s8, 12

In wet weather, large vehicles throw up a lot of spray. This can affect your view, and your vision, if your visor becomes smeared or dirty. Drop back further until you can see better. If the conditions make it difficult for you to see or be seen, use dipped headlights. If visibility is reduced to less than 100 metres (328 feet), you may use fog lights (if fitted).

If your visor or goggles mist up, stop and clean them to make sure that your vision isn't restricted before continuing.

HC r226 **RES** s11, 12

If you're riding downhill and a large vehicle coming uphill needs to move out to pass a parked car, slow down and give way if possible. It's much more difficult for large vehicles to stop and then start up again if they're going uphill.

RES s8

Stay well back and give large vehicles plenty of room as they approach or negotiate

- road junctions
- crossroads
- mini-roundabouts.

To get around a corner, long vehicles may need to move in the opposite direction to the one they're indicating. If they want to turn left, they may indicate left but move over to the right before making the turn, and vice versa.

HC r221 **RES** s9

If you're waiting to turn left from a minor road and a large vehicle is approaching from the right, think. It may seem as if there's time to turn but there could be an overtaking vehicle hidden from view.

 Buses

Bus drivers need to make frequent stops to pick up and set down passengers. If a bus pulls up at a bus stop, watch out for pedestrians who may get off and cross the road in front of or behind the bus. Be prepared to give way to a bus that's trying to move off from a bus stop, as long as it's safe to do so.

HC r223 **RES** s10

> Trams

Some cities have trams. Take extra care around them because they

- are very quiet
- move quickly
- can't steer to avoid you.

HC r223–224 **RES** s7, 8

In these cities there may be extra white light signals at some traffic lights, which are for tram drivers. When you're riding in an area where trams run, take care when crossing tram tracks, particularly in bad weather, as they can become very slippery.

RES s7, 8

> Powered vehicles used by disabled people

Powered vehicles used by disabled people, such as wheelchairs and mobility scooters, have a maximum speed limit of 8 mph (12 km/h) when used on the road.

HC r36, 220

Meeting the standards

You must be able to

look out for other road users and predict what they may do

monitor and manage your own reactions to other road users.

You must know and understand

the rules that apply to other road users and the positions they may select on the road as a result. For example

- drivers of large vehicles
- bus and coach drivers
- cyclists
- car drivers

the importance of predicting the actions of other road users, especially as many motorcycle crashes involve claims of 'I just didn't see you!' from others.

Notes

You can use this page to make your own notes or diagrams about the key points you need to remember.

Think about

- What conditions could make you or another motorcyclist swerve unexpectedly?
- When do you need to give large vehicles plenty of space?
- What should you watch out for when a bus has stopped at the side of the road?
- What do you need to be aware of when riding in an area that has trams?

Your notes

Things to discuss and practise with your trainer

These are just a few examples of what you could discuss and practise with your trainer. Read more about other types of vehicle to come up with your own ideas.

Discuss with your trainer

- how windy weather can affect the way that motorcyclists ride. What can you do to allow for this when you encounter another motorcyclist in these conditions?
- the maximum speed of powered wheelchairs and how you should behave when you need to overtake one
- how trams operate and what to look out for if you encounter a tram system.

Practise with your trainer

- how to behave when you're following a large vehicle, particularly at junctions and roundabouts
- overtaking large vehicles and noting how this differs from overtaking a car
- how to react to buses in a busy town centre.

Mark one answer RES s9, HC r221

You're riding behind a long vehicle. There's a mini-roundabout ahead. The vehicle is signalling left, but it's positioned to the right. What should you do?

☐ Sound your horn

☐ Overtake on the left

☑ Keep well back

☐ Flash your headlights

Long vehicles need more room than other vehicles to turn at junctions. The driver may take up a position that seems strange, but they have to do this to ensure their rear wheels don't mount the kerb as they turn. Don't overtake on the left – the driver won't expect you to be there and may not see you. Staying well back will also give you a better view ahead.

Mark one answer RES s7, HC r302

Why should you be careful when riding on roads where electric trams operate?

☑ They can't steer to avoid you

☐ They give off harmful exhaust fumes

☐ They're noisy and slow

☐ They can brake very quickly

Electric trams run on rails and can't deviate from the tracks. Keep a lookout for trams, as they move very quietly and can appear suddenly. Be particularly careful when crossing the rails – they can be very slippery, especially when wet.

Mark one answer RES s12, HC r213, p109, KYTS p12

You're about to overtake a slow-moving motorcyclist. Which one of these signs would make you take special care?

☑   ☐

☐   ☐

In windy weather, watch out for motorcyclists and also cyclists, as they can be blown sideways into your path. When you pass them, leave plenty of room and check their position in your mirror before pulling back in.

You're waiting to emerge left from a minor road. A large vehicle is approaching from the right. You have time to turn, but you should wait. Why?

☑ The large vehicle can easily hide an overtaking vehicle

☐ The large vehicle can turn suddenly

☐ The large vehicle is difficult to steer in a straight line

☐ The large vehicle can easily hide vehicles from the left

Large vehicles can hide other vehicles that are overtaking – especially motorcycles, which may be filtering past queuing traffic. You need to be aware of the possibility of hidden vehicles and not assume that it's safe to emerge.

You're following a long vehicle. As it approaches a crossroads, it signals left but moves out to the right. What should you do?

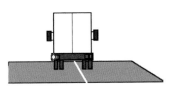

A long vehicle may need to swing out in the opposite direction as it approaches a turn, to allow the rear wheels to clear the kerb. Don't try to filter through if you see a gap; as the lorry turns, the gap will close.

☐ Get closer in order to pass it quickly

☑ Stay well back and give it room

☐ Assume the signal is wrong and that it's turning right

☐ Overtake it as it starts to slow down

You're following a long vehicle approaching a crossroads. The driver signals right but moves close to the left-hand kerb. What should you do?

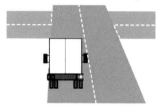

When a long vehicle is going to turn right, it may need to keep close to the left-hand kerb. This is to prevent the rear end of the trailer cutting the corner. You need to be aware of how long vehicles behave in such situations. Don't overtake the lorry, because it could turn as you're alongside. Stay behind and wait for it to turn.

☐ Warn the driver about the wrong signal

☑ Wait behind the long vehicle

☐ Report the driver to the police

☐ Overtake on the right-hand side

You're approaching a mini-roundabout. What should you do when you see the long vehicle in front signalling left but positioned over to the right?

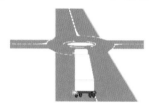

At mini-roundabouts, there isn't much room for a long vehicle to manoeuvre. It will have to swing out wide so that it can complete the turn safely. Keep well back and don't try to move up alongside it.

☐ Sound your horn

☐ Overtake on the left

☐ Follow the same course as the lorry

☑ Keep well back

7.8

Mark one answer RES s10, HC r164, 222

Before overtaking a large vehicle, you should keep well back. Why is this?

- ☐ To give acceleration space to overtake quickly on blind bends
- ☑ To get the best view of the road ahead
- ☐ To leave a gap in case the vehicle stops and rolls back
- ☐ To offer other drivers a safe gap if they want to overtake you

When following a large vehicle, keep well back. If you're too close, you won't be able to see the road ahead and the driver of the long vehicle might not be able to see you in their mirrors.

7.9

Mark one answer RES s10, HC r223

You're travelling behind a bus that pulls up at a bus stop. What should you do?

- ☐ Accelerate past the bus
- ☑ Watch carefully for pedestrians
- ☐ Sound your horn
- ☐ Pull in closely behind the bus

There might be pedestrians crossing from in front of the bus. Look out for them if you intend to pass. Consider how many people are waiting to get on the bus – check the queue if you can. The bus might move off straight away if no-one is waiting to get on.

If a bus is signalling to pull out, give it priority if it's safe to do so.

7.10

Mark one answer RES s10, HC r222, 227

You're following a lorry on a wet road. What should you do when spray makes it difficult to see the road ahead?

- ☑ Drop back until you can see better
- ☐ Put your headlights on full beam
- ☐ Keep close to the lorry, away from the spray
- ☐ Speed up and overtake quickly

Large vehicles throw up a lot of spray when it's wet. This makes it difficult for following drivers to see the road ahead. You'll be able to see more by dropping back further, out of the spray. This will also increase your separation distance, giving you more room to stop if you have to.

Mark one answer — RES s10, HC r164, 222

You keep well back while waiting to overtake a large vehicle. What should you do if a car moves into the gap?

☐ Sound your horn

☑ Drop back further

☐ Flash your headlights

☐ Start to overtake

Sometimes your separation distance is shortened by a driver moving into the gap you've allowed. When this happens, react positively, stay calm and drop further back to re-establish a safe following distance.

Mark one answer — RES s10, HC r223

What should you do when you're approaching a bus that's signalling to move away from a bus stop?

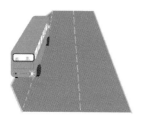

☐ Get past before it moves

☑ Allow it to pull away, if it's safe to do so

☐ Flash your headlights as you approach

☐ Signal left and wave the bus on

Try to give way to buses if you can do so safely, especially when the driver signals to pull away from a bus stop. Look out for people getting off the bus or running to catch it, because they may cross the road without looking. Don't accelerate to get past the bus, and don't flash your lights, as this could mislead other road users.

Mark one answer — RES s10, HC r164

How should you overtake a long, slow-moving vehicle on a busy road?

☐ Follow it closely and keep moving out to see the road ahead

☐ Flash your headlights for the oncoming traffic to give way

☐ Stay behind until the driver waves you past

☑ Keep well back until you can see that it's clear

When you're following a long vehicle, stay well back so that you can get a better view of the road ahead. The closer you get, the less you'll be able to see of the road. Be patient and don't take a gamble. Only overtake when you're certain that you can complete the manoeuvre safely.

7.14
Mark one answer RES s12, HC r232–233

Which of these is least likely to be affected by side winds?

☐ Cyclists

☐ Motorcyclists

☐ High-sided vehicles

☑ Cars

Although cars are the least likely to be affected, side winds can take anyone by surprise. This is most likely to happen after overtaking a large vehicle, when passing gaps between hedges or buildings, and on exposed sections of road.

7.15
Mark one answer RES s9, HC r221

What should you do as you approach this lorry?

When turning, long vehicles need much more room on the road than other vehicles. At junctions, they may take up the whole of the road space, so be patient and allow them the room they need.

☑ Slow down and be prepared to wait

☐ Make the lorry wait for you

☐ Flash your lights at the lorry

☐ Move to the right-hand side of the road

7.16
Mark one answer RES s9, HC r221

You're following a large vehicle approaching a crossroads. The driver signals to turn left. What should you do?

☐ Overtake if you can leave plenty of room

☐ Overtake only if there are no oncoming vehicles

☐ Don't overtake until the vehicle begins to turn

☑ Don't overtake as you approach or at the junction

Hold back and wait until the vehicle has turned before proceeding. Don't overtake, because the vehicle turning left could hide a vehicle emerging from the same junction.

What's the maximum speed of powered wheelchairs or scooters used by disabled people?

☑ 8 mph

☐ 12 mph

☐ 16 mph

☐ 20 mph

Some powered wheelchairs and mobility scooters are designed for use on the pavement only and cannot exceed 4 mph (6 km/h). Others can go on the road as well, and this category cannot exceed 8 mph (12 km/h). Take great care around these vehicles. They're extremely vulnerable because of their low speed and small size.

Why is it more difficult to overtake a large vehicle than a car?

☑ It will take longer to pass one

☐ It will be fitted with a speed limiter

☐ It will have air brakes

☐ It will be slow climbing hills

Depending on relative speed, it will usually take you longer to pass a lorry than other vehicles. Hazards to watch for include oncoming traffic, junctions ahead, bends or dips that could restrict your view, and signs or road markings that prohibit overtaking. Make sure you can see that it's safe to complete the manoeuvre before you start to overtake.

Case study practice – 7 Other types of vehicle

You travel to work in the town centre on your 1000 cc motorcycle. It's a dull, wet day.

There are many trams in town, and a bus is indicating to pull out from a bus stop.

At the first junction, you have to cross tramlines.

On the main high street, you see specifically shaped signs for tram drivers.

Ahead, you see a large vehicle indicating to turn left.

7.1 How can you improve your visibility in this weather?
Mark **one** answer

- ☐ By using main-beam headlights
- ☐ By using hazard warning lights
- ☑ By using dipped headlights
- ☐ By using front and rear fog lights

RES s4 **HC** r86

7.2 How should you react to the bus?
Mark **one** answer

- ☐ Rev the engine and sound the horn
- ☐ Keep going past but slow down a little
- ☐ Speed up quickly to get past the bus
- ☐ Allow it to pull out if it's safe to do so

HC r223

7.3 Why should you take care at the first junction?

Mark **one** answer

- ☐ The tyres could get stuck between the tracks
- ☑ The lines could be very slippery
- ☐ The motorcycle's tyres could stick to the metal
- ☐ The gaps in the lines could be full of water

RES s8 **HC** r306

7.4 What shape are the signs you see?

Mark **one** answer

- ☐ Triangle
- ☑ Diamond
- ☐ Hexagon
- ☐ Rectangle

KYTS p31

7.5 What might the large vehicle do next?

Mark **one** answer

- ☑ Pull a little over to the right
- ☐ Use the horn to warn others
- ☐ Pull a little over to the left
- ☐ Run over the pavement area

RES s9 **HC** r170, 221

Section eight

Road conditions and motorcycle handling

In this section, you'll learn about

- how to ride safely in different weather conditions
- riding at night
- keeping control of your motorcycle
- traffic-calming measures and different road surfaces.

Road conditions and motorcycle handling

As well as being aware of other road users, you need to think about the conditions you're riding in and how they might affect your safety. The weather, the time of day, hills, traffic calming and different road surfaces can all change the way you need to ride.

> Weather conditions

The weather makes a big difference to how you ride and how your motorcycle will handle.

Rain and wet conditions

When it's raining or the road is wet, leave at least double the normal stopping distance between you and the vehicle in front. If you're following a vehicle at a safe distance and another vehicle pulls into the gap you've left, drop back until you're at a safe distance again. See section 4, Safety margins, for more information on stopping distances.

If visibility becomes seriously reduced, you **MUST** use dipped headlights. 'Seriously reduced' means you can't see for more than about 100 metres (328 feet).

HC r226 **RES** s12

When there's been heavy rainfall, a ford is likely to flood and become difficult to cross. There may be a depth gauge to help you decide whether you should go through. If you decide to cross it

- use a low gear
- ride through slowly
- test your brakes afterwards: wet brakes are less effective.

HC r121 **RES** s12

Fog

When visibility is seriously reduced, you **MUST** use headlights and you may also use fog lights if you have them.

Remember to switch off your fog lights when conditions improve. Never use front or rear fog lights unless visibility is seriously reduced because

- they can dazzle other road users
- road users behind you won't be able to see your brake lights clearly, so they may not react in time to stop safely
- road users behind you may mistake your fog lights for brake lights and slow unnecessarily.

It's hard to see what's happening ahead in foggy weather, so always keep your speed down. Increase your distance from the vehicle in front in case it stops or slows suddenly.

HC r114, 226 **RES** s11, 12

Always allow more time for your journey in bad weather.

When riding on motorways in fog, reflective studs help you to see the road ahead.

- Red studs mark the left-hand edge of the carriageway.
- Amber studs mark the central reservation.

For more details, see section 9, Motorway riding.

HC r132 **RES** s7, 11

If you're parking on the road in foggy conditions, leave the parking lights switched on.

Very bad weather

In very bad weather, such as heavy snow or thick fog, don't travel unless your journey is essential. If you must travel, take great care and allow plenty of time.

Before you start your journey, make sure

- your lights are working
- your screen (if fitted) and visor are clean.

HC r228–235 **RES** s11, 12

When you're on the road, keep well back from the vehicle in front in case it stops suddenly. In icy conditions your stopping distance can be 10 times what it would be in dry conditions.

If the road looks wet and your tyres are making hardly any noise, you could be on black ice. Keep your speed down and use the highest gear possible to reduce the risk of skidding.

See this website for advice on riding in extreme weather conditions.

- **bikesafe.co.uk/advice-centre/ winter-riding**

Windy weather

Windy weather can affect all vehicles, but high-sided vehicles, cyclists, motorcyclists and cars towing caravans are likely to be the worst affected. A sudden gust may catch your motorcycle when you're

- passing a large vehicle on a dual carriageway or motorway
- riding on an exposed stretch of road
- passing gaps between buildings or hedges.

Look out for other vehicles that may also be affected by the wind and make allowances for them.

HC r232 **RES** s11, 12

Riding at night

When you're riding at night, you need to think about how clearly you can see and be seen, as well as how your lights might affect other road users.

Make sure that your headlights don't dazzle the vehicle you're following or any oncoming traffic. If you're dazzled by the headlights of an oncoming vehicle, slow down or stop if necessary.

HC r114–115 **RES** s13

 If you meet other road users at night, including cyclists and pedestrians, dip your headlights so that you don't dazzle them.

When you overtake at night, you can't see a long way ahead and there may be bends in the road or other unseen hazards.

On a motorway, use

- dipped headlights, even if the road is well lit
- sidelights if you've broken down and are parked on the hard shoulder. This will help other road users to see you.

RES s11, 12, 13

Keeping control of your motorcycle

For safety, before starting your engine, push the motorcycle forward to check that the rear wheel turns freely: this shows that the gear selector is in neutral. Check that the neutral light on your instrument panel is showing too.

Apply the front brake before you get on the motorcycle. If you're parked on a two-way road, you should get on from the left.

When you're astride your motorcycle, you should be able to put both feet on the ground comfortably, to support yourself and your machine. Never ride with the side stand in the down position – this can be dangerous, especially when cornering. Always fold the stand away safely before setting off.

Once you're moving, the normal riding position should be about central in the lane you're using. Try not to look down at the front wheel as this can affect your balance.

RES s6

You need to have full control of your motorcycle at all times. Riding with the clutch disengaged or in neutral for any length of time (called coasting) reduces your control of the motorcycle, especially steering and braking. This is particularly dangerous when you're travelling downhill, as your motorcycle will speed up when there's no engine braking.

HC r122 **RES** s6, 8

Definition

engine braking
using the engine's resistance to help slow the vehicle

You can use your motorcycle's engine to help control your speed: for example, if you select a lower gear when you're riding down a steep hill, the engine will act as a brake. This helps avoid your brakes overheating and becoming less effective.

When you're riding up a steep hill, the engine has to work harder. If you close the throttle to reduce speed, you'll slow down sooner than usual. Changing down to a lower gear will help prevent the engine struggling as it delivers the power needed to climb the hill.

RES s8

On single-track roads, be aware of the limited space available. If you see a vehicle coming towards you, pull into (or opposite) a passing place.

HC r155

See the Don't Risk It website for advice on riding on country roads.

❯ **dontriskit.info/country-roads**

Always match your riding to the road and weather conditions. Your stopping distance will be affected by several factors, including

- your speed
- the condition of your tyres
- the road surface
- the weather.

HC r155 **RES** s8, 10

When riding normally, you should brake when the motorcycle is upright and moving in a straight line. Apply both brakes smoothly, the front brake just before the rear brake. If your motorcycle has linked brakes, check the motorcycle handbook for more details.

When stopping in an emergency, or on a wet road, there's an increased risk of skidding. Try to avoid braking so hard that you cause a skid, as it can be hard to get your motorcycle back under control once you've started skidding.

The main causes of a motorcycle skidding are

- changing direction suddenly or travelling too fast
- too much acceleration
- heavy or sharp braking
- any combination of the above.

If you don't have anti-lock brakes and your motorcycle begins to skid when you're braking on a wet road

- release the brake(s) causing the skid to allow the wheel(s) to turn
- re-apply the brakes, but avoid braking so hard that you skid again.

HC r119 **RES** s6, 8, 10

Traffic calming and road surfaces

Traffic calming is used to slow traffic and make the roads safer for vulnerable road users, especially pedestrians. One of the most common measures is road humps (sometimes called speed humps). Make sure that you stay within the speed limit and don't overtake other moving vehicles within traffic-calmed areas.

HC r153 **RES** s7

Rumble devices (raised markings across the road) may be used to warn you of a hazard, such as a roundabout, and to encourage you to reduce your speed.

KYTS p68, 75

In cities where trams operate, the areas used by the trams may have a different surface texture or colour, which may be edged with white line markings.

HC r300 **KYTS** p31

If it rains after a long, dry hot spell, the road surface can become unusually slippery. Loose chippings can also increase the risk of skidding, so slow down and be aware of the increased skid risk in these conditions.

HC r237 **RES** s12

Painted road markings, tar banding, tram rails and drain covers can all become very slippery in wet weather. Keep your motorcycle upright and avoid braking while riding over them. If this isn't possible, take great care as your tyres have very little grip on these surfaces.

Spilt diesel fuel is very slippery. It spills from overfilled fuel tanks and poorly fitting or missing filler caps. It's often found near filling stations, at roundabouts and on bends. If you see a rainbow pattern on the road surface, slow down in good time and avoid the area if possible.

HC r213, 306 **RES** s8, 12

Some motorcycles are fitted with traction control systems (TCS), which help to prevent the rear wheel spinning while accelerating. Slippery surfaces increase the risk of this happening.

Meeting the standards

You must be able to

use the throttle smoothly to reach and keep to a suitable speed

change gear smoothly and in good time

coordinate

- steering
- leaning
- the use of the brakes
- the use of the throttle

steer the machine safely and responsibly in all road and traffic conditions.

You must know and understand

why it's best not to over-rev your engine when moving away and while stationary

the benefits of changing gear at the right time when going up and down hills

that different machines may have different numbers of gears with different ratios

how to change the direction of the machine by coordinating

- throttle
- lean
- steering input.

Notes

You can use this page to make your own notes or diagrams about the key points you need to remember.

Think about

- By how much must visibility be reduced before you can use fog lights?
- Why must you make sure that your fog lights are turned off when visibility improves again?
- In which weather conditions should you increase the distance between your motorcycle and the vehicle in front?
- Which road users are most likely to be affected by very windy weather?
- When can you use engine braking, and why is it a good idea?
- What are rumble devices used for?

Your notes

Things to discuss and practise with your trainer

These are just a few examples of what you could discuss and practise with your trainer. Read more about road conditions and motorcycle handling to come up with your own ideas.

Discuss with your trainer
- your stopping distances in different weather conditions
- how to use your front and back brakes in different situations and weather conditions
- what you should do if you get a sudden puncture.

Practise with your trainer
- positioning your motorcycle correctly in various situations, eg when turning right or left, and riding straight ahead
- going out at night to get used to riding with reduced visibility
- your gear selection and clutch control while riding downhill.

What safety measure should you take before starting a motorcycle engine?

☑ Check that the neutral lamp shows when the ignition is switched on

☐ Select first gear and apply the rear brake lightly

☐ Select first gear and apply the front brake firmly

☐ Check that your dipped headlights and tail light are on

Before starting the engine, make sure the motorcycle is in neutral. Do this by checking that the neutral warning light is lit when you switch on the ignition. If no neutral light is fitted, push the motorcycle forward to check that the rear wheel turns freely.

You're the motorcyclist approaching this junction. What should you do?

Look out for road signs warning of side roads, even if you aren't turning off. A driver who's emerging may not be able to see you due to parked cars or heavy traffic. Slow down and be prepared to stop if necessary. Remember, no-one has priority at an unmarked crossroads.

☐ Stop, as the car has right of way

☑ Slow down and be ready to stop

☐ Dip your headlights and keep near the left-hand kerb

☐ Speed up to clear the junction without delay

What can motorcyclists do to improve their safety on the road?

☑ Anticipate the actions of others

☐ Stay just above the speed limit

☐ Keep positioned close to the kerb

☐ Remain well below the speed limit

Always ride defensively. This means looking and planning ahead, as well as anticipating the actions of other road users.

What can cause skidding?

☐ Braking too gently

☐ Feathering the throttle

☐ Staying upright when cornering

☑ Braking too hard

To keep control of your motorcycle and prevent skidding, you should plan well ahead and avoid late, harsh braking. Try to avoid braking while changing direction, as the tyres may not have enough grip to cope with both together. Always consider how the road and weather conditions may affect your tyres' grip.

It's very cold and the road looks wet. What should you do if you can't hear any road noise as you ride?

☐ Continue riding at the same speed

☑ Ride slowly in as high a gear as possible

☐ Ride in as low a gear as possible

☐ Brake sharply to see if the road is slippery

Frozen rain on the road is called black ice. It can be hard to see, but it can be indicated by a lack of road noise and your steering may also feel very light. Reduce your speed and avoid harsh braking or steering. Riding in as high a gear as possible can help reduce the risk of wheelspin.

When should you wear full protective clothing while riding a motorcycle?

☑ At all times

☐ Only on faster, open roads

☐ Just on long journeys

☐ Only during bad weather

Protective clothing is designed to protect you from the cold and wet. It also gives you some protection from injury, so it's important that you always wear protective clothing when you ride.

What should you do before you start a journey in foggy conditions?

☐ Make sure that you have a spare visor with you

☐ Make sure that you have a warm drink with you

☑ Check that your lights are working

☐ Check that the battery is fully charged

It's best to avoid riding in foggy weather. However, if you have to, there are some precautions you can take before setting off to help make your journey as safe as possible. These include checking that all your lights are clean and working, and that your visor is clean.

Mark one answer RES s8

Where's the best place to park your motorcycle?

☐ On soft tarmac

☐ On bumpy ground

☐ On grass

☑ On firm, level ground

Parking your motorcycle on soft ground might cause the stand to sink in, and the machine could fall over. The ground should be level, as well as firm, to keep the motorcycle stable. Use off-road parking or motorcycle parking areas when they're available.

Mark one answer RES s12

What should you do when riding in windy conditions?

☐ Stay close to large vehicles

☐ Keep your speed up

☑ Keep your speed down

☐ Stay close to the gutter

Strong winds can blow a motorcycle off course, and even across the road. In windy conditions, you need to slow down and avoid riding on exposed roads. You should also watch for gaps in buildings and hedges, where you may be affected by a sudden gust of wind.

Mark one answer RES s8

On the road, what should be your normal riding position?

☐ Close to the kerb

☑ In the centre of your lane

☐ On the right of your lane

☐ Near the centre of the road

When you're riding a motorcycle, it's very important to ride where other road users can see you. In normal weather, you should ride in the centre of your lane. This will help you avoid uneven road surfaces in the gutter, and allow others to overtake on the right if they wish.

Mark one answer RES s6

Your motorcycle is parked on a two-way road. How should you get on the machine?

☐ From the right and apply the rear brake

☐ From the left and leave the brakes alone

☑ From the left and apply the front brake

☐ From the right and leave the brakes alone

When you get onto a motorcycle, you should get on from the left side to avoid putting yourself in danger from passing traffic. You should also apply the front brake to prevent the motorcycle from rolling either forwards or backwards.

8.12   Mark one answer   RES s2

How should you gain basic skills in motorcycle riding?

☑ Practise off-road with an approved training body

☐ Ride on the road on the first dry day

☐ Practise off-road in a public park or in a quiet cul-de-sac

☐ Ride on the road as soon as possible

All new motorcyclists must complete a course of basic training with an approved training body before going on the road. This training is given on a site that's been authorised by the Driver and Vehicle Standards Agency as being suitable for off-road training.

8.13   Mark one answer   RES s6

What will happen if you ride with your clutch lever pulled in for longer than is necessary?

☐ It will increase wear on the gearbox

☐ It will increase petrol consumption

☑ It will reduce your control of the motorcycle

☐ It will reduce the grip of the tyres

Riding with the clutch lever pulled in is known as coasting. If you coast, you lose the benefits of engine braking and you'll have reduced control of your motorcycle.

8.14   Mark one answer   RES s8

You're approaching a road with a surface of loose chippings. What should you do?

☐ Ride normally

☐ Speed up

☑ Slow down

☐ Stop suddenly

The handling of your motorcycle will be greatly affected by the road surface. Look well ahead and be especially alert if the road looks uneven or has loose chippings. Slow down in good time, as braking harshly in these conditions will cause you to skid. For the same reason, avoid making sudden changes of direction.

8.15   Mark one answer   RES s12, HC r237

It rains after a long, dry, hot spell. How can this affect the road surface?

☑ It can become unusually slippery

☐ It can give better grip

☐ It can become covered in grit

☐ It can melt and break up

Oil and rubber can build up on the road during long spells of dry weather. When it rains, this can make the road surface very slippery.

Mark one answer RES s8

What's most likely to cause a motorcycle to skid?

☑ Riding in wet weather

☐ Catching your foot on the ground

☐ Cornering too fast

☐ Riding in the winter

Skids are a lot easier to get into than they are to get out of. Riding at a suitable speed for the conditions, planning, looking ahead for hazards and braking in good time will all help you to avoid skidding or losing control.

Mark one answer RES s6

Your motorcycle doesn't have linked brakes. In an emergency, what should you do to stop quickly?

☐ Apply the rear brake only

☐ Apply the front brake only

☑ Apply the front brake just before the rear brake

☐ Apply the rear brake just before the front brake

You should plan ahead to avoid the need to stop suddenly, but if an emergency arises, you must be able to stop safely. Applying the front brake just before the rear brake will help you to stop safely and quickly.

Mark one answer RES s6

What will happen if you look down at the front wheel while riding?

☐ It will make your steering lighter

☐ It will improve your balance

☐ You'll use less fuel

☑ You'll upset your balance

When riding, look ahead and around you. Don't look down at the front wheel, as this can severely upset your balance.

Mark one answer RES s6

In normal riding conditions, how should you brake?

☐ By using the rear brake first and then the front

☐ When the motorcycle is being turned or ridden through a bend

☐ By pulling in the clutch before using the front brake

☑ When the motorcycle is upright and moving in a straight line

A motorcycle is most stable when it's upright and moving in a straight line. This is the best time to brake. With independent front and rear brakes, both brakes should be used, with the front brake being applied just before the rear brake.

ction eight** Questions

8.20 — Mark one answer — RES s8, HC r126

Which of these will affect the stopping distance of your motorcycle?

- [ ] The drive-chain adjustment
- [x] The condition of the tyres
- [ ] The time of day
- [ ] The street lighting

Tyres are a major factor in the handling, stability and stopping distance of a motorcycle. Make sure they're in a safe and legal condition. The weather and road surface also play a part. Always anticipate well ahead and take account of the conditions when you're braking.

8.21 — Mark one answer — RES s11

You're on a motorway at night. In which situation may you have your headlights switched off?

- [ ] When there are vehicles close in front of you
- [ ] When you're travelling below 50 mph
- [ ] When the motorway is lit
- [x] When your motorcycle is broken down on the hard shoulder

Always use your headlights at night on a motorway, unless you've had to stop on the hard shoulder. If you have to use the hard shoulder, switch off your headlights but leave your parking lights on, so that your motorcycle can be seen by other road users.

8.22 — Mark one answer — RES s12

You have to park on the road in fog. What should you do?

- [x] Leave parking lights on
- [ ] Leave no lights on
- [ ] Leave dipped headlights on
- [ ] Leave main-beam headlights on

If you have to park on the road in foggy conditions, it's important that your motorcycle can be seen by other road users. Try to find a place to park off the road. If this isn't possible, leave your motorcycle facing in the same direction as the traffic. Make sure that your lights are clean and leave your parking lights on.

8.23 — Mark one answer — RES s15

You ride over broken glass and get a puncture. What should you do?

- [x] Close the throttle and roll to a stop
- [ ] Brake to a stop as quickly as possible
- [ ] Release your grip on the handlebars
- [ ] Steer from side to side to keep your balance

Your motorcycle will be very unstable if a tyre bursts. Try to keep a straight course and stop as gently as possible.

247

Spilt fuel on the road can be very dangerous for a motorcyclist. How can this hazard be seen?

☑ By a rainbow-coloured pattern on the road surface

☐ By a series of skid marks on the road surface

☐ By a pitted road surface

☐ By a highly polished road surface

This rainbow-coloured pattern can be seen much more easily on a wet road. You should avoid riding over spilt fuel if possible. If you have to go over it, do so with extreme caution, knowing the surface will be slippery.

Which type of road surface increases the risk of skidding for motorcyclists?

☑ Tar banding

☐ Dry tarmac

☐ Concrete

☐ Asphalt

When riding, it's important to look for

- potholes
- drain covers (especially when they're wet)
- tar banding
- oily and greasy surfaces
- road markings
- tram tracks
- wet mud and leaves.

Keen observation will give you more time to brake or change course if you need to avoid these slippery surfaces.

You're riding on a wet road. What technique should you use when braking?

☐ Apply the rear brake well before the front brake

☑ Apply the front brake just before the rear brake

☐ Avoid using the front brake at all

☐ Avoid using the rear brake at all

On wet roads, you'll need to brake earlier and more smoothly than on dry roads. Always try to brake when the motorcycle is upright. This is particularly important in wet conditions.

8.27 — Mark one answer — RES s8

The road is wet. You're passing a line of queuing traffic and riding on the painted road markings. What should you take particular care in doing?

- ☐ Signalling
- ☑ Braking
- ☐ Carrying a passenger
- ☐ Checking your mirrors

When they're wet, painted road markings can be more slippery than the normal road surface. Other road-surface hazards that become slippery when wet include drain covers, leaves and mud. Take extra care when braking or cornering on these wet surfaces.

8.28 — Mark one answer — RES s8

Why should you be careful when crossing tram lines?

- ☐ Tram lines are always 'live'
- ☐ Trams will be stopping here
- ☐ Pedestrians will be crossing here
- ☑ The steel rails can be slippery

The smooth steel surface can be slippery and dangerous for motorcyclists, especially when it's wet. Try to cross tram lines at right angles.

8.29 — Mark one answer — RES s8

You have to brake sharply and your motorcycle starts to skid. What should you do?

- ☐ Continue braking and select a low gear
- ☐ Apply the brakes harder for better grip
- ☐ Select neutral and use the front brake only
- ☑ Release and reapply the brakes

If you skid as a result of braking harshly, you need to ease off the brakes to stop the skid. You should then reapply them progressively to stop.

8.30 — Mark one answer — RES s8

You see a rainbow-coloured pattern on the road. What will this warn you of?

- ☐ A soft, uneven road surface
- ☐ A polished road surface
- ☑ Fuel spilt on the road
- ☐ Water on the road

If fuel, especially diesel, is spilt on the road, it will make the surface very slippery. In wet weather, it can be seen as a rainbow-coloured pattern on the road.

Traction control systems (TCS) are fitted to some motorcycles. What do they help to prevent?

☑ Wheelspin when accelerating

☐ Skidding when braking too hard

☐ Uneven front tyre wear

☐ Uneven rear tyre wear

TCS helps to prevent the rear wheel from spinning, especially when accelerating on a slippery surface.

Braking too hard has caused both wheels to skid. What should you do?

☑ Release both brakes together

☐ Release the front brake, then the rear brake

☐ Release the front brake only

☐ Release the rear brake only

Braking too hard will cause a skid. Release the brakes immediately to allow the wheels to turn, then reapply them as firmly as the road surface and conditions will allow.

Your motorcycle doesn't have linked brakes. What should you do when braking normally to a stop?

☐ Apply only the front brake

☐ Apply only the rear brake

☑ Apply both brakes smoothly

☐ Apply either of the brakes gently

In normal riding, you should always use both brakes. Braking when the motorcycle is upright and travelling in a straight line helps you to keep control. If your motorcycle has linked brakes, refer to the vehicle handbook.

You're sitting on a stationary motorcycle and checking your riding position. What should you be able to do?

☐ Just touch the ground with your toes

☑ Place both feet on the ground

☐ Operate the centre stand

☐ Adjust your mirrors by stretching

When sitting astride a stationary motorcycle, you should be able to place both feet on the ground. This should enable you to keep your balance while using one foot to operate the foot controls.

8.35
Mark one answer RES s12, HC r237

It's been raining after a long dry spell. How will this affect the road surface?

- [ ] It will be rough
- [ ] It will be flooded
- [ ] It will be sticky
- [x] It will be slippery

During a long spell of hot, dry weather, the road surface will become coated with rubber and dust. When it rains after this, the road surface will be unusually slippery. Take extra care, particularly at junctions, bends and roundabouts, and allow double the usual stopping distance.

8.36
Mark one answer RES s6

Riding with the side stand down could cause you to crash. When is this most likely to happen?

Cornering with the side stand down could lead to a serious crash. Many motorcycles have a device that stops the engine if you try to ride off with the side stand down, but don't rely on this.

- [ ] When you're going uphill
- [ ] When you're accelerating
- [ ] When you're braking
- [x] When you're cornering

8.37
Mark one answer RES s8, HC r143

When may you overtake another vehicle on the left?

- [x] When you're in a one-way street
- [ ] When approaching a motorway slip road where you'll be turning off
- [ ] When the vehicle in front is signalling to turn left
- [ ] When a slower vehicle is travelling in the right-hand lane of a dual carriageway

You may pass slower vehicles on their left while travelling along a one-way street. Be aware of drivers who may need to change lanes and may not expect faster traffic passing on their left.

You're travelling in very heavy rain. How is this likely to affect your overall stopping distance?

☑ It will be doubled

☐ It will be halved

☐ It will be ten times greater

☐ It will be no different

The road will be very wet and spray from other vehicles will reduce your visibility. Tyre grip will also be reduced, increasing your stopping distance. You should at least double your separation distance.

What should you do when you're overtaking at night?

☐ Wait until a bend so that you can see oncoming headlights

☐ Sound your horn twice before moving out

☐ Put your headlights on full beam

☑ Beware of bends in the road ahead

Don't overtake if there's a possibility of a road junction, bend or brow of a bridge or hill ahead. There are many hazards that are difficult to see in the dark. Only overtake if you're certain that the road ahead is clear. Don't take a chance.

When may you wait in a box junction?

The purpose of a box junction is to keep the junction clear by preventing vehicles from stopping in the path of crossing traffic.

You mustn't enter a box junction unless your exit is clear. However, you may enter the box and wait if you want to turn right and are only prevented from doing so by oncoming traffic.

☐ When you're stationary in a queue of traffic

☐ When approaching a pelican crossing

☐ When approaching a zebra crossing

☑ When oncoming traffic prevents you turning right

Which of these plates normally appears with this road sign?

☑ Humps for ½ mile

☐ Hump Bridge

☐ Low Bridge

☐ Soft Verge

Road humps are used to slow down traffic. They're found in places where there are often pedestrians, such as

- shopping areas
- near schools
- residential areas.

Watch out for people close to the kerb or crossing the road.

What do traffic-calming measures do?

☐ Stop road rage

☐ Make overtaking easier

☑ Slow traffic down

☐ Make parking easier

Traffic-calming measures make the roads safer for vulnerable road users, such as cyclists, pedestrians and children. These can be designed as chicanes, road humps or other obstacles that encourage drivers and riders to slow down.

You're on a motorway in fog. The left-hand edge of the motorway can be identified by reflective studs. What colour are they?

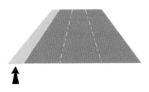

☐ Green

☐ Amber

☑ Red

☐ White

Be especially careful if you're on a motorway in fog. Reflective studs are there to help you in poor visibility. Different colours are used so that you'll know which lane you're in. These are

- red on the left-hand edge of the carriageway
- white between lanes
- amber on the right-hand edge of the carriageway
- green between the carriageway and slip roads.

What's a rumble device designed to do?

- [ ] Give directions
- [ ] Prevent cattle escaping
- [ ] Alert you to low tyre pressure
- [x] Alert you to a hazard

A rumble device consists of raised markings or strips across the road, designed to give drivers an audible, visual and tactile warning. These devices are used in various locations, including in the line separating the hard shoulder and the left-hand lane on the motorway and on the approach to some hazards, to alert drivers to the need to slow down.

What should you do when making a journey in foggy conditions?

- [ ] Follow other vehicles' tail lights closely
- [ ] Avoid using dipped headlights
- [x] Leave plenty of time for your journey
- [ ] Keep two seconds behind the vehicle ahead

If you're planning to make a journey when it's foggy, listen to the weather reports. If visibility is very poor, avoid making unnecessary journeys. If you do travel, leave plenty of time – and if someone is waiting for you to arrive, let them know that your journey will take longer than normal. This will also take off any pressure you may feel to rush.

What must you do when overtaking a car at night?

- [ ] Flash your headlights before overtaking
- [ ] Select a higher gear
- [ ] Switch your lights to full beam before overtaking
- [x] Make sure you don't dazzle other road users

To prevent your lights from dazzling the driver of the car in front, wait until you've passed them before switching to full beam.

8.47 Mark one answer HC r153

You're travelling on a road that has speed humps. What should you do when the driver in front is travelling more slowly than you?

☐ Sound your horn

☐ Overtake as soon as you can

☐ Flash your headlights

☑ Slow down and stay behind

Be patient and stay behind the car in front. You shouldn't normally overtake other vehicles in areas subject to traffic calming. If you overtake here, you may easily exceed the speed limit, defeating the purpose of the traffic-calming measures.

8.48 Mark one answer KYTS p68

You see these markings on the road. Why are they there?

These lines may be painted on the road on the approach to a roundabout, a village or a particular hazard. The lines are raised and painted yellow, and their purpose is to make you aware of your speed. Reduce your speed in good time so that you avoid having to brake harshly over the last few metres before reaching the junction.

☐ To show a safe distance between vehicles

☐ To keep the area clear of traffic

☑ To make you aware of your speed

☐ To warn you to change direction

8.49 Mark one answer HC r300, KYTS p30

How would you identify a section of road used by trams?

☐ There would be metal studs around it

☐ There would be zigzag markings alongside it

☑ There would be a different surface texture

☐ There would be yellow hatch markings around it

Trams may run on roads used by other vehicles and pedestrians. The section of road used by trams is known as the reserved area and should be kept clear. It usually has a different surface, edged with white lane markings.

What should you do when you meet an oncoming vehicle on a single-track road?

☐ Reverse back to the main road

☐ Carry out an emergency stop

☑ Stop at a passing place

☐ Switch on your hazard warning lights

Take care when using single-track roads. It can be difficult to see around bends, because of hedges or fences, so expect to meet oncoming vehicles. Drive carefully and be ready to pull into or stop opposite a passing place, where you can pass each other safely.

The road is wet. Why might a motorcyclist steer round drain covers on a bend?

☐ To avoid puncturing the tyres on the edge of the drain covers

☑ To prevent the motorcycle sliding on the metal drain covers

☐ To help judge the bend using the drain covers as marker points

☐ To avoid splashing pedestrians on the pavement

Other drivers or riders may have to change course due to the size or characteristics of their vehicle. Understanding this will help you to anticipate their actions. Motorcyclists and cyclists will be checking the road ahead for uneven or slippery surfaces, especially in wet weather. They may need to move across their lane to avoid surface hazards such as potholes and drain covers.

8.52

Mark one answer

RES s12, HC r121

After this hazard you should test your brakes. Why is this?

- [ ] You'll be on a slippery road
- [x] Your brakes will be soaking wet
- [ ] You'll be going down a long hill
- [ ] You'll have just crossed a long bridge

A ford is a crossing over a stream that's shallow enough to drive or ride through. After you've gone through a ford or deep puddle, your brakes will be wet and they won't work as well as usual. To dry them out, apply a light brake pressure while moving slowly. Don't travel at normal speeds until you're sure your brakes are working properly again.

8.53

Mark one answer

RES s12, HC r234

Why should you always reduce your speed when travelling in fog?

- [ ] The brakes don't work as well
- [ ] You'll be dazzled by other headlights
- [ ] The engine will take longer to warm up
- [x] It's more difficult to see what's ahead

You won't be able to see as far ahead in fog as you can on a clear day. You'll need to reduce your speed so that, if a hazard looms out of the fog, you have the time and space to take avoiding action.

Travelling in fog is hazardous. If you can, try to delay your journey until it has cleared.

> Case study practice – 8 Road conditions and motorcycle handling

> You're carrying a friend on the back of your motorcycle.
>
> You buy fuel at the service station, then make various checks, including your tyre pressures.
>
> You want to turn left when you leave the forecourt. There are parked cars obscuring your view.
>
> It begins to snow just before you reach your destination.

8.1 How will your friend affect your journey?
Mark one answer

- ☑ The extra weight can affect your balance
- ☐ Your stopping distance will be shorter
- ☐ It will be easier for you to accelerate
- ☐ They can help with observation

RES s14

8.2 What should you ask your friend to do during the journey?
Mark one answer

- ☐ Lean to the side in order to see ahead
- ☑ Lean with you when going round bends
- ☐ Look behind and then signal for you
- ☐ Keep upright when going round bends

RES s14

8.3 Other than tyre pressures, what might need adjusting under these circumstances?

Mark one answer

- ☐ Brakes
- ☑ Headlights
- ☐ Handlebars
- ☐ Seating

RES s14

8.4 What should you do as you leave the service-station forecourt?

Mark one answer

- ☐ Stop and wait until some of the parked cars move away
- ☐ Keep moving and merge with the traffic
- ☐ Stop and make your passenger signal to oncoming traffic
- ☑ Edge forward slowly until you can see clearly

RES s9 **HC** r170

8.5 Why would you choose to leave a larger gap towards the end of your journey?

Mark one answer

- ☐ So your passenger can see more clearly
- ☐ To keep away from exhaust fumes
- ☐ Your passenger told you to keep further back
- ☑ You'll need more room in which to stop safely

RES s14

> Section nine
Motorway riding

In this section, you'll learn about

- > how to ride safely on motorways
- > the speed limits that apply on motorways and how they're used to avoid congestion
- > the markings used on motorway lanes
- > what to do if your motorcycle breaks down on the motorway.

Motorway riding

Motorways are designed to help traffic travel at constant, higher speeds than on single carriageways. Due to the traffic's speed, situations on motorways can change more quickly than on other roads, so you need to be especially alert at all times.

Check your motorcycle thoroughly before starting a long motorway journey. Riding at high speeds for long periods of time may increase the risk of a breakdown. See section 3, Safety and your motorcycle, for more information about what to check.

RES s11

As a learner you can't drive a car or ride a motorcycle on the motorway but you can drive or ride on dual carriageways.
HC r253

Remember, to ride on a motorway, your motorcycle **MUST** have an engine capacity of 50 cc or more.

Pedestrians and horse riders can't use a motorway. The following vehicles can't be used on a motorway

* bicycles
* motorcycles under 50 cc
* powered wheelchairs/mobility scooters
* agricultural vehicles
* some slow-moving vehicles.

HC r253

❯ Riding on the motorway

When you join the motorway

* use the slip road to adjust your speed to match the traffic already on the motorway
* give way to traffic already on the motorway.

HC r259 RES s11

All traffic, whatever its speed, should normally use the left-hand lane of the motorway. Use the middle and right-hand lanes only for overtaking other vehicles and return to the left lane when you've finished overtaking.

HC r264, 267 **RES** s11

You should normally only overtake on the right. However, you may overtake on the left if traffic is moving slowly in queues and the queue on your right is moving more slowly than the one you're in.

HC r268 **RES** s11

Where the motorway goes uphill steeply, there may be a separate lane for slow-moving vehicles. This helps the faster-moving traffic to flow more easily.

HC r139 **RES** s11

If you're travelling in the left-hand lane and traffic is joining from a slip road, move to another lane if you're able to do so safely. This helps the flow of traffic joining the motorway, especially at peak times.

RES s11

Take care when filtering through queuing traffic as a driver may change lane into your path.

Countdown markers on the left-hand verge show that you're approaching the next exit. If you want to leave the motorway, try to get into the left-hand lane in good time. If you accidentally go past the exit you wanted, carry on to the next one. Never try to stop and go back.

HC r272 **RES** s11

⊖ Speed limits

The national speed limit for cars and motorcycles on a motorway is 70 mph (112 km/h). The same limit applies to all lanes. Obey any signs showing a lower speed limit.

HC r261, p40 **RES** s11

A vehicle towing a trailer

- is restricted to a lower speed limit of 60 mph (96 km/h)
- isn't allowed to travel in the right-hand lane of a motorway with three or more lanes, unless there are lane closures
- in Northern Ireland shouldn't use the right-hand lane of a three-lane motorway.

You can use your hazard lights to warn traffic behind you that the traffic ahead is slowing down or stopping suddenly. Switch them off as soon as following traffic has reacted to your signal.

HC r116 **RES** s11

When you're approaching roadworks, watch for lower speed limits, especially if there's a contraflow system. You should

- obey all speed limits
- keep a safe distance from the vehicle ahead.

HC r289–290 **RES** s11

See section 4, Safety margins, for more information about contraflow systems.

⊖ Reducing congestion

Active traffic management (ATM), also known as 'smart motorways', tries to reduce congestion and make journey times more reliable. Where this is in use, **mandatory speed limit** signs will show on the gantries. The speed limit helps to keep the traffic speed constant so that traffic is less likely to bunch up and journey times can be improved.

RES s18

Definition

mandatory speed limit
the maximum speed at which you may travel

In ATM areas, the hard shoulder is sometimes used as a normal traffic lane. You'll know when you can use this because a speed-limit sign will be shown above all lanes, including the hard shoulder. A red cross showing above the hard shoulder means that you shouldn't travel in this lane and it should be used only in an emergency or breakdown.

Emergency refuge areas have been built in these areas for use in cases of emergency or breakdown.

Find out more about ATM here.

❯ **www.gov.uk/government/
collections/smart-motorways**

Traffic officers only operate in England, covering motorways and some 'A' class roads. They

- can stop and direct anyone on a motorway or an 'A' road
- respond to calls made on roadside emergency telephones.

`HC` r105, 108 `RES` s18

❯ Lane markings

Reflective studs help you to see where you are on the carriageway, especially at night or in fog. Different colours are used in different places.

`HC` r132 `RES` s11

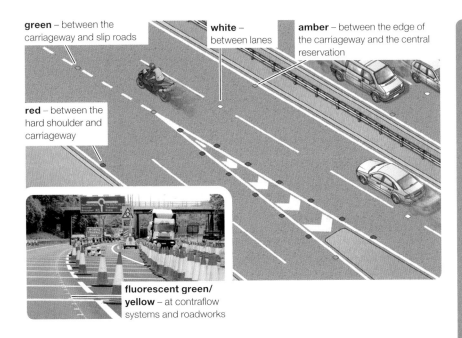

green – between the carriageway and slip roads

white – between lanes

amber – between the edge of the carriageway and the central reservation

red – between the hard shoulder and carriageway

fluorescent green/ yellow – at contraflow systems and roadworks

⊗ Stopping and breakdowns

Motorways are designed to keep traffic moving, so you mustn't stop on the motorway unless you have to.

Only stop on the motorway

- if flashing red lights show above every lane
- when told to do so by the police, Driver and Vehicle Standards Agency (DVSA) officers or traffic officers
- in a traffic jam
- in an emergency or breakdown.

Move over if signals on the overhead gantries advise you to do so.

HC r258, 270 **RES** s11 **KYTS** p90

Should you need to stop for any other reason, such as to have a rest, make a phone call or look at a map, either leave at the next exit or go to a service area.

HC r270 **RES** s11

If your motorcycle breaks down or a tyre has a puncture, try to get onto the hard shoulder and call for help. If you can, use one of the emergency telephones. These are

- normally at one-mile intervals. Marker posts at 100-metre intervals point you in the direction of the nearest phone
- connected directly to a control centre, where the operator will deal with your call and direct the appropriate services to help you.

HC r275 **RES** s11, 16

When you're using an emergency phone, stand facing the oncoming traffic so that you can see any hazards approaching – for example, the draught from a large vehicle driving past could take you by surprise.

If you decide to use your mobile phone

- make a note of your location (the number on the nearest marker post) before you make the call
- give this information to the emergency services.

HC r275 **RES** s11, 16

While your motorcycle is on the hard shoulder

- switch on the hazard lights, if fitted
- switch on the parking lights at night or if visibility is poor.

RES s11

When you're ready to return to the carriageway, wait for a safe gap in the traffic and then ride along the hard shoulder to gain speed before moving out onto the main carriageway.

HC r276 **RES** s16

Meeting the standards

You must be able to

join a motorway or dual carriageway safely and responsibly from the left or the right

allow for other road users joining or leaving the motorway

change lanes safely and responsibly.

You must know and understand

that you mustn't stop on a motorway except in an emergency

that you mustn't

- pick anybody up on a motorway
- set anybody down on a motorway
- walk on a motorway, except in an emergency

the need to look well ahead for other road users joining or leaving the motorway or for queuing traffic

that some stretches of motorway may have

- local, active traffic management (sometimes called smart motorways)
- control systems installed, which will change speed limits and the direction of flow in particular lanes.

You must obey the instructions given by these systems.

Notes

You can use this page to make your own notes or diagrams about the key points you need to remember.

Think about

- At what speed should you be riding when you join the motorway?
- What should you do if you miss the exit that you want to take off the motorway?
- What information do the marker posts give you?
- What should you do if your motorcycle breaks down on the motorway?

Your notes

Things to discuss and practise with your trainer

These are just a few examples of what you could discuss and practise with your trainer. Read more about motorway riding to come up with your own ideas.

Discuss with your trainer

- how you should join the motorway and what to look out for as you do so
- the different national speed limits for various vehicles on the motorway, and in which lanes these vehicles may travel
- what you should do if you break down on the motorway
- what ATM stands for and its purpose on the motorway.

Practise with your trainer

Until you hold a full motorcycle licence, you won't be able to ride on the motorway, so practising your riding there won't be possible. Instead, practise with your trainer

- on a dual carriageway, some of the techniques of riding on the motorway eg joining from a slip road, lane discipline and riding at higher speeds
- identifying motorway signs, signals and road markings from *Know Your Traffic Signs* and *The Official Highway Code*.

9.1
Mark one answer

RES s11, HC r270

When may you stop on the hard shoulder of a motorway?

☑ Only in an emergency

☐ If you feel tired and need to rest

☐ If you've gone past your exit

☐ To answer your mobile phone

You mustn't stop on the hard shoulder, except in an emergency. Never use the hard shoulder to have a rest or a picnic, answer a mobile phone or check a road map. Also, you mustn't travel back along the hard shoulder if you've gone past your exit.

9.2
Mark one answer

RES s11, HC r272

You're riding on the motorway. Well before you reach your intended exit, where should you position your motorcycle?

☐ In the middle lane

☑ In the left-hand lane

☐ On the hard shoulder

☐ In any lane

You'll see the first advance direction sign one mile from a motorway exit. If you're travelling at 60 mph, you'll only have about 50 seconds before you reach the countdown markers. There'll be another sign at the half-mile point. Move to the left-hand lane in good time. Don't cut across traffic at the last moment and don't risk missing your exit.

9.3
Mark one answer

RES s11

You're joining a motorway from a slip road. What should you do?

☑ Adjust your speed to the speed of the traffic on the motorway

☐ Accelerate as quickly as you can and ride straight out

☐ Ride onto the hard shoulder until a gap appears

☐ Expect drivers on the motorway to give way to you

Give way to vehicles that are already on the motorway, and join the left-hand lane when there's a suitable gap in the traffic. Don't expect traffic on the motorway to give way to you, but try to avoid stopping at the end of the slip road.

9.4
Mark one answer

RES s11, HC r253

If you want to ride on the motorway, what's the minimum engine size your motorcycle must have?

☑ 50 cc

☐ 125 cc

☐ 150 cc

☐ 250 cc

Riders of motorcycles with an engine smaller than 50 cc aren't allowed to use motorways, due to their restricted speed. They may cause a hazard – both for the rider and for drivers of other vehicles.

9.5 | Mark one answer | RES s11, HC r264

You're riding at 70 mph on a three-lane motorway. There's no traffic ahead. Which lane should you use?

☐ Any lane
☐ The middle lane
☐ The right-hand lane
☐ The left-hand lane

Use the left-hand lane if it's free, regardless of the speed at which you're travelling.

9.6 | NI EXEMPT | Mark one answer | RES s11, HC p40

You're riding on a motorway. Unless signs show otherwise, what's the national speed limit?

☐ 50 mph
☐ 60 mph
☑ 70 mph
☐ 80 mph

The national speed limit of 70 mph applies to cars and motorcycles on the motorway, unless they're towing a trailer. On smart motorways, this speed limit can be reduced and overhead signs will show the new limit in force.

9.7 | Mark one answer | RES s11

Why is it particularly important to carry out a check of your motorcycle before making a long motorway journey?

☐ You'll have to do more harsh braking on motorways
☐ Motorway service stations don't deal with breakdowns
☐ The road surface will wear down the tyres faster
☑ Continuous high speeds increase the risk of your motorcycle breaking down

Before starting a motorway journey, make sure your motorcycle can cope with the demands of high-speed riding. Things you need to check include oil, water, tyres and fuel. When you're travelling a long way, it's a good idea to plan rest stops in advance.

9.8 | Mark one answer | RES s11, HC r259

What should you do when you're joining a motorway?

☐ Use the hard shoulder
☐ Stop at the end of the acceleration lane
☐ Slow to a stop before joining the motorway
☑ Give way to traffic already on the motorway

You should give way to traffic already on the motorway. Where possible, traffic may move over to let you in, but don't force your way into the traffic stream. Traffic could be travelling at high speed, so try to match your speed to filter in without affecting the traffic flow.

What's the national speed limit on motorways for cars and motorcycles?

☐ 30 mph

☐ 50 mph

☐ 60 mph

☐ 70 mph

Travelling at the national speed limit doesn't allow you to hog the right-hand lane. Always use the left-hand lane whenever possible. When leaving a motorway, get into the left-hand lane well before your exit. Reduce your speed on the slip road and look out for sharp bends or curves and traffic queuing at roundabouts.

Which vehicles should use the left-hand lane on a three-lane motorway?

On a motorway, all traffic should use the left-hand lane unless overtaking. When overtaking a number of slower vehicles, move back to the left-hand lane when you're safely past. Check your mirrors frequently and don't stay in the middle or right-hand lane if the left-hand lane is free.

☑ Any vehicle

☐ Large vehicles only

☐ Emergency vehicles only

☐ Slow vehicles only

Which of these isn't allowed to travel in the right-hand lane of a three-lane motorway?

☐ A small delivery van

☐ A motorcycle

☑ A vehicle towing a trailer

☐ A motorcycle and sidecar

A vehicle with a trailer is restricted to 60 mph. For this reason, it isn't allowed in the right-hand lane, as it might hold up faster-moving traffic that wishes to overtake in that lane.

9.12

Mark one answer RES s11, HC r275

You break down on a motorway. You need to call for help. Why may it be better to use an emergency roadside telephone rather than a mobile phone?

☐ It connects you to a local garage

☐ Using a mobile phone will distract other drivers

☑ It allows easy location by the emergency services

☐ Mobile phones don't work on motorways

On a motorway, it's best to use a roadside emergency telephone so that the emergency services are able to find you easily. The location of the nearest telephone is shown by an arrow on marker posts at the edge of the hard shoulder. If you use a mobile, the operator will need to know your exact location. Before you call, find out the number on the nearest marker post. This number will identify your exact location.

9.13

Mark one answer RES s11, HC r276

You've had a breakdown on the hard shoulder of a motorway. When the problem has been fixed, how should you rejoin the main carriageway?

☐ Move out onto the carriageway, then build up your speed

☐ Move out onto the carriageway using your hazard warning lights

☑ Gain speed on the hard shoulder before moving out onto the carriageway

☐ Wait on the hard shoulder until someone flashes their headlights at you

Signal your intention and build up sufficient speed on the hard shoulder so that you can filter into a safe gap in the traffic. Don't push your way in, causing other traffic to alter speed or direction.

9.14

Mark one answer RES s11

You're travelling along a motorway. Where would you find a crawler or climbing lane?

☑ On a steep gradient

☐ Before a service area

☐ Before a junction

☐ Along the hard shoulder

Large, slow-moving vehicles can hinder the progress of other traffic. On a steep gradient, an extra crawler lane may be provided for slow-moving vehicles to allow faster-moving traffic to flow more easily.

273

What do these motorway signs show?

The exit from a motorway is indicated by countdown markers. These are positioned 90 metres (100 yards) apart, the first being 270 metres (300 yards) from the start of the slip road. Move into the left-hand lane well before you reach the start of the slip road.

- [ ] They're countdown markers to a bridge
- [ ] They're distance markers to the next telephone
- [ ] They're countdown markers to the next exit
- [ ] They warn of a police control ahead

On which part of a motorway are amber reflective studs found?

- [ ] Between the hard shoulder and the carriageway
- [ ] Between the acceleration lane and the carriageway
- [x] Between the central reservation and the carriageway
- [ ] Between each pair of lanes

On motorways, reflective studs of various colours are fixed in the road between the lanes. These help you to identify which lane you're in when it's dark or in poor visibility. Amber-coloured studs are found on the right-hand edge of the main carriageway, next to the central reservation.

9.17
Mark one answer RES s7, HC r132

What colour are the reflective studs between the lanes on a motorway?

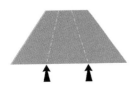

White studs are found between the lanes on motorways. They reflect back the light from your headlights. This is especially useful in bad weather, when visibility is restricted.

☐ Green
☐ Amber
☑ White
☐ Red

9.18
Mark one answer RES s7, HC r132

What colour are the reflective studs between a motorway and its slip road?

☐ Amber
☐ White
☑ Green
☐ Red

The studs between the carriageway and the hard shoulder are normally red. These change to green where there's a slip road, helping you to identify slip roads when visibility is poor or when it's dark.

9.19
Mark one answer RES s11, HC r275

You've broken down on a motorway. In which direction should you walk to find the nearest emergency telephone?

☐ With the traffic flow
☐ Facing oncoming traffic
☐ In the direction shown on the marker posts
☐ In the direction of the nearest exit

Along the hard shoulder there are marker posts at 100-metre intervals. These will direct you to the nearest emergency telephone.

Mark one answer

You're joining a motorway. Why is it important to make full use of the slip road?

☐ Because there is space available to turn round if you need to

☐ To allow you direct access to the overtaking lanes

☐ To build up a speed similar to traffic on the motorway

☐ Because you can continue on the hard shoulder

Try to join the motorway without affecting the progress of the traffic already travelling on it. Always give way to traffic already on the motorway. At busy times you may have to slow down to merge into slow-moving traffic.

Mark one answer

How should you use the emergency telephone on a motorway?

☐ Stay close to the carriageway

☐ Face the oncoming traffic

☐ Keep your back to the traffic

☐ Stand on the hard shoulder

Traffic is passing you at speed. If the draught from a large lorry catches you by surprise, it could blow you off balance and even onto the carriageway. By facing the oncoming traffic, you can see approaching lorries and so be prepared for their draught. You'll also be in a position to see other hazards approaching.

Mark one answer

You're on a motorway. What colour are the reflective studs on the left of the carriageway?

☐ Green

☑ Red

☐ White

☐ Amber

Red studs are placed between the edge of the carriageway and the hard shoulder. Where slip roads leave or join the motorway, the studs are green.

Mark one answer

On a three-lane motorway, which lane should you normally use?

☑ Left

☐ Right

☐ Centre

☐ Either the right or centre

On a three-lane motorway, you should travel in the left-hand lane unless you're overtaking. This applies regardless of the speed at which you're travelling.

What should you do when going through a contraflow system on a motorway?

☐ Ensure that you don't exceed 30 mph

☐ Keep a good distance from the vehicle ahead

☐ Switch lanes to keep the traffic flowing

☐ Stay close to the vehicle ahead to reduce queues

At roadworks, and especially where a contraflow system is operating, a speed restriction is likely to be in place. Keep to the lower speed limit and don't

- switch lanes
- get too close to the vehicle in front of you.

Be aware that there will be no permanent barrier between you and the oncoming traffic.

You're on a three-lane motorway. There are red reflective studs on your left and white ones to your right. Which lane are you in?

☐ In the right-hand lane

☐ In the middle lane

☐ On the hard shoulder

☑ In the left-hand lane

The colours of the reflective studs on the motorway and their locations are

- red – between the hard shoulder and the carriageway
- white – between lanes
- amber – between the carriageway and the central reservation
- green – along slip-road exits and entrances
- bright green/yellow – at roadworks and contraflow systems.

9.26
Mark one answer
RES s11, HC r288

You're approaching roadworks on a motorway. What should you do?

☐ Speed up to clear the area quickly

☐ Always use the hard shoulder

☐ Obey all speed limits

☐ Stay very close to the vehicle in front

Collisions often happen at roadworks. Be aware of the speed limits, slow down in good time and keep your distance from the vehicle in front.

9.27
Mark one answer
HC r253

Which of these mustn't use motorways?

☐ Cars driven by learner drivers

☐ Motorcycles over 50 cc

☐ Double-deck buses

☐ Cars with automatic transmission

Motorways mustn't be used by learner drivers, pedestrians, cyclists, motorcycles under 50 cc, certain slow-moving vehicles without permission, and invalid carriages weighing less than 254 kg (560 lbs).

9.28
Mark one answer
HC r254

What should you do when driving or riding along a motorway?

☐ Look much further ahead than you would on other roads

☐ Travel much faster than you would on other roads

☐ Maintain a shorter separation distance than you would on other roads

☐ Concentrate more than you would on other roads

Traffic on motorways usually travels faster than on other roads. You need to be looking further ahead to give yourself more time to react to any hazard that may develop.

9.29
Mark one answer
RES s11, HC r264

What should you do immediately after joining a motorway?

☐ Try to overtake

☐ Re-adjust your mirrors

☐ Position your vehicle in the centre lane

☑ Keep in the left-hand lane

Stay in the left-hand lane long enough to get used to the higher speeds of motorway traffic before considering overtaking.

278

9.30   Mark one answer   RES s11, HC r265

What's the right-hand lane used for on a three-lane motorway?

☐ Emergency vehicles only

☐ Overtaking

☐ Vehicles towing trailers

☐ Coaches only

You should keep to the left and only use the right-hand lane if you're passing slower-moving traffic.

9.31   Mark one answer   RES s11, HC r269, 270

What should you use the hard shoulder of a motorway for?

Don't use the hard shoulder for stopping unless it's an emergency. If you want to stop for any other reason, go to the next exit or service station.

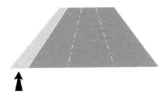

☐ Stopping in an emergency

☐ Leaving the motorway

☐ Stopping when you're tired

☐ Joining the motorway

You're in the right-hand lane of a three-lane motorway. What do these overhead signs mean?

You must obey these signs even if there appear to be no problems ahead. There could be queuing traffic or another hazard which you can't yet see.

- ☐ Move to the left and reduce your speed to 50 mph
- ☐ There are roadworks 50 metres (55 yards) ahead
- ☐ Use the hard shoulder until you've passed the hazard
- ☐ Leave the motorway at the next exit

When are you allowed to stop on a motorway?

- ☐ When you need to walk and get fresh air
- ☐ When you wish to pick up hitchhikers
- ☑ When you're signalled to do so by flashing red lights
- ☐ When you need to use a mobile telephone

You must stop if overhead gantry signs show flashing red lights above every lane on the motorway. If any of the other lanes doesn't show flashing red lights or a red cross, you may move into that lane and continue if it's safe to do so.

You're travelling in the left-hand lane of a three-lane motorway. How should you react to traffic joining from a slip road?

- ☐ Race the other vehicles
- ☑ Move to another lane
- ☐ Maintain a steady speed
- ☐ Switch on your hazard warning lights

Plan well ahead when approaching a slip road. If you see traffic joining the motorway, move to another lane if it's safe to do so. This can help the flow of traffic joining the motorway, especially at peak times.

9.35

Mark one answer

RES s11, HC r264

What basic rule applies when you're using a motorway?

☐ Use the lane that has the least traffic

☑ Keep to the left-hand lane unless overtaking

☐ Overtake on the side that's clearest

☐ Try to keep above 50 mph to prevent congestion

You should normally travel in the left-hand lane unless you're overtaking a slower-moving vehicle. When you've finished overtaking, move back into the left-hand lane, but don't cut across in front of the vehicle that you've overtaken.

9.36

Mark one answer

RES s11, HC r268

You're travelling along a motorway. When are you allowed to overtake on the left?

☐ When you can see well ahead that the hard shoulder is clear

☐ When the traffic in the right-hand lane is signalling right

☐ When you warn drivers behind by signalling left

☑ When in queues and traffic to your right is moving more slowly than you are

Never overtake on the left, unless the traffic is moving in queues and the queue on your right is moving more slowly than the one you're in.

9.37

Mark one answer

RES s18

On a motorway, what's an emergency refuge area used for?

☑ In cases of emergency or breakdown

☐ If you think you'll be involved in a road rage incident

☐ For a police patrol to park and watch traffic

☐ For construction and road workers to store emergency equipment

Emergency refuge areas are built at the side of the hard shoulder. If you break down, try to get your vehicle into the refuge, where there's an emergency telephone. The phone connects directly to a control centre. Remember to take care when rejoining the motorway, especially if the hard shoulder is being used as a running lane.

Traffic officers operate on motorways and some primary routes in England. What are they authorised to do?

☐ Stop and arrest drivers who break the law

☐ Repair broken-down vehicles on the motorway

☐ Issue fixed penalty notices

☐ Stop and direct anyone on a motorway

Traffic officers don't have enforcement powers but are able to stop and direct people on motorways and some 'A' class roads. They only operate in England and work in partnership with the police at incidents, providing a highly trained and visible service. They're recognised by an orange-and-yellow jacket and their vehicle has yellow-and-black markings.

You're on a motorway. A red cross is displayed above the hard shoulder. What does this mean?

Active traffic management operates on some motorways. Within these areas, at certain times, the hard shoulder will be used as a running lane. A red cross above the hard shoulder shows that this lane should only be used for emergencies and breakdowns.

☐ Pull up in this lane to answer your mobile phone

☐ Use this lane as a running lane

☐ This lane can be used if you need a rest

☐ You shouldn't travel in this lane

9.40

Mark one answer

RES s18, HC r269

You're on a smart motorway. A mandatory speed limit is displayed above the hard shoulder. What does this mean?

A mandatory speed-limit sign above the hard shoulder shows that this part of the road can be used as a running lane between junctions. You must stay within the speed limit. Look out for vehicles that may have broken down and could be blocking the hard shoulder.

☐ You shouldn't travel in this lane

☑ The hard shoulder can be used as a running lane

☐ You can park on the hard shoulder if you feel tired

☐ You can pull up in this lane to answer a mobile phone

9.41

Mark one answer

RES s18

What's the aim of a smart motorway?

☐ To prevent overtaking

☐ To reduce rest stops

☐ To prevent tailgating

☐ To reduce congestion

Smart motorway schemes are intended to reduce congestion and make journey times more reliable. In these areas, the hard shoulder may be used as a running lane to ease congestion at peak times or in the event of an incident. Variable speed limits are used to help keep the traffic moving and to avoid bunching.

9.42

Mark one answer

RES s18, HC r269

You're using a smart motorway. What happens when it's operating?

☐ Speed limits above lanes are advisory

☐ The national speed limit will apply

☐ The speed limit is always 30 mph

☐ You must obey the speed limits shown

When a smart motorway is operating, you must follow the mandatory signs on the gantries above each lane, including the hard shoulder. Variable speed limits help keep the traffic moving and also help to prevent bunching.

9.43
Mark one answer
RES s18, HC r269

Why can it be an advantage for traffic speed to stay constant over a longer distance?

☐ You'll do more stop–start driving

☐ You'll use far more fuel

☐ You'll be able to use more direct routes

☑ Your overall journey time will normally improve

When traffic travels at a constant speed over a longer distance, journey times normally improve. You may feel that you could travel faster for short periods, but this generally leads to bunching and increased overall journey time.

9.44
Mark one answer
RES s18, HC r269

You shouldn't normally travel on the hard shoulder of a motorway. When can you use it?

☐ When taking the next exit

☐ When traffic is stopped

☑ When signs direct you to

☐ When traffic is slow moving

Normally, you should only use the hard shoulder for emergencies and breakdowns, and at roadworks when signs direct you to do so. Smart motorways use active traffic management to ease congestion. In these areas, the hard shoulder may be used as a running lane when speed-limit signs are shown directly above.

9.45
Mark one answer
RES s18, HC r261

What's used to reduce traffic bunching on a motorway?

☑ Variable speed limits

☐ Contraflow systems

☐ National speed limits

☐ Lane closures

Congestion can be reduced by keeping traffic at a constant speed. At busy times, maximum speed limits are displayed on overhead gantries. These can be varied quickly, depending on the amount of traffic. By keeping to a constant speed on busy sections of motorway, overall journey times are normally improved.

9.46
Mark one answer
RES s11, HC r270

When may you stop on a motorway?

☐ If you have to read a map

☐ When you're tired and need a rest

☐ If your mobile phone rings

☑ In an emergency or breakdown

You shouldn't normally stop on a motorway, but there may be occasions when you need to do so. If you're unfortunate enough to break down, make every effort to pull up on the hard shoulder.

9.47
Mark one answer   HC r261, p40

Unless signs show otherwise, what's the national speed limit for a car or motorcycle on a motorway?

☐ 50 mph

☐ 60 mph

☑ 70 mph

☐ 80 mph

The national speed limit for a car or motorcycle on a motorway is 70 mph. Lower speed limits may be in force; for example, at roadworks. Variable speed limits also operate in some areas when the motorway is very busy. Cars or motorcycles towing trailers are subject to a lower speed limit.

9.48
Mark one answer   RES s11, HC r275

You stop on the hard shoulder of a motorway and use the emergency telephone. Where's the best place to wait for help to arrive?

☐ Next to the phone

☑ Well away from the carriageway

☐ With your vehicle

☐ On the hard shoulder

When you're on the hard shoulder, you're at risk of being injured by motorway traffic. The safest place to wait is away from the carriageway, but near enough to see the emergency services arriving.

9.49
Mark one answer   RES s11, HC r270

You're on a motorway and there are red flashing lights above every lane. What must you do?

☐ Pull onto the hard shoulder

☐ Slow down and watch for further signals

☐ Leave at the next exit

☑ Stop and wait

Red flashing lights above all lanes mean you must stop and wait. You'll also see a red cross lit up. Don't change lanes, don't continue and don't pull onto the hard shoulder (unless in an emergency).

You're on a three-lane motorway. A red cross is showing above the hard shoulder and mandatory speed limits above all other lanes. What does this mean?

A red cross above the hard shoulder shows that it's closed as a running lane and should only be used for emergencies or breakdowns. On a smart motorway, the hard shoulder may be used as a running lane at busy times. This will be shown by a mandatory speed limit on the gantry above the hard shoulder.

☐ The hard shoulder can be used as a rest area if you feel tired

☑ The hard shoulder is for emergency or breakdown use only

☐ The hard shoulder can be used as a normal running lane

☐ The hard shoulder has a speed limit of 50 mph

On a three-lane motorway, what does this sign mean?

You must obey mandatory speed-limit signs above motorway lanes, including the hard shoulder. In this case, you can use the hard shoulder as a running lane but you should look for any vehicles that may have broken down and may be blocking the hard shoulder.

☐ Use any lane except the hard shoulder

☐ Use the hard shoulder only

☐ Use the three right-hand lanes only

☑ Use all the lanes, including the hard shoulder

You're travelling along a motorway and feel tired. Where should you stop to rest?

☐ On the hard shoulder

☑ At the nearest service area

☐ On a slip road

☐ On the central reservation

If you feel tired, stop at the nearest service area. If that's too far away, leave the motorway at the next exit and find a safe place to stop. You mustn't stop on the carriageway or hard shoulder of a motorway except in an emergency, when in a traffic queue, or when signalled to do so by a police officer, a traffic officer or traffic signals. Plan your journey so that you have regular rest stops.

Case study practice – 9 Motorway riding

> It's raining. You're riding your motorcycle and newly fitted sidecar.
>
> On the motorway, you ride in the left-hand lane. You see flashing amber lights on the central reservation, with a sign showing '50'.
>
> Later, you need to exit at the next junction, so you watch for countdown markers.
>
> You then reach the marker showing three bars.

9.1 What would be affected by the new addition to your motorcycle?
Mark **one** answer

- ☑ Steering and braking
- ☐ Your speed limits
- ☐ Vehicle tax
- ☐ Fuel type and exhaust

RES s14

9.2 Why would you take this position on the motorway?
Mark **one** answer

- ☐ It's the only lane which is empty of other traffic
- ☐ You're not allowed in the other two lanes
- ☑ All traffic should do so unless they're overtaking
- ☐ You're only licensed to use this lane

RES s11 **HC** r264

9.3 What gap should you leave between your motorcycle and the vehicle in front?

Mark **one** answer

☐ One second
☐ Two seconds
☑ Four seconds
☐ Ten seconds

HC r126

9.4 What's meant by the sign and the lights?

Mark **one** answer

☐ Temporary minimum speed advised
☐ Temporary maximum distance advised
☑ Temporary maximum speed advised
☐ Temporary minimum distance advised

RES s11

9.5 At the marker, how far are you from the exit you need?

Mark **one** answer

☑ 400 yards
☐ 300 yards
☐ 200 yards
☐ 100 yards

RES s11 **HC** p112

Section ten
Rules of the road

In this section, you'll learn about

- ❯ the speed limits that you need to obey
- ❯ how to use junctions and lanes safely
- ❯ rules about overtaking
- ❯ riding over pedestrian crossings and level crossings
- ❯ where you can stop and park safely and legally.

Rules of the road

It's important that everyone knows and follows the rules of the road. Some are legal requirements and some are recommended best practice, but they all help to make the roads safer.

❯ Speed limits

You **MUST NOT** ride faster than the speed limit for the road you're on or your vehicle type. Where no other limit is shown, the national speed limit for cars and motorcycles is

- 60 mph (96 km/h) on a single carriageway road
- 70 mph (112 km/h) on a dual carriageway or motorway.

There are lower speed limits for these vehicles when towing a trailer or caravan

- 50 mph (80 km/h) on a single carriageway road
- 60 mph (96 km/h) on a dual carriageway or motorway.

HC r124, p40

Where there are street lights, there's normally a 30 mph (48 km/h) speed limit for all vehicles unless signs show otherwise.

HC r124, p40

On some roads you may see a sign showing a minimum speed limit. You should travel above the limit shown on the sign unless it's not safe to do so.

HC p107

Speed limits

Type of vehicle	Built-up areas* mph (km/h)	Single carriage-ways mph (km/h)	Dual carriage-ways mph (km/h)	Motorways mph (km/h)
Cars and motorcycles (including car-derived vans up to 2 tonnes maximum laden weight)	30 (48)	60 (96)	70 (112)	70 (112)
Cars towing caravans or trailers (including car-derived vans and motorcycles)	30 (48)	50 (80)	60 (96)	60 (96)
Buses, coaches and minibuses (not exceeding 12 metres in overall length)	30 (48)	50 (80)	60 (96)	70 (112)
Goods vehicles (not exceeding 7.5 tonnes maximum laden weight)	30 (48)	50 (80)	60 (96)	70† (112)
Goods vehicles (exceeding 7.5 tonnes maximum laden weight)	30 (48)	40 (64)	50 (80)	60 (96)

*The 30 mph limit usually applies to all traffic on all roads with street lighting unless signs show otherwise.
†60 mph (96 km/h) if articulated or towing a trailer.

Be aware that large vehicles may have speed limiters – buses and coaches are restricted to 62 mph and large goods vehicles to 56 mph.

Always ride with care and take account of the road and weather conditions. If you're riding along a street where cars are parked, keep your speed down and beware of

pedestrians (especially children) stepping out from behind parked vehicles

vehicles pulling out

drivers' doors opening.

HC r152 **RES** s10

At roadworks, there may be temporary speed limits to slow traffic down. These are mandatory speed limits and may be enforced by cameras.

HC r288 KYTS p90

The Think! road safety website has more advice on speed and speed limits.

❯ **http://think.direct.gov.uk/ speed.html**

❯ Lanes and junctions

Some roads have lanes reserved for specific vehicles, such as cycles, buses, trams or, in some places, motorcycles. These are marked by signs and road markings, and should be used only by those vehicles during the lanes' hours of operation, unless signs indicate otherwise.

HC r141

Never ride or park in a cycle lane marked by a solid white line during its hours of operation. Don't ride or park in a cycle lane marked by a broken line unless it's unavoidable.

HC r140–141 **KYTS** p32–36

You should only ride over a footpath when it's necessary in order to reach a property.

HC r145

On a dual carriageway, the right-hand lane is only for turning right or overtaking. The same rule applies to three-lane dual carriageways.

If you want to turn right onto a dual carriageway that has a central reservation that's too narrow to fit the length of your vehicle, wait until the road is clear in both directions before you emerge. If you emerge into the central reservation but your vehicle is too long, it could obstruct traffic coming from your right.

HC r173 **RES** s9

Always be careful at junctions. As you approach a junction, move into the correct position in plenty of time.

When you're turning left, keep well to the left as you approach the junction. In slow-moving traffic, remember to check for cyclists to your left before you turn.

HC r181–183 **RES** s9

If you're on a busy road and you find you're travelling in the wrong direction, or you're in the wrong lane at a busy junction, keep going until you can find somewhere safe, such as a quiet side road, where you can turn around.

HC r200 **RES** s6, 9

A box junction is marked by yellow hatched lines, and should be kept clear. Only enter it if your exit road is clear – otherwise, wait on your side of the junction. You can, however, wait in the box if you want to turn right and are waiting for a gap in the oncoming traffic before you can turn.

HC r174 **RES** s7, 9

If something is blocking your side of the road, such as a parked car, you should give way to oncoming traffic if there isn't room for you both to continue safely.

RES s8

Crossroads

If you're turning right at a crossroads when an oncoming road user is also turning right, it's normally safer to keep the other vehicle to your right and turn behind it. If you have to pass in front of the other vehicle, take extra care as your view may be blocked.

HC r181

At crossroads where there aren't any signs or markings, no-one has priority. Check very carefully in all directions before you proceed.

HC r146 **RES** s9

Roundabouts

Roundabouts are designed to help traffic flow smoothly. Follow signs and road markings as you approach and ride around them. Normally, if you're going straight ahead

- don't signal as you approach
- signal left just after you pass the exit before the one you want.

HC r185–186 **RES** s9

Some vehicles may not follow the normal rules.

- Cyclists and horse riders may stay in the left-hand lane even if they're turning right.
- Long vehicles may take up a different position to stop the rear of the vehicle hitting the kerb.

HC r187

❯ Overtaking

Overtaking can be dangerous. Ask yourself if you really need to do it, and never overtake if you're in any doubt as to whether it's safe.

HC r163 **RES** s8

You should normally overtake other vehicles on the right, but in a one-way street you can pass slower traffic on the left. Take extra care if you're overtaking on a dual carriageway, as the right-hand lane can also be used by traffic turning right.

HC r137 138 **RES** s8

At night, if a vehicle overtakes you, dip your headlights as soon as it passes you, otherwise your lights could dazzle the other driver.

HC r115

❯ Pedestrian crossings

If someone is standing on the pavement waiting to cross at a zebra crossing, stop and let them cross if it's safe to do so.

Pelican crossings are controlled by traffic lights. When the red light changes to flashing amber, wait for any pedestrians to finish crossing before you move off.

On toucan crossings, cyclists are allowed to cycle across at the same time as pedestrians.

HC r195–199 **RES** s8 **KYTS** p124

For more information on pedestrian crossings, see section 6, Vulnerable road users.

❯ Level crossings

A level crossing is where a railway line crosses the road.

It may have countdown markers to warn you if the crossing is hidden, such as around a bend.

Controlled crossings have traffic-light signals with twin flashing red lights, plus a warning alarm for pedestrians.

Crossings may or may not have barriers.

If this happens ...	you should do this
 The warning lights come on as you're approaching the crossing.	Stop. You **MUST** obey the red lights, by law.
 You're already on the crossing when the warning lights come on or a bell rings.	Keep going and clear the crossing.

You're waiting at a level crossing and a train has passed but the red lights keep flashing.

You **MUST** wait: there may be another train coming.

HC r293, p109 **RES** s7 **KYTS** p26–29

Some types of level crossing don't have lights. These include crossings with user-operated gates or barriers, and open crossings. Be careful at all level crossings, and take particular care when crossing rails – they may be slippery, particularly in wet weather.

HC r295–299 **RES** s8

See the Network Rail guide to using level crossings safely.

❯ **networkrail.co.uk/level-crossings**

❯ Stopping and parking

Always think carefully about where you stop and park your motorcycle, to make sure it's safe and legal.

At night, the safest place to park your motorcycle is in your garage, if you have one. If you're away from home, try to find a secure car park, or park in a well-lit area.

HC r239, p131 **RES** s8

If you have to park on a road at night, you **MUST** leave your parking lights on if the speed limit on that road is over 30 mph (48 km/h). You should normally park on the left-hand side of the road so that other road users can see your reflectors, but in a one-way street you can park on either side.

HC r248–250 **RES** s13

You **MUST NOT** stop on a **clearway**. On an urban clearway, you may stop only to drop off and pick up passengers. On a road marked with double white lines (even where one of the lines is broken), you may stop only to drop off and pick up passengers or to load/unload goods.

HC r240 **RES** s7

Definition

clearway
a stretch of road or street where stopping isn't allowed

Don't park where you would cause a danger or get in the way of other road users, such as

- on or near the brow of a hill
- at a bus stop
- opposite a traffic island
- in front of someone else's drive
- near a school entrance
- opposite or within 10 metres (32 feet) of a junction (in Northern Ireland, within 15 metres or 48 feet of a junction), unless there's an authorised parking space.

HC r242–243

You also need to make sure that you don't cause an obstruction by stopping or parking where there are restrictions shown by signs and yellow lines. In a controlled parking zone, you'll have to pay to park. Make sure you park within marked bays on the days and times shown on the zone entry signs.

HC r238, 245 **RES** s7 **KYTS** p39–50

By law, you **MUST** stop
- if you're involved in a road traffic incident
- at a red traffic light
- when signalled to do so by a police officer, traffic warden, Driver and Vehicle Standards Agency (DVSA) officer, traffic officer or school crossing patrol.

HC r105, 109, 286

Meeting the standards

You must be able to

apply a safe, systematic procedure to safely and responsibly negotiate

- junctions
- roundabouts
- crossings

turn left and right and go ahead safely and responsibly

emerge safely and responsibly into streams of traffic

cross the path of traffic safely when turning right.

You must know and understand

the rules that apply to particular junctions and roundabouts; for example, priority rules

the rules about

- merging into a stream of traffic
- crossing the path of an approaching stream of traffic
- all types of pedestrian crossing
- train and tram crossings

how to work out the speed limit where you can't see speed-limit signs.

> Notes

You can use this page to make your own notes or diagrams about the key points you need to remember.

Think about

- Where might you see a minimum-speed-limit sign?
- When can you ride in a bus lane?
- What's a box junction? What mustn't you do at one of these junctions?
- Where could you park your motorcycle when you're away from home?
- What should you do if you've just ridden onto a level crossing and the warning lights start flashing?
- How close to a junction are you allowed to park?

Your notes

Things to discuss and practise with your trainer

These are just a few examples of what you could discuss and practise with your trainer. Read more about rules of the road to come up with your own ideas.

Discuss with your trainer

- what the 'national speed limit applies' sign looks like. What does this mean in mph on different roads and for different vehicles?
- what the speed limit will usually be if there are street lights along the road
- what the different lanes are used for on
  - a two-lane dual carriageway
  - a three-lane dual carriageway
  - a motorway.

Practise with your trainer

- negotiating roundabouts with several lanes on approach
- riding in areas with changing speed limits
- entering, exiting and overtaking on busy dual carriageways.

You're riding slowly in a town centre. Why should you glance over your left shoulder before turning left?

- ☑ To check for cyclists
- ☐ To help keep your balance
- ☐ To look for traffic signs
- ☐ To check for potholes

When riding slowly, you must remember to look out for cyclists – they can travel quickly and fit through surprisingly narrow spaces. Before you turn left in slow-moving traffic, it's important to check that a cyclist isn't trying to filter past on your left.

Which lane mustn't you use when you're riding your motorcycle?

- ☐ Crawler lane
- ☐ Overtaking lane
- ☐ Acceleration lane
- ☑ Tram lane

Always plan ahead and be aware of lanes and areas designated for specific road users only. The restrictions are sometimes in force only at certain times of day, and signs will show when they apply. In some towns, motorcycles are permitted to use bus lanes – check the signs carefully.

What does this sign mean?

In some towns and cities there are special areas reserved for parking motorcycles. Look out for these signs.

- ☐ No parking for solo motorcycles
- ☑ Parking for solo motorcycles
- ☐ Passing place for motorcycles
- ☐ Police motorcycles only

10.4

Mark one answer

RES s8

You're riding on a busy dual carriageway. What should you do before you change lanes?

☐ Rely totally on your mirrors

☐ Always increase your speed

☐ Signal so that others will give way

☐ Use mirrors and shoulder checks

Before changing direction, as well as using your mirrors, you may need to take a quick sideways glance to check for vehicles in your blind spots. These are the areas behind and to the side of you that aren't covered by your mirrors.

10.5

Mark one answer

RES s8, HC r241

You're looking for somewhere to park your motorcycle. The area is full except for spaces marked 'disabled use'. What can you do?

☐ You can use these spaces when elsewhere is full

☐ You can park in one of these spaces if you stay with your motorcycle

☐ You can use one of the spaces as long as one is kept free

☐ You can't park there, unless you're permitted to do so

It's illegal to park in a space reserved for disabled users unless you're permitted to do so. These spaces are provided for people with limited mobility, who may need extra space to get into and out of their vehicle.

10.6

Mark one answer

RES s10, HC r155–156

You're on a road with passing places. It's only wide enough for one vehicle. A car is coming towards you. What should you do?

☐ Pull into a passing place on your right

☐ Force the other driver to reverse

☐ Turn round and ride back to the main road

☐ Pull into a passing place on your left

If you meet another vehicle on a narrow road and the passing place is on your left, pull into it. If the passing place is on your right, wait opposite it.

Mark one answer

RES s9, HC r181

You're both turning right at this crossroads. Why is it safer to keep the car to your right?

When turning right at this crossroads, you should keep the oncoming car to your right. This will give you a clear view of the road ahead and any oncoming traffic.

☑ So you can see approaching traffic

☐ So you can keep close to the kerb

☐ So you can keep clear of following traffic

☐ So you can make oncoming vehicles stop

10.8

Mark one answer

HC r88

What should you do when filtering through slow-moving or stationary traffic?

☑ Watch for vehicles emerging from side roads

☐ Continually use your horn as a warning

☐ Stand up on the footrests for a good view ahead

☐ Ride with your hazard warning lights on

Other road users may not expect or look for motorcycles filtering through slow-moving or stationary traffic. Your view will be reduced by the vehicles around you. Watch out for pedestrians walking between the vehicles, vehicles suddenly changing direction and vehicles turning into or out of side roads.

10.9

Mark one answer

RES s8, HC r109

You're riding towards roadworks. The temporary traffic lights are on red. The road ahead is clear. What should you do?

☐ Ride on with extreme caution

☐ Ride on at normal speed

☐ Carry on if approaching cars have stopped

☐ Wait for the green light

You must obey all traffic signs and signals. Just because the lights are temporary, it doesn't mean that you can disregard them.

10.10 — Mark one answer — RES s19

You intend to go abroad and will be riding on the right-hand side of the road. What should you fit to your motorcycle?

☐ Twin headlights
☐ Headlight deflectors
☐ Tinted yellow brake lights
☐ Tinted red indicator lenses

When abroad and riding on the right, deflectors are usually required to prevent your headlights from dazzling approaching drivers.

10.11 — Mark one answer — RES s14

You want to tow a trailer with your motorcycle. What's the minimum engine size required to do this?

☐ 50 cc
☑ 125 cc
☐ 525 cc
☐ 1000 cc

Towing a trailer requires special care. You must obey the restrictions that apply when towing – including the 125 cc minimum size of your motorcycle engine and the reduced national speed limits. Don't forget the trailer is there, especially when negotiating bends and junctions.

10.12 — Mark one answer — HC r124, p40

What's the national speed limit on a single carriageway?

☐ 40 mph
☐ 50 mph
☑ 60 mph
☐ 70 mph

You don't have to ride at the speed limit. Use your own judgement and ride at a speed that suits the prevailing road, weather and traffic conditions.

10.13 — Mark one answer — HC r105, 109, 286

When must you stop your motorcycle?

☐ At a clear pelican crossing when the amber light is flashing
☐ At an empty zebra crossing
☐ When signalled to do so by a police officer
☐ At a junction with double broken white lines

Don't stop or hold up traffic unnecessarily. However, there are occasions when you must stop by law. These include

- when signalled to do so by a school crossing patrol, police officer or traffic officer
- at a red traffic light
- at a junction with a 'stop' sign.

10.14

What's the meaning of this sign?

This sign doesn't tell you the speed limit in figures. You should know the speed limit for the type of road that you're on and the type of vehicle that you're driving. Study your copy of The Highway Code.

- ☐ Local speed limit applies
- ☐ No waiting on the carriageway
- ☑ National speed limit applies
- ☐ No entry for vehicles

10.15

What's the national speed limit for cars and motorcycles on a dual carriageway?

- ☐ 30 mph
- ☐ 50 mph
- ☐ 60 mph
- ☑ 70 mph

Make sure that you know the speed limit for the road that you're on. The speed limit on a dual carriageway or motorway is 70 mph for cars and motorcycles, unless signs indicate otherwise. The speed limits for different types of vehicle are listed in The Highway Code.

10.16

There are no speed-limit signs on the road. How is a 30 mph limit indicated?

- ☐ By hazard warning lines
- ☑ By street lighting
- ☐ By pedestrian islands
- ☐ By double or single yellow lines

There's a 30 mph speed limit where there are street lights unless signs show another limit.

10.17

You see street lights but no speed-limit signs. What will the speed limit usually be?

- ☐ 30 mph
- ☐ 40 mph
- ☐ 50 mph
- ☐ 60 mph

The presence of street lights generally indicates that there's a 30 mph speed limit, unless signs tell you otherwise.

10.18 — Mark one answer — KYTS p21

What does this sign mean?

The red slash through the sign indicates that the restriction has ended. In this case, the restriction was a minimum speed limit of 30 mph.

- ☐ Minimum speed 30 mph
- ☐ End of maximum speed
- ☑ End of minimum speed
- ☐ Maximum speed 30 mph

10.19 — Mark one answer — RES s8, HC r163

There's a tractor ahead. You want to overtake but you aren't sure whether it's safe. What should you do?

- ☐ Follow another vehicle as it overtakes the tractor
- ☐ Sound your horn to make the tractor pull over
- ☐ Speed past, flashing your lights at oncoming traffic
- ☑ Stay behind the tractor if you're in any doubt

Following a tractor can be frustrating, but never overtake if you're unsure whether it's safe. Ask yourself: 'Can I see far enough down the road to ensure that I can complete the manoeuvre safely?' It's better to be delayed for a minute or two than to take a chance that may cause a collision.

10.20 — Mark one answer — HC r187

Which vehicle is most likely to take an unusual course at a roundabout?

- ☐ Estate car
- ☐ Milk float
- ☐ Delivery van
- ☑ Long lorry

Long vehicles might have to take a slightly different position when approaching the roundabout or going around it. This is to stop the rear of the vehicle cutting in and mounting the kerb.

When mustn't you stop on a clearway?

☑ At any time

☐ When it's busy

☐ In the rush hour

☐ During daylight hours

Clearways are in place so that traffic can flow without the obstruction of parked vehicles. Just one parked vehicle can cause an obstruction for all other traffic. You mustn't stop where a clearway is in force, not even to pick up or set down passengers.

What's the meaning of this sign?

☐ No entry

☑ Waiting restrictions

☐ National speed limit

☐ School crossing patrol

This sign indicates that there are waiting restrictions. It's normally accompanied by details of when the restrictions are in force.

Details of most signs in common use are shown in The Highway Code. For more comprehensive coverage, see Know Your Traffic Signs.

When can you park on the right-hand side of a road at night?

☐ When you're in a one-way street

☐ When you have your sidelights on

☐ When you're more than 10 metres (32 feet) from a junction

☐ When you're under a lamppost

Red rear reflectors show up when headlights shine on them. These are useful when you're parked at night, but they'll only reflect if you park in the same direction as the traffic flow. Normally you should park on the left, but in a one-way street you may also park on the right-hand side.

10.24　Mark one answer　RES s8, HC r137–138

On a three-lane dual carriageway, what can the right-hand lane be used for?

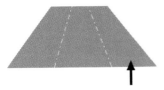

☐ Overtaking only, never turning right

☑ Overtaking or turning right

☐ Fast-moving traffic only

☐ Turning right only, never overtaking

You should normally use the left-hand lane on any dual carriageway unless you're overtaking or turning right.

When overtaking on a dual carriageway, look for vehicles ahead that are turning right. They may be slowing or stopped. You need to see them in good time so that you can take appropriate action.

10.25　Mark one answer　RES s8

You're approaching a busy junction. What should you do when, at the last moment, you realise you're in the wrong lane?

☑ Continue in that lane

☐ Force your way across

☐ Stop until the area has cleared

☐ Use clear arm signals to cut across

There are times when road markings are obscured by queuing traffic, or you're unsure which lane to use. If, at the last moment, you find you're in the wrong lane, don't cut across or bully other drivers to let you in. Follow the lane you're in and find somewhere safe to turn around and rejoin your route.

10.26　Mark one answer　RES s8, HC r143

Where may you overtake on a one-way street?

☐ Only on the left-hand side

☐ Overtaking isn't allowed

☐ Only on the right-hand side

☑ On either the right or the left

You can overtake other traffic on either side when travelling in a one-way street. Make full use of your mirrors and ensure it's clear all around before you attempt to overtake. Look for signs and road markings, and use the most suitable lane for your destination.

How should you signal when going straight ahead at a roundabout?

- ☑ Indicate left before leaving the roundabout
- ☐ Don't indicate at any time
- ☐ Indicate right when approaching the roundabout
- ☐ Indicate left when approaching the roundabout

When going straight ahead at a roundabout, don't signal as you approach it. Indicate left just after passing the exit before the one you wish to take.

Which vehicle might have to take a different course from normal at roundabouts?

- ☐ Sports car
- ☐ Van
- ☐ Estate car
- ☑ Long vehicle

A long vehicle may have to straddle lanes either on or approaching a roundabout so that the rear wheels don't hit the kerb.

If you're following a long vehicle, stay well back and give it plenty of room.

On which occasion may you enter a box junction?

Yellow box junctions are marked on the road to prevent the road becoming blocked. Don't enter the box unless your exit road is clear. You may wait in the box if you want to turn right and your exit road is clear but oncoming traffic or other vehicles waiting to turn right are preventing you from making the turn.

- ☐ When there are fewer than two vehicles ahead
- ☐ When signalled by another road user
- ☑ When your exit road is clear
- ☐ When traffic signs direct you

10.30   Mark one answer   RES s7, HC r174

When may you stop and wait in a box junction?

The purpose of yellow box markings is to keep junctions clear of queuing traffic. You may only wait in the marked area when you're turning right and your exit lane is clear but you can't complete the turn because of oncoming traffic or other traffic waiting to turning right.

- ☑ When oncoming traffic prevents you from turning right
- ☐ When you're in a queue of traffic turning left
- ☐ When you're in a queue of traffic going ahead
- ☐ When you're on a roundabout

10.31   Mark one answer   HC r105–109

Which person's signal to stop must you obey?

- ☐ A motorcyclist
- ☐ A pedestrian
- ☑ A police officer
- ☐ A bus driver

You must obey signals to stop given by police and traffic officers, traffic wardens and school crossing patrols. Failure to do so is an offence and could lead to prosecution.

10.32   Mark one answer   RES s8, HC r195

You see a pedestrian waiting at a zebra crossing. What should you normally do?

- ☐ Go on quickly before they step onto the crossing
- ☐ Stop before you reach the zigzag lines and let them cross
- ☑ Stop to let them cross and wait patiently
- ☐ Ignore them as they're still on the pavement

By standing on the pavement, the pedestrian is showing an intention to cross. By looking well ahead, you'll give yourself time to see the pedestrian, check your mirrors and respond safely.

10.33

Who can use a toucan crossing?

☐ Cars and motorcycles

☑ Cyclists and pedestrians

☐ Buses and lorries

☐ Trams and trains

Toucan crossings are similar to pelican crossings but there's no flashing amber phase. Cyclists share the crossing with pedestrians and are allowed to cycle across when the green cycle symbol is shown.

10.34

You're waiting at a pelican crossing. What does it mean when the red light changes to flashing amber?

☑ Wait for pedestrians on the crossing to clear

☐ Move off immediately without any hesitation

☐ Wait for the green light before moving off

☐ Get ready and go when the continuous amber light shows

This light allows pedestrians already on the crossing to get to the other side in their own time, without being rushed. Don't rev your engine or start to move off while they're still crossing.

10.35

When can you park on the left opposite these road markings?

You mustn't park or stop on a road marked with double white lines (even where one of the lines is broken) except to pick up or set down passengers.

☐ If the line nearest to you is broken

☐ When there are no yellow lines

☑ To pick up or set down passengers

☐ During daylight hours only

10.36 — Mark one answer — HC r181

You're turning right at a crossroads. An oncoming driver is also turning right. How should you normally deal with this?

☑ Keep the other vehicle to your right and turn behind it (offside to offside)

☐ Keep the other vehicle to your left and turn in front of it (nearside to nearside)

☐ Carry on and turn at the next junction instead

☐ Hold back and wait for the other driver to turn first

At crossroads, traffic normally turns offside to offside. This is the safest way to turn, but sometimes the layout or road markings indicate drivers should pass nearside to nearside. Take extra care at these crossroads because, as you turn, your view ahead will be obscured by the oncoming vehicle crossing in front of you.

10.37 — Mark one answer — RES s10, HC r152

You're travelling along a street with parked vehicles on the left-hand side. Why should you keep your speed down?

☐ So that oncoming traffic can see you more clearly

☐ You may set off car alarms

☐ There may be delivery lorries on the street

☑ Children may run out from between the vehicles

Travel slowly and carefully near parked vehicles. Beware of

- vehicles pulling out, especially bicycles and motorcycles
- pedestrians, especially children, who may run out from between cars
- drivers opening their doors.

10.38 — Mark one answer — RES s7

What should you do when you meet an obstruction on your side of the road?

☐ Carry on, as you have priority

☑ Give way to oncoming traffic

☐ Wave oncoming vehicles through

☐ Accelerate to get past first

Take care if you have to pass a parked vehicle on your side of the road. Give way to oncoming traffic if there isn't enough room for you both to continue safely.

10.39 — Mark one answer — HC r137

You're on a two-lane dual carriageway. Why would you use the right-hand lane?

☑ To overtake slower traffic

☐ For normal progress

☐ When staying at the minimum allowed speed

☐ To keep driving at a constant high speed

Normally you should travel in the left-hand lane and only use the right-hand lane for overtaking or turning right. Move back into the left lane as soon as it's safe but don't cut in across the path of the vehicle you've just passed.

10.40 Mark one answer RES s9, HC r146

Who has priority at an unmarked crossroads?

☐ The larger vehicle

☑ No-one has priority

☐ The faster vehicle

☐ The smaller vehicle

Practise good observation in all directions before you emerge or make a turn. Proceed only when you're sure it's safe to do so.

10.41 NI EXEMPT Mark one answer HC r243

What's the nearest you may park to a junction?

☑ 10 metres (32 feet)

☐ 12 metres (39 feet)

☐ 15 metres (49 feet)

☐ 20 metres (66 feet)

Don't park within 10 metres (32 feet) of a junction (unless in an authorised parking place). This is to allow drivers emerging from, or turning into, the junction a clear view of the road they're joining. It also allows them to see hazards such as pedestrians or cyclists at the junction.

10.42 NI EXEMPT Mark one answer HC r243

Where shouldn't you park?

☐ On a road with a 40 mph speed limit

☐ At or near a bus stop

☐ Where there's no pavement

☐ Within 20 metres (65 feet) of a junction

It may be tempting to park where you shouldn't while you run a quick errand. Careless parking is a selfish act and could endanger other road users. It's important not to park at or near a bus stop, as this could inconvenience passengers and may put them at risk as they get on or off the bus.

10.43 Mark one answer RES s7, HC r293, KYTS p27

You're waiting at a level crossing. A train passes but the lights keep flashing. What must you do?

☑ Carry on waiting

☐ Phone the signal operator

☐ Edge over the stop line and look for trains

☐ Park and investigate

If the lights at a level crossing keep flashing after a train has passed, you should continue to wait, because another train might be coming. Time seems to pass slowly when you're held up in a queue. Be patient and wait until the lights stop flashing.

10.44

Mark one answer   HC p107

What does this sign tell you?

The blue-and-red circular sign on its own means that waiting restrictions are in force. This sign shows that you're leaving the controlled zone and waiting restrictions no longer apply.

☐ No through road

☐ End of traffic-calming zone

☐ Free-parking zone ends

☑ No-waiting zone ends

10.45

Mark one answer   HC r288, KYTS p139

What must you do when entering roadworks where a temporary speed limit is displayed?

Where there are extra hazards, such as at roadworks, it's often necessary to slow traffic down by imposing a lower speed limit. These speed limits aren't advisory; they must be obeyed.

☑ Obey the speed limit

☐ Obey the limit, but only during rush hour

☐ Ignore the displayed limit

☐ Use your own judgment; the limit is only advisory

10.46

Mark one answer   HC r115

You're on a well-lit road at night, in a built-up area. How will using dipped headlights help?

You may be difficult to see when you're travelling at night, even on a well-lit road. If you use dipped headlights rather than sidelights, other road users should be able to see you more easily.

☐ You can see further along the road

☐ You can go at a much faster speed

☐ You can switch to main beam quickly

☑ You can be easily seen by others

Mark one answer

The dual carriageway you're turning right onto has a very narrow central reservation. What should you do?

☐ Proceed to the central reservation and wait

☑ Wait until the road is clear in both directions

☐ Stop in the first lane so that other vehicles give way

☐ Emerge slightly to show your intentions

When the central reservation is narrow, you should treat a dual carriageway as one road. Wait until the road is clear in both directions before emerging to turn right. If you try to treat it as two separate roads and wait in the middle, you're likely to cause an obstruction and possibly a collision.

Mark one answer

What's the national speed limit on a single carriageway road for cars and motorcycles?

☐ 30 mph

☐ 50 mph

☑ 60 mph

☐ 70 mph

Exceeding the speed limit is dangerous and can result in you receiving penalty points on your licence. It isn't worth it. You should know the speed limit for the road that you're on by observing the road signs. Different speed limits apply if you're towing a trailer.

Mark one answer

You park at night on a road with a 40 mph speed limit. What should you do?

☐ Park facing the traffic

☑ Park with parking lights on

☐ Park with dipped headlights on

☐ Park near a street light

You must use parking lights when parking at night on a road or in a lay-by on a road with a speed limit greater than 30 mph. You must also park in the direction of the traffic flow and not close to a junction.

10.50

Mark one answer

KYTS p27

Where will you see these red and white markers?

☐ Approaching the end of a motorway

☑ Approaching a concealed level crossing

☐ Approaching a concealed speed-limit sign

☐ Approaching the end of a dual carriageway

If there's a bend just before a level crossing, you may not be able to see the level-crossing barriers or waiting traffic. These signs give you an early warning that you may find these hazards just around the bend.

10.51

Mark one answer

RES s18, HC r108

You're travelling on a motorway in England. You must stop when signalled to do so by which of these?

☐ Flashing amber lights above your lane

☐ A traffic officer

☐ Pedestrians on the hard shoulder

☐ A driver who has broken down

You'll find traffic officers on England's motorways. They work in partnership with the police, helping to keep traffic moving and helping to make your journey as safe as possible. It's an offence not to comply with the directions given by a traffic officer.

10.52

Mark one answer

RES s9, HC r186

You're going straight ahead at a roundabout. How should you signal?

☐ Signal right on the approach and then left to leave the roundabout

☐ Signal left after you leave the roundabout and enter the new road

☐ Signal right on the approach to the roundabout and keep the signal on

☑ Signal left just after you pass the exit before the one you're going to take

To go straight ahead at a roundabout, you should normally approach in the left-hand lane, but check the road markings. At some roundabouts, the left lane on approach is marked 'left turn only', so make sure you use the correct lane to go ahead. You won't normally need to signal as you approach, but signal before you leave the roundabout, as other road users need to know your intentions.

> Case study practice – 10 Rules of the road

> You're riding your motorcycle in a residential area.
>
> At a signed mini-roundabout, you turn right.
>
> Later, you come to roadworks. There are temporary traffic lights showing red, but no oncoming traffic.
>
> Once past, you turn right into a residential street containing road humps. You see a sign showing red-and-black arrows, asking road users to give way to oncoming traffic.

10.1 What colour is the roundabout sign?

Mark **one** answer

- ☑ Blue and white
- ☐ Red and white
- ☐ Green and white
- ☐ Black and white

HC p107 **KYTS** p19, 69

10.2 What should you do at the traffic lights?

Mark **one** answer

- ☐ Ride past the lights quickly as there's no oncoming traffic
- ☑ Stop and wait until the green light shows
- ☐ Get off and wheel your motorcycle through the roadworks
- ☐ Call the helpline because the lights must be faulty

HC p109

10.3 What should you do before making the turn?

Mark **one** answer

- ☐ Check that your hazard warning lights are working
- ☐ Turn and look back over your left shoulder
- ☐ Position yourself by the left-hand kerb
- ☑ Take a look over your right shoulder

RES s8, 9

10.4 What are the features in the residential street for?

Mark **one** answer

- ☐ To increase reaction time
- ☐ To monitor tyre pressure
- ☑ To slow down the traffic
- ☐ To test the suspension

RES s7 **HC** r153

10.5 What shape is the arrowed sign?

Mark **one** answer

- ☑ Circular
- ☐ Triangular
- ☐ Rectangular
- ☐ Square

KYTS p18

Road and traffic signs

In this section, you'll learn about

- ❯ what the shapes of road sign can tell you
- ❯ what road markings mean
- ❯ the sequence and meaning of traffic lights
- ❯ motorway warning lights
- ❯ the signals used by other drivers and by police officers.

Road and traffic signs

Road and traffic signs give important information to keep you safe on the road, so it's essential that you know what they mean and what you need to do when you see them.

> Signs

The shape and colour of a road sign tell you about its meaning.

Circular signs give orders.

Blue circles give an instruction or show which sort of road user can use a route, eg cyclists, pedestrians, trams.

Red rings or circles tell you what you mustn't do.

Triangular signs give warnings.

Rectangular signs give information.

Signs with a brown background give tourist information.

 **KYTS** p9, 84, 100–104

The exception to the shape rule is the 'stop' sign: this is octagonal so that it stands out and can be understood even if it's partly covered, eg by snow.

HC r109 **RES** s7 **KYTS** p9

Maximum speed limits are shown inside red circles: you **MUST NOT** go faster than the speed shown. Where no speed limit is shown, the national speed limits (given on page 294) apply. Speed-limit signs may be combined with other signs, such as those indicating a traffic-calmed area.

HC p106 **KYTS** p20

It's impossible to mention all the signs here. *Know Your Traffic Signs* shows all the signs you're likely to see and *The Official Highway Code* contains important advice, information on current laws in Great Britain, and best practice in road safety. It's important that you get to know these to make sure that you don't break the law.

Test your knowledge of signs using the activity on the Safe Driving for Life website.

❯ **safedrivingforlife.info/signsquiz**

❯ Road markings

Markings on the road give information, orders or warnings. As a general rule, the more paint there is, the more important the message.

HC r127–131 **RES** s7 **KYTS** p62–64

There are three types of road markings.

Along the middle of the road

Short broken white lines mark the centre of the road.

Longer broken white lines show that a hazard is ahead: only overtake if the road ahead is clear.

You **MUST NOT** cross or straddle double white lines with a solid white line on your side of the road unless

- you're turning into a junction or an entrance
- you need to pass a stationary vehicle
- you need to overtake a cyclist, horse or road maintenance vehicle if they're moving at 10 mph or less.

White diagonal stripes or chevrons separate lanes of traffic or protect traffic turning right.

Sometimes red tarmac is used within a block of white lines or diagonals. This highlights the area that separates traffic flowing in opposite directions.

HC p114 RES s7 KYTS p62–64

Along the side of the road

A white line shows the edge of the carriageway.

Yellow lines show waiting and stopping restrictions.

Zigzag lines (white at pedestrian crossings, yellow outside schools) mean no stopping or parking at any time.

HC p115, 116 RES s7 KYTS p39–44, 56, 65, 122

Lines on or across the road

Broken lines across the road mean 'give way'. At a roundabout, give way to traffic from the right.

A single solid line means 'stop'.

Various markings on the road, for example 'give way' triangles, road-hump markings and rumble strips, warn of a hazard.

HC p114–116 **KYTS** p62–75

As with signs, you should look at *Know Your Traffic Signs* and *The Official Highway Code* to learn more about road markings.

You may see reflective studs on motorways and other roads. These are especially useful at night and when visibility is poor, as they help to make the lanes and edges of the road easier to see. Different coloured studs are used on motorways to help drivers and riders identify which lane they're using. See section 9, Motorway riding, for more details.

HC r132

❯ Traffic lights and warning lights

Traffic lights work in a sequence.

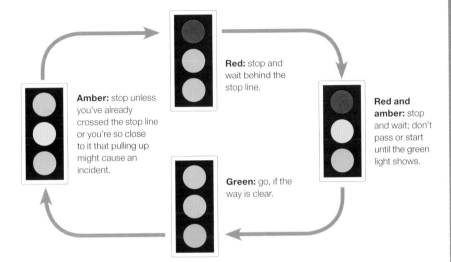

Red: stop and wait behind the stop line.

Amber: stop unless you've already crossed the stop line or you're so close to it that pulling up might cause an incident.

Red and amber: stop and wait; don't pass or start until the green light shows.

Green: go, if the way is clear.

HC p102 **RES** s7 **KYTS** p119–120

On some traffic lights there's a green filter arrow. This means you can go in the direction of the arrow, even if the main light isn't showing green.

If a set of traffic lights is out of order, ride very carefully: nobody has priority. There may be a sign telling you that the lights aren't working.

RES s7

Red flashing lights are used at level crossings and other locations, such as lifting bridges and outside some fire stations. You **MUST** stop when these show.

HC r293, p102 **KYTS** p13, 26–29, 120

At roadworks, traffic can be controlled by

- a police officer
- traffic lights
- a 'stop/go' board.

HC r288 **KYTS** p136

Amber warns you of a hazard (eg lane closures, to leave at the next exit, fog) or a temporary maximum speed advised for the conditions.

Red above your lane tells you that the lane is closed beyond this point, and you should move into another lane.

Red above all the lanes, on the central reservation or on the roadside tells you to stop. You **MUST NOT** go beyond that point in any lane.

HC r255–258, p102 KYTS p89–91

> Signals given by drivers and the police

Road users normally signal where they're intending to turn by using their indicators. Make sure that you cancel your indicators after you've turned, to avoid confusing other road users. Be aware that another driver may have left their indicator on by mistake.

If you're emerging from a junction and a driver coming along the main road from the right is close to you and indicating left, wait until the vehicle starts to turn before you emerge.

HC r103–104 RES s5

You may need to use an arm signal to strengthen or clarify the message given by your indicators, such as when you're

- signalling to turn right in busy traffic
- slowing down to give way at a zebra crossing.

However, don't keep signalling with your arm while you're turning left or right, because you'll have less control over the steering.

If you're slowing down and stopping just after a junction, wait to signal until you're passing the junction, or just after it.

You can use the horn to warn others that you're there. You **MUST NOT** use it between 11.30 pm and 7.00 am when riding in a built-up area, except when another road user puts you in danger. You **MUST NOT** use your horn when stationary unless another vehicle is likely to cause a danger.

The only reason you should flash your headlights is to warn other road users that you're there.

HC r110–112 **RES** s6

If you're riding on a motorway or unrestricted dual carriageway, you can briefly use your hazard warning lights to warn drivers behind you that there's an obstruction ahead.

HC r116 **RES** s5, 11

Police or traffic officers may signal to you if they're directing traffic. Make sure that you know all the official arm signals in case you need to use or react to them.

HC p103–105

A police or traffic officer following you in a patrol vehicle may flash their headlights, indicate left and point to the left to direct you to stop. Pull up on the left as soon as it's safe to do so.

HC r106

Remember, you **MUST** obey any signals given by police or traffic officers, traffic wardens and signs used by school crossing patrols.

HC r105–108, p104–105

⊛ Road lanes

Contraflow lanes are lanes that flow in the opposite direction to most of the traffic. Bus and cycle contraflow lanes may be found in one-way streets. They'll be signed and marked on the road. Don't try to ride against the flow of traffic in these lanes.

HC r140–141, 143 **RES** s7

You may also see contraflow lanes at roadworks. When you see the signs

* reduce your speed and comply with any temporary speed limits
* choose an appropriate lane in good time
* keep the correct distance from the vehicle in front.

RES s11 **KYTS** p128–133

The centre and right-hand lanes of a three-lane motorway are overtaking lanes. Always move back to a lane on your left after overtaking, to allow other vehicles to overtake. On a free-flowing motorway or dual carriageway, you mustn't overtake other vehicles on their left.

HC r264, 268 **RES** s11

Meeting the standards

You must be able to

respond correctly to all

- permanent traffic signals, signs and road markings
- temporary traffic signals, signs and road markings.

You must know and understand

the meaning of all mandatory traffic signs and how to respond to them

the meaning of all warning signs and how to respond to them

the meaning of all road markings and how to respond to them.

> Notes

You can use this page to make your own notes or diagrams about the key points you need to remember.

Think about

- When are you allowed to cross double white lines along the centre of the road?
- What must you never do on zigzag lines?
- What shape is the 'stop' sign?
- What should you do at an amber traffic light?
- When might you need to use arm signals?

Your notes

Things to discuss and practise with your trainer

These are just a few examples of what you could discuss and practise with your trainer. Read more about road and traffic signs to come up with your own ideas.

Discuss with your trainer

- which is the only octagonal road sign and why it's unique
- what these shapes of sign tell you
  - round
  - triangular
  - rectangular
- what signs are relevant to solo motorcycles and what they mean.

Practise with your trainer

- identifying signs, from *The Official Highway Code* and *Know Your Traffic Signs*
- riding through a busy town centre and identifying all the warning signs that you see. Discuss these after your lesson
- riding to a level crossing and identifying the signs and signals that you find there.

Mark one answer

How should you give an arm signal to turn left?

☐   ☐

☑   ☐

Arm signals can be effective during daylight, especially when you're wearing bright clothing. Practise giving arm signals when you're learning. You need to be able to keep full control of your motorcycle with one hand off the handlebars.

Mark one answer

You're giving an arm signal, ready to turn left. Why shouldn't you continue with the arm signal while you turn?

Consider giving an arm signal if it will help other road users; for example, in bright sunshine, when your indicators may be difficult to see. Don't maintain an arm signal when turning, but return your hand to the handlebars to help you steer through the turn.

☐ Because you might hit a pedestrian on the corner

☑ Because you'll have less steering control

☐ Because you'll need to keep the clutch applied

☐ Because other motorists will think that you're stopping on the corner

11.3

Mark one answer

RES s12, HC p109, KYTS p12

What does this sign mean?

☑ Side winds
☐ Airport
☐ Slippery road
☐ Service area

Strong side winds can suddenly blow you off course. Keep your speed down when it's very windy, especially on exposed roads.

11.4

Mark one answer

RES s7, HC p106, KYTS p17

Which of these signs are you allowed to ride past on a solo motorcycle?

Most regulatory signs are circular. A red circle tells you what you mustn't do.

11.5

Mark one answer

RES s6, HC r103, p103

Which of these signals should you give when slowing or stopping your motorcycle?

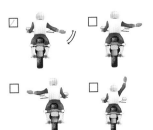

Arm signals can be given to reinforce your flashing indicators, especially if the indicator signal could cause confusion; for example, if you intend to pull up close to a side road.

Mark one answer RES s6, HC r103–104

Why should you make sure that you cancel your indicators after turning?

☐ To avoid flattening the battery

☑ To avoid misleading other road users

☐ To avoid dazzling other road users

☐ To avoid damage to the indicator relay

Always check that you've cancelled your indicators after turning. Failing to cancel your indicators could lead to a serious or even fatal collision. Other road users might pull out in front of you if they think you're going to turn off before you reach them.

11.7 **Mark one answer** RES s6, HC p103

Your indicators are difficult to see due to bright sunshine. What should you do to let other road users know your intentions?

☑ Give an arm signal

☐ Sound your horn

☐ Flash your headlights

☐ Keep both hands on the handlebars

Arm signals should be used to confirm your intentions when you aren't sure that your indicators can be seen by other road users. Use the signals shown in The Highway Code and return your hand to the handlebars before you turn.

11.8 **Mark one answer** RES s11, HC p113

You're riding on a motorway. There's a slow-moving vehicle ahead. On the back, you see this sign. What should you do?

☐ Pass on the right

☑ Pass on the left

☐ Leave at the next exit

☐ Drive no further

If this vehicle is in your lane, you'll have to move to the left. Use your mirrors and signal if necessary. When it's safe, move into the lane on your left. You should always look well ahead so that you can spot such hazards early, giving yourself time to react safely.

11.9 **Mark one answer** RES s7, HC p106, KYTS p9, 16

How can you identify traffic signs that give orders?

☐ They're rectangular with a yellow border

☐ They're triangular with a blue border

☐ They're square with a brown border

☑ They're circular with a red border

There are three basic types of traffic sign: those that warn, those that inform and those that give orders. Generally, triangular signs warn, rectangular signs give information or directions, and circular signs give orders. An exception is the eight-sided 'stop' sign.

11.10

Mark one answer

RES s7, HC p106, KYTS p9, 16

Traffic signs giving orders are generally which shape?

Road signs in the shape of a circle give orders. Those with a red circle are mostly prohibitive. The 'stop' sign is octagonal to give it greater prominence. Signs giving orders must always be obeyed.

11.11

Mark one answer

RES s7, HC p106, KYTS p9, 16

Which type of sign tells you not to do something?

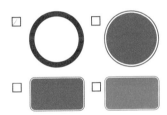

Signs in the shape of a circle give orders. A sign with a red circle means that you aren't allowed to do something. Study Know Your Traffic Signs to ensure that you understand what the different traffic signs mean.

11.12

Mark one answer

RES s7, HC p106, KYTS p20

What does this sign mean?

☑ Maximum speed limit with traffic calming

☐ Minimum speed limit with traffic calming

☐ '20 cars only' parking zone

☐ Only 20 cars allowed at any one time

If you're in a place where there are likely to be pedestrians (for example, outside a school, near a park, in a residential area or in a shopping area), you should be cautious and keep your speed down.

Many local authorities have taken steps to slow traffic down by creating traffic-calming measures such as speed humps. They're there for a reason; slow down.

Which sign means no motor vehicles are allowed?

You'll generally see this sign at the approach to a pedestrian-only zone.

What does this sign mean?

Where you see this sign, the 20 mph restriction ends. Check all around for possible hazards and only increase your speed if it's safe to do so.

- ☐ New speed limit 20 mph
- ☐ No vehicles over 30 tonnes
- ☐ Minimum speed limit 30 mph
- ☑ End of 20 mph zone

What does this sign mean?

A sign will indicate which types of vehicles are prohibited from certain roads. Make sure that you know which signs apply to the vehicle you're using.

- ☐ No overtaking
- ☑ No motor vehicles
- ☐ Clearway (no stopping)
- ☐ Cars and motorcycles only

11.16

Mark one answer

RES s7, HC p106, KYTS p17

What does this sign mean?

☐ No parking

☐ No road markings

☐ No through road

☑ No entry

'No entry' signs are used in places such as one-way streets to prevent vehicles driving against the traffic. To ignore one would be dangerous, both for yourself and for other road users, as well as being against the law.

11.17

Mark one answer

RES s7, HC p106, KYTS p18

What does this sign mean?

☐ Bend to the right

☐ Road on the right closed

☐ No traffic from the right

☑ No right turn

The 'no right turn' sign may be used to warn road users that there's a 'no entry' prohibition on a road to the right ahead.

11.18

Mark one answer

RES s7, HC p106, KYTS p17

Which sign means 'no entry'?

Look for and obey traffic signs. Disobeying or not seeing a sign could be dangerous. It may also be an offence for which you could be prosecuted.

What does this sign mean?

Avoid blocking tram routes. Trams are fixed on their route and can't manoeuvre around other vehicles or pedestrians. Modern trams travel quickly and are quiet, so you might not hear them approaching.

- ☑ Route for trams only
- ☐ Route for buses only
- ☐ Parking for buses only
- ☐ Parking for trams only

Which type of vehicle does this sign apply to?

The triangular shapes above and below the dimensions indicate a height restriction that applies to the road ahead.

- ☐ Wide vehicles
- ☐ Long vehicles
- ☑ High vehicles
- ☐ Heavy vehicles

Which sign means no motor vehicles allowed?

This sign is used to enable pedestrians to walk free from traffic. It's often found in shopping areas.

☐   ☑

☐   ☐

11.22

Mark one answer

RES s7, HC p106, KYTS p18

What does this sign mean?

Road signs that prohibit overtaking are placed in locations where passing the vehicle in front is dangerous. If you see this sign, don't attempt to overtake. The sign is there for a reason; you must obey it.

☐ You have priority

☐ No motor vehicles

☐ Two-way traffic

☐ No overtaking

11.23

Mark one answer

RES s7, HC p107, KYTS p54

What does this sign mean?

There'll be a plate or additional sign to tell you when the restrictions apply.

☐ Waiting restrictions apply

☐ Waiting permitted

☐ National speed limit applies

☐ Clearway (no stopping)

11.24

Mark one answer

RES s7, HC p112, KYTS p54

What does this sign mean?

Even though you've left the restricted area, make sure that you park where you won't endanger other road users or cause an obstruction.

☐ End of restricted speed area

☐ End of restricted parking area

☐ End of clearway

☐ End of cycle route

Which sign means 'no stopping'?

Stopping where this clearway restriction applies is likely to cause congestion. Allow the traffic to flow by obeying the signs.

You see this sign ahead. What does it mean?

Clearways are stretches of road where you aren't allowed to stop unless it's an emergency. Stopping where these restrictions apply may be dangerous and is likely to cause an obstruction. Restrictions might apply for several miles and this may be indicated on the sign.

- ☐ National speed limit applies
- ☐ Waiting restrictions apply
- ☑ No stopping
- ☐ No entry

What does this sign mean?

If you intend to stop and rest, this sign allows you time to reduce speed and pull over safely.

- ☑ Distance to parking place ahead
- ☐ Distance to public telephone ahead
- ☐ Distance to public house ahead
- ☐ Distance to passing place ahead

11.28

Mark one answer

RES s7, KYTS p50

What does this sign mean?

In order to keep roads free from parked cars, there are some areas where you're allowed to park on the verge. Only do this where you see the sign. Parking on verges or footways anywhere else could lead to a fine.

☐ Vehicles may not park on the verge or footway

☐ Vehicles may park on the left-hand side of the road only

☑ Vehicles may park fully on the verge or footway

☐ Vehicles may park on the right-hand side of the road only

11.29

Mark one answer

RES s7, HC p106, KYTS p18

What does this traffic sign mean?

Priority signs are normally shown where the road is narrow and there isn't enough room for two vehicles to pass. Examples are narrow bridges, roadworks and where there's a width restriction.

Make sure you know who has priority; don't force your way through. Show courtesy and consideration to other road users.

☐ No overtaking allowed

☑ Give priority to oncoming traffic

☐ Two-way traffic

☐ One-way traffic only

What's the meaning of this traffic sign?

Don't force your way through. Show courtesy and consideration to other road users. Although you have priority, make sure oncoming traffic is going to give way before you continue.

☐ End of two-way road

☐ Give priority to vehicles coming towards you

☐ You have priority over vehicles coming towards you

☐ Bus lane ahead

What shape is a 'stop' sign at a junction?

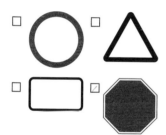

To make it easy to recognise, the 'stop' sign is the only sign of this shape. You must stop and take effective observation before proceeding.

At a junction, you see this sign partly covered by snow. What does it mean?

The 'stop' sign is the only road sign that's octagonal. This is so that it can be recognised and obeyed even if it's obscured (for example, by snow).

☐ Crossroads

☐ Give way

☑ Stop

☐ Turn right

11.33
Mark one answer   RES s7, HC p107, KYTS p21

What does this sign mean?

This sign is shown where slow-moving vehicles would impede the flow of traffic; for example, in tunnels. However, if you need to slow down or even stop to avoid an incident or potential collision, you should do so.

- [ ] Service area 30 miles ahead
- [ ] Maximum speed 30 mph
- [x] Minimum speed 30 mph
- [ ] Lay-by 30 miles ahead

11.34
Mark one answer   RES s7, HC p107, KYTS p19

What does this sign mean?

These signs are often seen in one-way streets that have more than one lane. When you see this sign, use the route that's the most convenient and doesn't require a late change of direction.

- [ ] Give way to oncoming vehicles
- [ ] Approaching traffic passes you on both sides
- [ ] Turn off at the next available junction
- [ ] Pass either side to get to the same destination

11.35
Mark one answer   RES s7, HC p107, KYTS p30

What does this sign mean?

Take extra care when you encounter trams. Look out for road markings and signs that alert you to them. Modern trams are very quiet and you may not hear them approaching.

- [ ] Route for trams
- [ ] Give way to trams
- [ ] Route for buses
- [ ] Give way to buses

What does a circular traffic sign with a blue background do?

Signs with blue circles mostly give a positive instruction. These are often found in urban areas and include signs for mini-roundabouts and directional arrows.

☐ Give warning of a motorway ahead

☐ Give directions to a car park

☐ Give motorway information

☐ Give an instruction

Where would you see a contraflow bus and cycle lane?

☐ On a dual carriageway

☐ On a roundabout

☐ On an urban motorway

☑ On a one-way street

The traffic permitted to use a contraflow lane travels in the opposite direction to traffic in the other lanes on the road.

What does this sign mean?

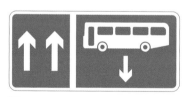

There will also be markings on the road surface to indicate the bus lane. You mustn't use this lane for parking or overtaking.

☐ Bus station on the right

☑ Contraflow bus lane

☐ With-flow bus lane

☐ Give way to buses

11.39
Mark one answer
RES s7, KYTS p84

What does a sign with a brown background show?

Signs with a brown background give directions to places of interest. They're often seen on a motorway, directing you along the easiest route to the attraction.

☐ Tourist directions
☐ Primary roads
☐ Motorway routes
☐ Minor roads

11.40
Mark one answer
RES s7, KYTS p100

What does this sign mean?

These signs indicate places of interest and are designed to guide you by the easiest route. They're particularly useful when you're unfamiliar with the area.

☐ Tourist attraction
☐ Beware of trains
☐ Level crossing
☐ Beware of trams

11.41
Mark one answer
RES s7, HC p108, KYTS p10

What are triangular signs for?

This type of sign warns you of hazards ahead. Make sure you look at each sign that you pass on the road, so that you don't miss any vital instructions or information.

☑ To give warnings
☐ To give information
☐ To give orders
☐ To give directions

What does this sign mean?

This type of sign warns you of hazards ahead. Make sure you look at each sign and road marking that you pass, so that you don't miss any vital instructions or information. This particular sign shows there's a T-junction with priority over vehicles from the right.

☐ Turn left ahead
☑ T-junction
☐ No through road
☐ Give way

What does this sign mean?

It will take up to ten times longer to stop when it's icy. Where there's a risk of icy conditions, you need to be aware of this and take extra care. If you think the road may be icy, don't brake or steer harshly, as your tyres could lose their grip on the road.

☐ Multi-exit roundabout
☑ Risk of ice
☐ Six roads converge
☐ Place of historical interest

What does this sign mean?

The priority through the junction is shown by the broader line. You need to be aware of the hazard posed by traffic crossing or pulling out onto a major road.

☑ Crossroads
☐ Level crossing with gate
☐ Level crossing without gate
☐ Ahead only

11.45

Mark one answer

RES s7, HC p108, KYTS p10

What does this sign mean?

As you approach a roundabout, look well ahead and check all signs. Decide which exit you wish to take and move into the correct position as you approach the roundabout, signalling as required.

☐ Ring road

☐ Mini-roundabout

☐ No vehicles

☑ Roundabout

11.46

Mark one answer

RES s7, HC p108–109, KYTS p10–14

What information would be shown in a triangular road sign?

Warning signs are there to make you aware of potential hazards on the road ahead. Take note of the signs so you're prepared and can take whatever action is necessary.

☑ Road narrows

☐ Ahead only

☐ Keep left

☐ Minimum speed

What does this sign mean?

☐ Cyclists must dismount
☐ Cycles aren't allowed
☑ Cycle route ahead
☐ Cycle in single file

Where there's a cycle route ahead, a sign will show a bicycle in a red warning triangle. Watch out for children on bicycles and cyclists rejoining the main road.

Which sign means that pedestrians may be walking along the road?

☑   ☐

☐   ☐

When you pass pedestrians in the road, leave plenty of room. You might have to use the right-hand side of the road, so look well ahead, as well as in your mirrors, before pulling out. Take great care if a bend in the road obscures your view ahead.

Which of these signs means there's a double bend ahead?

☐   ☑

☐   ☐

Triangular signs give you a warning of hazards ahead. They're there to give you time to prepare for the hazard; for example, by adjusting your speed.

11.50 Mark one answer — RES s7, KYTS p30

What does this sign mean?

Obey the 'give way' signs. Trams are unable to steer around you if you misjudge when it's safe to enter the junction.

☐ Wait at the barriers
☐ Wait at the crossroads
☑ Give way to trams
☐ Give way to farm vehicles

11.51 Mark one answer — RES s7, HC p109, KYTS p72

What does this sign mean?

These humps have been put in place to slow the traffic down. They're usually found in residential areas. Slow down to an appropriate speed.

☐ Hump bridge
☑ Humps in the road
☐ Entrance to tunnel
☐ Soft verges

11.52 Mark one answer — RES s7, HC p108, KYTS p11

Which of these signs means the end of a dual carriageway?

If you're overtaking, make sure you move back safely into the left-hand lane before you reach the end of the dual carriageway.

☐ ☐

☐ ☑

What does this sign mean?

Don't wait until the last moment before moving into the left-hand lane. Plan ahead and don't rely on other traffic letting you in.

☑ End of dual carriageway

☐ Tall bridge

☐ Road narrows

☐ End of narrow bridge

What does this sign mean?

A warning sign with a picture of a windsock indicates that there may be strong side winds. This sign is often found on exposed roads.

☑ Side winds

☐ Road noise

☐ Airport

☐ Adverse camber

What does this traffic sign mean?

This sign is there to alert you to the likelihood of danger ahead. It may be accompanied by a plate indicating the type of hazard. Be ready to reduce your speed and take avoiding action.

☐ Slippery road ahead

☐ Tyres liable to punctures ahead

☑ Danger ahead

☐ Service area ahead

11.56

Mark one answer

RES s7, HC p109, KYTS p13–14

You're about to overtake. What should you do when you see this sign?

Hidden dip

You won't be able to see any hazards that might be hidden in the dip. As well as oncoming traffic, the dip may conceal

• cyclists
• horse riders
• parked vehicles
• pedestrians

in the road.

☐ Overtake the other driver as quickly as possible

☐ Move to the right to get a better view

☐ Switch your headlights on before overtaking

☑ Hold back until you can see clearly ahead

11.57

Mark one answer

RES s7, HC p108, KYTS p26

What does this sign mean?

Some crossings have gates but no attendant or signals. You should stop, look both ways, listen and make sure that no train is approaching. If there's a telephone, contact the signal operator to make sure it's safe to cross.

☑ Level crossing with gate or barrier

☐ Gated road ahead

☐ Level crossing without gate or barrier

☐ Cattle grid ahead

11.58

What does this sign mean?

This sign tells you to beware of trams. If you don't usually drive in a town where there are trams, remember to look out for them at junctions and look for tram rails, signs and signals.

☐ No trams ahead
☐ Oncoming trams
☑ Trams crossing ahead
☐ Trams only

11.59

What does this sign mean?

This sign gives you an early warning that the road ahead will slope downhill. Prepare to alter your speed and gear. Looking at the sign from left to right will show you whether the road slopes uphill or downhill.

☐ Adverse camber
☐ Steep hill downwards
☐ Uneven road
☐ Steep hill upwards

11.60

What does this sign mean?

This sign is found where a shallow stream crosses the road. Heavy rainfall could increase the flow of water. If the water looks too deep or the stream has spread over a large distance, stop and find another route.

☐ Uneven road surface
☐ Bridge over the road
☐ Road ahead ends
☑ Water across the road

11.61

Mark one answer

RES s7, KYTS p114

What does this sign mean?

This sign shows you that you can't get through to another route by turning left at the junction ahead.

☐ Turn left for parking area

☑ No through road on the left

☐ No entry for traffic turning left

☐ Turn left for ferry terminal

11.62

Mark one answer

RES s7, HC p113, KYTS p114

What does this sign mean?

You won't be able to find a through route to another road. Use this road only for access.

☐ T-junction

☑ No through road

☐ Telephone box ahead

☐ Toilet ahead

11.63

Mark one answer

RES s7, HC p113, KYTS p114

Which sign means 'no through road'?

This sign is found at the entrance to a road that can only be used for access.

☐   ☐

☑   ☐

11.64

Mark one answer

Which is the sign for a ring road?

☐   ☐

☑   ☐

Ring roads are designed to relieve congestion in towns and city centres.

11.65

Mark one answer

What does this sign mean?

Yellow-and-black temporary signs may be used to inform you about roadworks or lane restrictions. Look well ahead. If you have to change lanes, do so in good time.

☐ The right-hand lane ahead is narrow
☐ Right-hand lane for buses only
☐ Right-hand lane for turning right
☑ The right-hand lane is closed

11.66

Mark one answer

What does this sign mean?

If you use the right-hand lane in a contraflow system, you'll be travelling with no permanent barrier between you and the oncoming traffic. Observe speed limits and keep a good distance from the vehicle ahead.

☐ Change to the left lane
☐ Leave at the next exit
☑ Contraflow system
☐ One-way street

11.67

Mark one answer

RES s7, 11, HC r139

What does this sign mean?

Where there's a long, steep, uphill gradient on a motorway, a crawler lane may be provided. This helps the traffic to flow by diverting the slower heavy vehicles into a dedicated lane on the left.

☐ Leave motorway at next exit

☑ Lane for heavy and slow vehicles

☐ All lorries use the hard shoulder

☐ Rest area for lorries

11.68

Mark one answer

RES s7, HC p102, KYTS p119

What does a red traffic light mean?

Whatever light is showing, you should know which light is going to appear next and be able to take appropriate action. For example, when amber is showing on its own, you'll know that red will appear next. This should give you ample time to anticipate and respond safely.

☐ You should stop unless turning left

☐ Stop, if you're able to brake safely

☑ You must stop and wait behind the stop line

☐ Proceed with care

Mark one answer

At traffic lights, what does it mean when the amber light shows on its own?

When the amber light is showing on its own, the red light will follow next. The amber light means stop, unless you've already crossed the stop line or you're so close to it that stopping may cause a collision.

- ☐ Prepare to go
- ☐ Go if the way is clear
- ☐ Go if no pedestrians are crossing
- ☑ Stop at the stop line

Mark one answer

You're at a junction controlled by traffic lights. When shouldn't you proceed at green?

As you approach the lights, look into the road you wish to take. Only proceed if your exit road is clear. If the road is blocked, hold back, even if you have to wait for the next green signal.

- ☐ When pedestrians are waiting to cross
- ☑ When your exit from the junction is blocked
- ☐ When you think the lights may be about to change
- ☐ When you intend to turn right

11.71
Mark one answer RES s7, HC p102, KYTS p119

You're in the left-hand lane at traffic lights, waiting to turn left. At which of these traffic lights mustn't you move on?

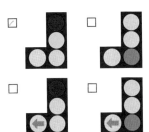

At some junctions, there may be separate signals for different lanes. These are called 'filter' lights. They're designed to help traffic flow at major junctions. Make sure that you're in the correct lane and proceed if the way is clear and the green light shows for your lane.

11.72
Mark one answer RES s7, HC p108, KYTS p139

What does this sign mean?

You might see this sign where traffic lights are out of order. Proceed with caution, as nobody has priority at the junction.

- ☑ Traffic lights out of order
- ☐ Amber signal out of order
- ☐ Temporary traffic lights ahead
- ☐ New traffic lights ahead

11.73
Mark one answer RES s7

When traffic lights are out of order, who has priority?

- ☐ Traffic going straight on
- ☐ Traffic turning right
- ☑ Nobody
- ☐ Traffic turning left

When traffic lights are out of order, you should treat the junction as an unmarked crossroads. Be cautious, as you may need to give way or stop. Look for traffic attempting to cross the junction, unaware that it doesn't have priority.

11.74

These flashing red lights mean that you must stop. Where would you find them?

These signals are found at level crossings, swing or lifting bridges, some airfields and emergency access sites. The flashing red lights mean stop whether or not the way seems to be clear.

- ☐ Pelican crossings
- ☐ Motorway exits
- ☐ Zebra crossings
- ☐ Level crossings

11.75

What do these zigzag lines at pedestrian crossings mean?

The approach to, and exit from, a pedestrian crossing is marked with zigzag lines. You mustn't park on them or overtake the leading vehicle when approaching the crossing. Parking here would block the view for pedestrians and approaching traffic.

- ☑ No parking at any time
- ☐ Parking allowed only for a short time
- ☐ Slow down to 20 mph
- ☐ Sounding horns isn't allowed

When may you cross a double solid white line in the middle of the road?

You may cross the solid white line to pass a stationary vehicle or to pass a pedal cycle, horse or road maintenance vehicle if it's travelling at 10 mph or less. You may also cross the solid white line to enter a side road or access a property.

☐ To pass traffic that's queuing back at a junction

☐ To pass a car signalling to turn left ahead

☐ To pass a road maintenance vehicle travelling at 10 mph or less

☐ To pass a vehicle that's towing a trailer

What does this road marking mean?

Road markings will warn you of a hazard ahead. A single broken line along the centre of the road, with long markings and short gaps, is a hazard warning line. Don't cross it unless you can see that the road is clear well ahead.

☐ Don't cross the line

☐ No stopping allowed

☑ You're approaching a hazard

☐ No overtaking allowed

Where would you see this road marking?

Because the road has a dark colour, changes in level aren't easily seen. White triangles painted on the road surface give you an indication of where there are road humps.

- ☐ At traffic lights
- ☐ On road humps
- ☐ Near a level crossing
- ☐ At a box junction

Which of these is a hazard warning line?

☐   ☑

You need to know the difference between the normal centre line and a hazard warning line. If there's a hazard ahead, the markings are longer and the gaps shorter. This gives you advance warning of an unspecified hazard.

☐   ☐

At this junction, there's a 'stop' sign and a solid white line on the road surface. Why is there a 'stop' sign here?

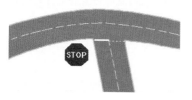

If your view at a road junction is restricted, you must stop. There may also be a 'stop' sign. Don't emerge until you're sure no traffic is approaching. If you don't know, don't go.

- ☐ Speed on the major road is derestricted
- ☐ It's a busy junction
- ☑ Visibility along the major road is restricted
- ☐ There are hazard warning lines in the centre of the road

11.81

Mark one answer

RES s7, HC p114, KYTS p68

You see this line across the road at the entrance to a roundabout. What does it mean?

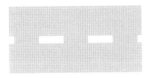

☐ Give way to traffic from the right

☐ Traffic from the left has right of way

☐ You have right of way

☐ Stop at the line

Slow down as you approach the roundabout and check for traffic from the right. If you need to stop and give way, stay behind the broken line until it's safe to emerge onto the roundabout.

11.82

Mark one answer

RES s7, HC r106

How will a police officer in a patrol vehicle normally get you to stop?

☑ Flash the headlights, indicate left and point to the left

☐ Wait until you stop, then approach you

☐ Use the siren, overtake, cut in front and stop

☐ Pull alongside you, use the siren and wave you to stop

You must obey signals given by the police. If a police officer in a patrol vehicle wants you to pull over, they'll indicate this without causing danger to you or other traffic.

11.83

Mark one answer

HC p104

You're approaching a junction where the traffic lights aren't working. What should you do when a police officer gives this signal?

☐ Turn left only

☐ Turn right only

☐ Continue ahead only

☑ Stop at the stop line

When a police officer or traffic warden is directing traffic, you must obey them. They'll use the arm signals shown in The Highway Code. Learn what these signals mean and obey them.

The driver of the car in front is giving this arm signal. What does it mean?

There might be an occasion where another driver uses an arm signal. This may be because the vehicle's indicators are obscured by other traffic. In order for such signals to be effective, all drivers should know their meaning. Be aware that the 'left turn' signal might look similar to the 'slowing down' signal.

☐ The driver is slowing down
☐ The driver intends to turn right
☐ The driver wishes to overtake
☐ The driver intends to turn left

Where would you see these road markings?

When driving on a motorway or slip road, you mustn't enter an area marked with chevrons and bordered by a solid white line for any reason, except in an emergency.

☐ At a level crossing
☑ On a motorway slip road
☐ At a pedestrian crossing
☐ On a single-track road

What does this motorway sign mean?

On the motorway, signs sometimes show temporary warnings due to traffic or weather conditions. They may be used to indicate

• lane closures
• temporary speed limits
• weather warnings.

☑ Change to the lane on your left
☐ Leave the motorway at the next exit
☐ Change to the opposite carriageway
☐ Pull up on the hard shoulder

11.87

Mark one answer — RES s11, HC p102, KYTS p91

What does this motorway sign mean?

Look out for signs above your lane or on the central reservation. These will give you important information or warnings about the road ahead. To allow for the high speed of motorway traffic, these signs may light up some distance from any hazard. Don't ignore the signs just because the road looks clear to you.

☐ Temporary minimum speed 50 mph

☐ No services for 50 miles

☐ Obstruction 50 metres (164 feet) ahead

☑ Temporary maximum speed 50 mph

11.88

Mark one answer — RES s11, HC p102, KYTS p90

What does this sign mean?

You should change lanes as directed by the sign. Here, the right-hand lane is closed but the left-hand and centre lanes are available. Merging in turn is recommended when it's safe and traffic is going slowly; for example, at roadworks or a road traffic incident. When vehicles are travelling at speed, this isn't advisable and you should move into the appropriate lane in good time.

☐ Through traffic to use left lane

☐ Right-hand lane T-junction only

☑ Right-hand lane closed ahead

☐ 11 tonne weight limit

11.89

Mark one answer — RES s11, HC p110, KYTS p79

What does '25' mean on this motorway sign?

Nottingham
A46
25

Before you set out on your journey, use a road map to plan your route. When you see an advance warning of your junction, make sure you get into the correct lane in plenty of time. Last-minute harsh braking and cutting across lanes at speed is extremely hazardous.

☐ The distance to the nearest town

☐ The route number of the road

☑ The number of the next junction

☐ The speed limit on the slip road

11.90
Mark one answer

RES s11

How should the right-hand lane of a three-lane motorway be used?

☐ As a high-speed lane
☐ As an overtaking lane
☐ As a right-turn lane
☐ As an acceleration lane

You should stay in the left-hand lane of a motorway unless you're overtaking another vehicle. The right-hand lane of a motorway is an overtaking lane; it isn't the 'fast lane'. After overtaking, move back to the left when it's safe to do so.

11.91
Mark one answer

RES s11, HC r132, KYTS p71

Where can you find reflective amber studs on a motorway?

☐ Separating the slip road from the motorway
☐ On the left-hand edge of the road
☑ On the right-hand edge of the road
☐ Separating the lanes

At night or in poor visibility, reflective studs on the road help you to judge your position on the carriageway.

11.92
Mark one answer

RES s11, HC r132, KYTS p71

Where on a motorway would you find green reflective studs?

☐ Separating driving lanes
☐ Between the hard shoulder and the carriageway
☑ At slip-road entrances and exits
☐ Between the carriageway and the central reservation

Knowing the colours of the reflective studs on the road will help you judge your position, especially at night, in foggy conditions or when visibility is poor.

11.93
Mark one answer

RES s11, HC p102, KYTS p90

What should you do when you see this sign as you travel along a motorway?

You'll see this sign if the motorway is closed ahead. Pull into the left-hand lane as soon as it's safe to do so. Don't wait until the last moment before you move across, because the lane may be busy and you'll have to rely on another driver making room for you.

☑ Leave the motorway at the next exit
☐ Turn left immediately
☐ Change lane
☐ Move onto the hard shoulder

11.94
Mark one answer | RES s11, HC p112, KYTS p89

What does this sign mean?

When you leave the motorway, make sure that you check your speedometer. You may be going faster than you realise. Slow down and look for speed-limit signs.

- ☐ No motor vehicles
- ☑ End of motorway
- ☐ No through road
- ☐ End of bus lane

11.95
Mark one answer | RES s7, HC p106, KYTS p20

Which of these signs means that the national speed limit applies?

You should know the speed limit for the road on which you're travelling and the vehicle that you're driving. The different speed limits are shown in The Highway Code.

11.96
Mark one answer | HC p40

What's the maximum speed on a single carriageway road?

- ☐ 50 mph
- ☑ 60 mph
- ☐ 40 mph
- ☐ 70 mph

If you're travelling on a dual carriageway that becomes a single carriageway road, reduce your speed gradually so that you aren't exceeding the limit as you enter. There might not be a sign to remind you of the limit, so make sure you know the speed limits for different types of road and vehicle.

What does this sign mean?

Temporary restrictions on motorways are shown on signs that have flashing amber lights. At the end of the restriction, you'll see this sign without any flashing lights.

☐ End of motorway
☐ End of restriction
☐ Lane ends ahead
☐ Free recovery ends

What does this sign indicate?

When a diversion route has been put in place, drivers are advised to follow a symbol, which may be a black triangle, square, circle or diamond shape on a yellow background.

☑ A diversion route
☐ A picnic area
☐ A pedestrian zone
☐ A cycle route

What does this temporary sign indicate?

In the interests of road safety, temporary mandatory speed limits are imposed at all major roadworks. Signs like this, giving advance warning of the speed limit, are normally placed about three-quarters of a mile ahead of where the speed limit comes into force.

☐ The speed-limit change at the end of the motorway
☐ An advisory change of speed limit ahead
☐ A variable speed limit ahead
☑ A mandatory speed-limit change ahead

Mark one answer

What does this traffic sign mean?

The sign gives you an early warning of a speed restriction. If you're travelling at a higher speed, slow down in good time. You could come across queuing traffic due to roadworks or a temporary obstruction.

☑ Compulsory maximum speed limit

☐ Advisory maximum speed limit

☐ Compulsory minimum speed limit

☐ Advised separation distance

Mark one answer

What should you do when you see this sign at a crossroads?

When traffic lights are out of order, treat the junction as an unmarked crossroads. Be very careful and be prepared to stop; no-one has priority.

☐ Maintain the same speed

☐ Carry on with great care

☐ Find another route

☐ Telephone the police

Mark one answer

You're signalling to turn right in busy traffic. How would you confirm your intention safely?

☐ Sound the horn

☑ Give an arm signal

☐ Flash your headlights

☐ Position over the centre line

In some situations, you may feel your indicators can't be seen by other road users. If you think you need to make your intention more obvious, give the arm signal shown in The Highway Code.

Section eleven Questions

Mark one answer

What does this sign mean?

You must comply with all traffic signs and be especially aware of those signs that apply specifically to the type of vehicle you're using.

☐ Motorcycles only

☐ No cars

☐ Cars only

☐ No motorcycles

Mark one answer

You're on a motorway. A lorry has stopped in the right-hand lane. What should you do when you see this sign on the lorry?

Sometimes work is carried out on the motorway without closing the lanes. When this happens, signs are mounted on the back of lorries to warn other road users of the roadworks ahead.

☐ Move into the right-hand lane

☐ Stop behind the flashing lights

☐ Pass the lorry on the left

☐ Leave the motorway at the next exit

Mark one answer

You're on a motorway. Red flashing lights appear above your lane only. What should you do?

☐ Continue in that lane and look for further information

☑ Move into another lane in good time

☐ Pull onto the hard shoulder

☐ Stop and wait for an instruction to proceed

Flashing red lights above your lane show that your lane is closed. You should move into another lane as soon as you can do so safely.

11.106

Mark one answer

RES s6, HC r112

When may you sound the horn?

- ☐ To give you right of way
- ☐ To attract a friend's attention
- ☑ To warn others of your presence
- ☐ To make slower drivers move over

Never sound the horn aggressively. You mustn't sound it when driving in a built-up area between 11.30 pm and 7.00 am, or when you're stationary, unless another road user poses a danger. Don't scare animals by sounding your horn.

11.107

Mark one answer

RES s6, HC r112

Your vehicle is stationary. When may you use its horn?

- ☑ When another road user poses a danger
- ☐ When the road is blocked by queuing traffic
- ☐ When it's used only briefly
- ☐ When signalling that you've just arrived

When your vehicle is stationary, only sound the horn if you think there's a risk of danger from another road user. Don't use it just to attract someone's attention. This causes unnecessary noise and could be misleading.

11.108

Mark one answer

RES s7, HC p107, KYTS p55

What does this sign mean?

🚫 **URBAN CLEARWAY**
Monday to Friday

am	pm
8.00 - 9.30	4.30 - 6.30

- ☐ You can park on the days and times shown
- ☑ No parking on the days and times shown
- ☐ No parking at all from Monday to Friday
- ☐ End of the urban clearway restrictions

Urban clearways are provided to keep traffic flowing at busy times. You may stop only briefly to set down or pick up passengers. Times of operation will vary from place to place, so always check the signs.

11.109

Mark one answer   RES s7, HC p109, KYTS p12

What does this sign mean?

You should be careful in these locations, as the road surface is likely to be wet and slippery. There may be a steep drop to the water, and there may not be a barrier along the edge of the road.

- ☑ Quayside or river bank
- ☐ Steep hill downwards
- ☐ Uneven road surface
- ☐ Road liable to flooding

11.110

Mark one answer   RES s7, HC p113, KYTS p73

Which sign means you have priority over oncoming vehicles?

☐   ☐

☑   ☐

Even though you have priority, be prepared to give way if other drivers don't. This will help to avoid congestion, confrontation or even a collision.

11.111

Mark one answer   RES s7, HC r127, p114, KYTS p62

What does this white line along the centre of the road mean?

The centre of the road is usually marked by a broken white line, with lines that are shorter than the gaps. When the lines become longer than the gaps, this is a hazard warning line. Look well ahead for these, especially when you're planning to overtake or turn off.

- ☐ Bus lane marking
- ☑ Hazard warning
- ☐ Give way warning
- ☐ Lane marking

What's the reason for the yellow crisscross lines painted on the road here?

Yellow 'box junctions' like this are often used where it's busy. Their purpose is to keep the junction clear for crossing traffic. Don't enter the painted area unless your exit is clear. The one exception is when you're turning right and are only prevented from doing so by oncoming traffic or by other vehicles waiting to turn right.

- ☐ To mark out an area for trams only
- ☑ To prevent queuing traffic from blocking the junction on the left
- ☐ To mark the entrance lane to a car park
- ☐ To warn you of the tram lines crossing the road

What's the reason for the area marked in red and white along the centre of this road?

Areas of 'hatched markings' such as these separate traffic streams that could be a danger to each other. They're often seen on bends or where the road becomes narrow. If the area is bordered by a solid white line, you mustn't enter it except in an emergency.

- ☑ It separates traffic flowing in opposite directions
- ☐ It marks an area to be used by overtaking motorcyclists
- ☐ It's a temporary marking to warn of the roadworks
- ☐ It separates the two sides of the dual carriageway

11.114

Mark one answer

RES s6, HC r110

Other drivers may sometimes flash their headlights at you. In which situation are they allowed to do this?

☐ To warn of a radar speed trap ahead

☐ To show that they're giving way to you

☐ To warn you of their presence

☐ To let you know there's a fault with your vehicle

If other drivers flash their headlights, this isn't a signal to show priority. The flashing of headlights has the same meaning as sounding the horn: it's a warning of their presence.

11.115

Mark one answer

RES s7, HC r152

What speed limit is often found in narrow residential streets?

☑ 20 mph

☐ 25 mph

☐ 35 mph

☐ 40 mph

In some built-up areas, you may find the speed limit reduced to 20 mph. Driving at a slower speed will help give you the time and space to see and deal safely with hazards such as pedestrians and other vulnerable road users.

11.116

Mark one answer

RES s7, HC p102, KYTS p31

What does this signal mean?

☐ Cars must stop

☑ Trams must stop

☐ Both trams and cars must stop

☐ Both trams and cars can continue

The white light shows that trams must stop. The green light shows that other vehicles can go if the way is clear. Trams are being introduced into more cities, so you're likely to come across them and you should learn which signs apply to them.

11.117
Mark one answer | **KYTS p69**

Where would you find these road markings?

These markings show the direction in which the traffic should go at a mini-roundabout.

☐ At a railway crossing
☑ At a mini-roundabout
☐ On a motorway
☐ On a pedestrian crossing

11.118
Mark one answer | **RES s8, HC r106**

A police car is following you. The police officer flashes the headlights and points to the left. What should you do?

You must pull up on the left as soon as it's safe to do so and switch off your engine.

☐ Turn left at the next junction
☑ Pull up on the left
☐ Stop immediately
☐ Move over to the left

11.119
Mark one answer | **RES s7, HC p102, KYTS p119**

You see this amber traffic light ahead. Which light, or lights, will come on next?

At junctions controlled by traffic lights, you must stop behind the white line until the lights change to green. A red light, an amber light, and red and amber lights showing together all mean stop.

You may proceed when the light is green unless your exit road is blocked or pedestrians are crossing in front of you.

If you're approaching traffic lights that are visible from a distance and the light has been green for some time, be ready to slow down and stop, because the lights are likely to change.

☐ Red alone
☐ Red and amber together
☐ Green and amber together
☐ Green alone

You see this signal overhead on the motorway. What does it mean?

☑ Leave the motorway at the next exit

☐ All vehicles use the hard shoulder

☐ Sharp bend to the left ahead

☐ Stop: all lanes ahead closed

You'll see this sign if there has been an incident ahead and the motorway is closed. You must obey the sign. Make sure that you prepare to leave in good time.

Don't cause drivers to take avoiding action by cutting in at the last moment.

What must you do when you see this sign?

'Stop' signs are situated at junctions where visibility is restricted or where there's heavy traffic. They must be obeyed: you must stop.

Take good all-round observation before moving off.

☐ Stop only if traffic is approaching

☑ Stop even if the road is clear

☐ Stop only if children are waiting to cross

☐ Stop only if a red light is showing

Which shape is used for a 'give way' sign?

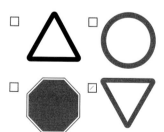

Other warning signs are the same shape and colour, but the 'give way' triangle points downwards. When you see this sign, you must give way to traffic on the road that you're about to enter.

11.123

Mark one answer RES s7, HC p107, KYTS p19

What does this sign mean?

When you see this sign, look out for any direction signs and judge whether you need to signal your intentions. Do this in good time so that other road users approaching the roundabout know what you're planning to do.

☐ Buses turning
☐ Ring road
☑ Mini-roundabout
☐ Keep right

11.124

Mark one answer RES s7, HC p108, KYTS p11

What does this sign mean?

Be prepared for traffic approaching from junctions on either side of you. Try to avoid unnecessary changing of lanes just before the junction.

☐ Two-way traffic straight ahead
☑ Two-way traffic crosses a one-way road
☐ Two-way traffic over a bridge
☐ Two-way traffic crosses a two-way road

11.125

Mark one answer RES s7, HC p108, KYTS p11

What does this sign mean?

This sign may be at the end of a dual carriageway or a one-way street. It's there to warn you of oncoming traffic.

☐ Two-way traffic crosses a one-way road
☐ Traffic approaching you has priority
☑ Two-way traffic straight ahead
☐ Motorway contraflow system ahead

What does this sign mean?

You'll need to slow down. At hump bridges, your view ahead will be restricted and the road will often be narrow. If the bridge is very steep, sound your horn to warn others of your approach. Going over the bridge too fast is highly dangerous to other road users and could even cause your wheels to leave the road, with a resulting loss of control.

☑ Hump bridge

☐ Traffic-calming hump

☐ Low bridge

☐ Uneven road

Which sign informs you that you're coming to a 'no through road'?

This sign is found at the entrance to a road that can only be used for access.

☐  ☐

☑ ☐

What does this sign mean?

To ease the congestion in town centres, some cities and towns provide park-and-ride schemes. These allow you to park in a designated area and ride by bus into the centre.

Park-and-ride schemes are usually cheaper and easier than car parking in the town centre.

☐ Direction to park-and-ride car park

☐ No parking for buses or coaches

☐ Direction to bus and coach park

☐ Parking area for cars and coaches

11.129 — Mark one answer — RES s7, HC p102, KYTS p119

What should you do when approaching traffic lights where red and amber are showing together?

Be aware that other traffic might still be clearing the junction as you approach. A green light means you may go on, but only if the way is clear.

☐ Pass the lights if the road is clear

☐ Take care because there's a fault with the lights

☑ Wait for the green light

☐ Stop because the lights are changing to red

11.130 — Mark one answer — RES s7, HC p116, KYTS p69

Where does this marking normally appear on a road?

This road marking means you should give way to traffic on the main road. It might not be used at junctions where there isn't much traffic. However, if there's a double broken line across the junction, the 'give way' rules still apply.

☐ Just before a 'no entry' sign

☑ Just before a 'give way' sign

☐ Just before a 'stop' sign

☐ Just before a 'no through road' sign

11.131 — Mark one answer — RES s7, HC r293, p102

At a railway level crossing, the red lights continue to flash after a train has gone by. What should you do?

☐ Phone the signal operator

☐ Alert drivers behind you

☑ Wait

☐ Proceed with caution

You must always obey red flashing stop lights. If a train passes but the lights continue to flash, another train will be passing soon. Cross only when the lights go off and the barriers open.

You're in a tunnel and you see this sign. What does it mean?

If you have to leave your vehicle and get out of a tunnel by an emergency exit, do so as quickly as you can. Follow the signs directing you to the nearest exit point. If there are several people using the exit, don't panic but try to leave in a calm and orderly manner.

- ☑ Direction to emergency pedestrian exit
- ☐ Beware of pedestrians: no footpath ahead
- ☐ No access for pedestrians
- ☐ Beware of pedestrians crossing ahead

Which of these signs shows that you're entering a one-way system?

☐   ☑

☐   ☐

If the road has two lanes, you can use either lane and overtake on either side. Use the lane that's more convenient for your destination unless signs or road markings indicate otherwise.

What does this sign mean?

- ☑ With-flow bus and cycle lane
- ☐ Contraflow bus and cycle lane
- ☐ No buses and cycles allowed
- ☐ No waiting for buses and cycles

Buses and cycles can travel in this lane. In this example, they'll flow in the same direction as other traffic. If it's busy, they may be passing you on the left, so watch out for them. Times on the sign will show the lane's hours of operation; if no times are shown, or there's no sign at all, this means the lane is in operation 24 hours a day. In some areas, other vehicles, such as taxis and motorcycles, are allowed to use bus lanes. The sign will show if this is the case.

11.135
Mark one answer
RES s7, HC p109, KYTS p13

Which of these signs warns you of a zebra crossing?

✓   ☐

☐   ☐

Look well ahead and check the pavements and surrounding areas for pedestrians. Look for anyone walking towards the crossing. Check your mirrors for traffic behind, in case you have to slow down or stop.

11.136
Mark one answer
RES s7, HC p109, KYTS p13

What does this sign mean?

☐ School crossing patrol
☐ No pedestrians allowed
☐ Pedestrian zone – no vehicles
☑ Zebra crossing ahead

Look well ahead and be ready to stop for any pedestrians crossing, or about to cross, the road. Also check the pavements for anyone who looks like they might step or run into the road.

11.137
Mark one answer
RES s7, HC p108, KYTS p11

Which sign means there will be two-way traffic crossing your route ahead?

☐   ☐

☐   ☐

This sign is found in or at the end of a one-way system. It warns you that traffic will be crossing your path from both directions.

11.138
Mark one answer RES s6, HC r103, p103

Which arm signal tells you that the car you're following is going to pull up?

There may be occasions when drivers need to give an arm signal to confirm their intentions. This could include in bright sunshine, at a complex road layout, when stopping at a pedestrian crossing or when turning right just after passing a parked vehicle. You should understand what each arm signal means. If you give arm signals, make them clear, correct and decisive.

11.139
Mark one answer RES s7, HC p107, KYTS p19

Which of these signs means turn left ahead?

Blue circles tell you what you must do and this sign gives a clear instruction to turn left ahead. You should be looking out for signs at all times and know what they mean.

11.140
Mark one answer RES s7, HC p107, KYTS p19

You've just driven past this sign. What should you be aware of?

In a one-way system, traffic may pass you on either side. Always be aware of all traffic signs and understand their meaning. Look well ahead and react to them in good time.

☐ This is a single-track road

☐ You can't stop on this road

☐ Only one lane is in use

☐ All traffic is going one way

11.141

Mark one answer

RES s7, HC p102, KYTS p119

You're approaching a red traffic light. What will the signal show next?

☑ Red and amber

☐ Green alone

☐ Amber alone

☐ Green and amber

If you know which light is going to show next, you can plan your approach accordingly. This can help prevent excessive braking or hesitation at the junction.

11.142

Mark one answer

RES s7, HC p108, KYTS p12

What does this sign mean?

☐ Low bridge ahead

☑ Tunnel ahead

☐ Ancient monument ahead

☐ Traffic danger spot ahead

When approaching a tunnel, switch on your dipped headlights. Be aware that your eyes might need to adjust to the sudden darkness. You may need to reduce your speed.

> Case study practice – 11 Road and traffic signs

You're riding in the town centre. As you approach the first junction, you see a staggered junction sign.

At the second junction there's a 'no entry' sign, while at the third is a one-way traffic sign.

At a large junction there are traffic lights with filter arrows for traffic going left.

Beyond the junction, there are bus lanes on either side of the road. There are no signs showing times of operation.

11.1 What describes the first junction?
Mark **one** answer

☐ Where the joining side roads are both narrow one-way streets
☐ Where the joining side roads are exactly opposite each other
☐ Where the joining side roads are reserved for pedestrians only
☑ Where the joining side roads are slightly offset from each other

RES s9 **HC** p108

11.2 What type of sign is at the second junction?
Mark **one** answer

☐ Advisory
☐ Warning
☑ Regulatory
☐ Information

HC p106 **KYTS** p16

11.3 What does the third sign look like?

Mark **one** answer

- ☐ White with red arrow
- ☑ Blue with white arrow
- ☐ Red with green arrow
- ☐ White with black arrow

HC p107 **KYTS** p19

11.4 What colour are the filter arrows?

Mark **one** answer

- ☐ White
- ☐ Amber
- ☑ Green
- ☐ Blue

RES s7 **HC** p102

11.5 When are the bus lanes in operation?

Mark **one** answer

- ☐ All the time
- ☐ During rush hour
- ☐ At the weekend
- ☐ They're not in operation

HC r141

> Section twelve

Essential documents

In this section, you'll learn about

- ❯ the documents you need when owning and keeping a motorcycle
- ❯ the driving licence
- ❯ buying insurance
- ❯ the MOT test.

Essential documents

Before you can ride as a learner on a public road, you **MUST** have

- successfully completed a compulsory basic training (CBT) course, given by a DVSA-approved training body
- checked that the vehicle tax has been paid on the motorcycle you're riding
- a valid provisional driving licence
- valid insurance cover
- L plates (D plates in Wales) correctly displayed at the front and rear of the motorcycle
- a valid MOT certificate, if it's required for the motorcycle you're using.

You won't be able to tax your motorcycle unless you have

- a valid MOT certificate (if your motorcycle requires one)
- appropriate, current insurance cover.

HC p120–123 **RES** s2

As a learner, you **MUST NOT** carry a **pillion passenger**, pull a trailer or ride your motorcycle on a motorway. You can do these things once you've passed your practical tests, provided your motorcycle has an engine capacity

- over 125 cc if you wish to tow a trailer
- of at least 50 cc if you wish to ride on the motorway.

HC r85, p120 **RES** s2

pillion passenger
a passenger who sits on the rear seat of a motorcycle, behind the rider

Definition

❯ Registering and owning a motorcycle

The vehicle registration certificate (V5C) contains details of

- the vehicle, including make, model, engine size and year of registration
- the registered keeper.

If you're the registered keeper, you **MUST** tell the Driver and Vehicle Licensing Agency (DVLA) when you change

- your motorcycle
- your name
- your permanent address.

If you buy a second-hand motorcycle, tell DVLA immediately that the keeper of the motorcycle has changed.

Find out more about the V5C at this website.

❯ **www.gov.uk**

Vehicle tax **MUST** be paid on all motor vehicles used or kept on public roads (unless the vehicle is exempt – see **www.gov.uk** for more details).
HC **p122** **RES** **s2**

If you're not going to use your motorcycle on public roads, you won't have to pay vehicle tax as long as you tell DVLA in advance. This is called a Statutory Off-Road Notification (SORN) and lasts until you tax, sell or scrap your vehicle.
RES **s2**

❯ Your motorcycle licence

Before riding on a public road, a learner **MUST** have a valid provisional driving licence and a CBT completion certificate. The CBT certificate is valid for two years. If you don't pass a practical test within that time, you'll have to retake the CBT.
HC **p118–119** **RES** **s2**

You **MUST** tell the licensing authority if

- your health is likely to affect your riding
- your eyesight doesn't meet the required standard.

`HC` r90 `RES` s1

> **Eyesight:** to be able to ride you **MUST** be able to read in good daylight, with glasses or contact lenses if you wear them, a vehicle number plate from 20 metres (about 66 feet) – which is about five car lengths.

For two years after you pass your first practical test (car or motorcycle), there's a probation period. This means that if you get six or more penalty points within this two-year probation period, you'll lose your licence. You'll then have to

- reapply for a provisional licence
- take your theory and practical tests, and your CBT, again.

Any points on your provisional licence will be transferred to your new licence when you pass your test.

`HC` p127, 134

Insurance

You **MUST** have at least third-party insurance cover before riding on public roads. This covers

- injury to another person
- damage to someone else's property
- damage to other vehicles.

Riding without insurance is a criminal offence. It can lead to an unlimited fine, and possibly disqualification.

`HC` p121–122 `RES` s2

You'll need to show your insurance certificate when you're taxing your motorcycle or if a police officer asks you for it. Your insurer may give you a temporary cover note until you receive your insurance certificate.

Remember, if your vehicle is unused or off the road it **MUST** have either a SORN or valid insurance. If you have neither, and ignore any subsequent reminders sent to you as the registered keeper, you risk

- a fixed-penalty fine of £100
- court prosecution and a fine of up to £1000
- having the vehicle clamped, seized and destroyed.

RES s2

If a police officer asks to see your documents and you don't have them with you, you can produce them at a police station within seven days.

HC p122 **RES** s16

Your insurance policy may have an excess of, for example, £100. This means you'll have to pay the first £100 of any claim for damage to your vehicle. The cost of your insurance is generally lower if you're over 25 years old.

Before you ride anyone else's motorcycle, make sure that it's insured for your use.

HC p121–122 **RES** s2

❯ MOT test

The MOT test makes sure your motorcycle meets road safety and environmental standards. Motorcycles **MUST** first have an MOT test when they're three years old (four in Northern Ireland). MOT certificates are valid for one year.

HC p121 **RES** s2

If your motorcycle has a sidecar, the MOT costs slightly more. Motorcycle trailers don't need an MOT, but they do need to be kept in good order.

Unless your motorcycle is exempt from MOT testing (see **www.gov.uk** for rules exempting vehicles from MOT testing), the only time when you can ride your motorcycle without an MOT certificate is when you're riding to or from an appointment at an MOT centre or to have MOT repairs carried out.

If your motorcycle needs an MOT certificate and you don't have one

- you won't be able to renew your vehicle tax
- you could be prosecuted
- your insurance may be invalid.

HC p121 **RES** s2

For more information about MOT tests, see this website.

❯ **www.gov.uk**

Meeting the standards

You must be able to

make sure that your driving licence is valid for the category of machine that you're riding

make sure that the machine is registered and the vehicle tax has been paid

make sure that you have valid insurance for your use of the machine

make sure that the machine has a current MOT certificate (if necessary).

You must know and understand

that you must have a valid driving licence for the machine you ride. You must also comply with any restrictions on your licence

that the machine must be registered with DVLA

that you must tell DVLA/DVA if you

- change your name
- change your address
- have or develop a medical condition that will affect your ability to ride

the MOT requirements for vehicles being used on the road.

> Notes

You can use this page to make your own notes or diagrams about the key points you need to remember.

Think about

- What documents do you need when taxing your motorcycle?
- You must tell DVLA/DVA when certain details change: what are they?
- What's a SORN?
- What's the minimum level of insurance you must have before riding on public roads?
- What does an MOT test cover?

Your notes

Things to discuss and practise with your trainer

These are just a few examples of what you could discuss and practise with your trainer. Read more about essential documents to come up with your own ideas.

Discuss with your trainer

- what the New Drivers Act means to someone whose first full licence is a motorcycle licence
- what the letters 'SORN' stand for and what this means to the keeper of a vehicle
- different types of insurance for your motorcycle and what they cover, eg third party, pillion passenger, etc.

Practise with your trainer

It's difficult to practise your knowledge and understanding of documents. Just remember that the safer and more responsibly you ride, the less likely you are to

- cause high wear and tear to your motorcycle
- accumulate penalty points
- be involved in an incident and damage your motorcycle.

This means that

- your motorcycle will be more likely to be roadworthy and pass its MOT test
- you'll be able to find cheaper insurance
- you won't lose your licence under the New Drivers Act and beyond.

12.1

Mark one answer

RES s2, HC p122

What information is found on a vehicle registration document?

- ☑ The make and model
- ☐ The service history
- ☐ The ignition-key security number
- ☐ The original purchase price

Every vehicle should have a registration document showing the registered keeper. It's your legal responsibility to make sure all the information is correct. This includes make, model and engine size. If you buy a new vehicle, the dealer will register it with DVLA, who will send the registration document to you.

12.2 NI EXEMPT

Mark one answer

RES s2, HC p118–119

Who can carry out compulsory basic training (CBT)?

- ☐ Any approved driving instructor (ADI)
- ☐ Any road safety officer
- ☑ Any Driver and Vehicle Standards Agency (DVSA)-approved training body
- ☐ Any motorcycle main dealer

CBT courses can only be given by training bodies that are approved by DVSA. The standard of training is monitored by DVSA examiners. The course is designed to give you basic skills before riding on the road.

12.3

Mark one answer

RES s2

What should you be sure of before riding anyone else's motorcycle?

- ☐ That the owner has third-party insurance cover
- ☐ That your own motorcycle has insurance cover
- ☑ That the motorcycle is insured for your use
- ☐ That the owner has the insurance documents with them

If you borrow a motorcycle, you must make sure that you're insured to ride it. It's better to find this out for yourself, rather than taking somebody else's word for it.

12.4 NI EXEMPT

Mark one answer

RES s2, HC p121

How long after first registration must a motorcycle have its first MOT test?

- ☐ One year
- ☑ Three years
- ☐ Five years
- ☐ Seven years

Any motorcycle you ride must be in good condition and roadworthy. If it's over three years old, it must have a valid MOT test certificate (unless it was made before 1960, in which case it will be exempt from the MOT test).

12.5

Mark one answer

RES s2, HC p122

What information can be found on a motorcycle's registration document?

☐ The registered keeper's name

☐ The type of insurance cover required

☐ The service history

☐ The date of the MOT

Every vehicle on the road has a registration document. This records any change of ownership and gives specific information relating to the vehicle and owner. This includes the date of first registration, the registration number, the make and colour of the vehicle, and the registered keeper's name.

12.6

Mark one answer

RES s2, HC p120, 122

You own a motorcycle licensed in the UK. When do you have a duty to contact the Driver and Vehicle Licensing Agency (DVLA)?

☐ When you go abroad on holiday

☐ When your job involves riding abroad

☑ When your permanent address changes

☐ When you change your job status

DVLA need to keep their records up to date. They'll send you a reminder when you need to tax your vehicle. To do this, they need your current address. Every vehicle in the country is registered so that its history can be traced.

12.7

Mark one answer

RES s2, HC p121

Your motorcycle is insured third-party only. What does this cover?

☐ Damage to your motorcycle

☐ All damage and injury

☐ Injury to yourself

☑ Injury to others

Third-party insurance is usually cheaper than comprehensive insurance. It covers injuries to other people and damage to their property, but it doesn't cover any damage to your own motorcycle or property. Nor does it provide cover if your motorcycle is stolen.

12.8

Mark one answer

RES s2, HC p121

What's the legal minimum insurance cover you must have to ride on public roads?

☐ Third-party, fire and theft

☐ Comprehensive

☑ Third-party only

☐ Personal injury cover

The minimum insurance cover required by law is third-party only. This covers the other people and vehicles involved in a collision, but not you or your vehicle. Also, basic third-party insurance won't cover you for theft or fire damage. Make sure you read your policy carefully and understand what it covers.

12.9
RES s2

What does a motorcycle registration document show?

☐ The service history

☑ The year of first registration

☐ The purchase price

☐ The tyre sizes

A motorcycle registration document contains a number of details that are unique to a particular vehicle. You must notify DVLA of any changes to, for example, the registered keeper or registration number. You must also tell them about any modifications made to the motorcycle.

12.10
Mark one answer RES s2, HC p121

What's the purpose of an MOT test?

☑ To make sure your motorcycle is roadworthy

☐ To certify how many miles per gallon it does

☐ To prove you own the motorcycle

☐ To allow you to park in restricted areas

It's your responsibility to make sure that any motorcycle you ride is in a roadworthy condition. Any faults that develop should be corrected promptly. If your motorcycle fails an MOT test, it shouldn't be used on the road unless you're taking it to have the faults repaired or for a previously arranged retest.

12.11 NI EXEMPT
Mark one answer RES s2, HC p118

What do you need before you can take a practical motorcycle test?

☐ A valid full moped licence

☐ A valid full car licence

☑ A valid compulsory basic training (CBT) certificate

☐ 12 months' riding experience

The purpose of a CBT course is to teach you basic theory and practical skills before you ride on the road, on your own, for the first time. CBT courses can only be given by approved training bodies (ATBs).

12.12
Mark one answer RES s2, HC r90, 92, p122

When must you notify the licensing authority?

☐ When your insurance is due for renewal

☑ When you have a medical condition that affects your riding

☐ When you intend to take your motorcycle abroad on holiday

☐ When you wish to renew your motorcycle's MOT certificate

The licensing authorities hold the records of all vehicles, drivers and riders in Great Britain and Northern Ireland. They need to keep their records up to date and you must notify them if any aspect of your health affects your ability to ride your motorcycle.

12.13

Mark one answer

RES s2, HC p127, 134

You've just passed your practical motorcycle test. This is your first full licence. What will you have to do if you gather six or more penalty points within the next two years?

☐ Retake only your theory test
☐ Reapply for your full licence immediately
☐ Retake only your practical test
☐ Reapply for your provisional licence

If the number of points on your licence reaches six or more during your first two years of holding a full licence, your licence will be revoked. This includes offences you committed before you passed your test. You may ride only as a learner until you pass both the theory and practical tests again.

12.14

Mark one answer

RES s2, HC r85, 253, p123

You hold a provisional motorcycle licence. What does this licence restrict you from doing?

☐ Exceeding 30 mph
☐ Riding on a dual carriageway
☐ Riding after dark
☑ Carrying a pillion passenger

Provisional entitlement means that restrictions apply to your use of motorcycles. For example, you may not ride on a motorway or carry a passenger. The requirements are there to protect you and other road users. Make sure you're aware of all the restrictions that apply before you ride your motorcycle on the road.

12.15

Mark one answer

RES s2, HC p118–120

What's the maximum engine size a full category A1 motorcycle licence will allow you to ride?

☐ 125 cc
☐ 250 cc
☐ 350 cc
☐ 425 cc

When you pass your test on a motorcycle between 120 cc and 125 cc, you'll be issued with a full light motorcycle licence of category A1. You'll then be allowed to ride any motorcycle up to 125 cc and with a power output not exceeding 11 kW (14.6 bhp).

Section twelve Questions

397

Do you need to display L plates when learning to ride a motorcycle under the direct access scheme?

☐ No, you don't need L plates if you've passed a car test

☐ Yes, you need L plates only when learning on your own machine

☑ Yes, you need L plates while learning with a qualified instructor

☐ No, you don't need L plates if you've passed a moped test

When training under the direct access scheme, you must be accompanied by an instructor on another motorcycle, who must be in radio contact with you. You must display red L plates to the front and rear of your motorcycle and follow all normal learner restrictions.

A motorcyclist is riding a motorcycle that has an engine larger than 50 cc. When may they carry a pillion passenger?

☐ When the rider has successfully completed CBT (compulsory basic training)

☑ When the rider holds a full licence for the category of motorcycle they're riding

☐ When no sidecar is fitted to the machine

☐ When the rider has a full car licence and is over 21

Before carrying a passenger on a motorcycle, the rider must hold a full licence for the category of motorcycle being ridden. They must also ensure that a proper passenger seat and footrests are fitted.

You have a CBT (compulsory basic training) certificate. How long is it valid?

☐ One year

☑ Two years

☐ Three years

☐ Four years

All new learner motorcycle and moped riders must complete a CBT course before riding on the road. This can only be given by an approved training body (ATB). If you don't pass your practical test within two years, you'll need to retake and pass CBT to continue riding.

12.19 — Mark one answer — RES s2

Your vehicle tax is due to expire. To renew it, you'll need a renewal form, the fee and a valid MOT (if applicable). What else will you need?

☐ Proof of purchase
☐ A CBT certificate
☑ A valid certificate of insurance
☐ A complete service record

You'll normally be sent a reminder automatically by DVLA close to the time of renewal. Make sure that all your documentation is correct, up to date and valid. You can renew online, by phone or at certain post offices.

12.20 — Mark one answer — RES s2, HC r85

What must you have to legally carry a pillion passenger on your motorcycle?

☐ A motorcycle with an engine larger than 125 cc
☐ A passenger who holds a full motorcycle licence
☐ A full motorcycle licence
☐ Three years' motorcycle riding experience

As a learner motorcyclist, you aren't allowed to carry a pillion passenger, even if they hold a full motorcycle licence. You mustn't carry a passenger, or tow a trailer, until you've passed your test.

12.21 — Mark one answer — RES s2, HC r85

A friend asks you to give them a lift on your motorcycle. What conditions apply?

☐ Your motorcycle must be larger than 125 cc
☐ You must have three years' motorcycle riding experience
☐ The pillion passenger must hold a full motorcycle licence
☐ You must have a full motorcycle licence

By law, you can only carry a pillion passenger after you've gained a full motorcycle licence. It makes no difference if the passenger holds a full licence. As a learner, you're also prohibited from towing a trailer or riding on motorways.

Mark one answer

Your motorcycle insurance policy has an excess of £100. What does this mean?

☐ The insurance company will pay the first £100 of any claim

☐ You'll be paid £100 if you don't have a crash

☐ Your motorcycle is insured for a value of £100 if it's stolen

☑ You'll have to pay the first £100 of any claim

This is a method used by insurance companies to keep annual premiums down. Generally, the higher the excess you choose to pay, the lower the annual premium you'll be charged.

Mark one answer

For how long is an MOT certificate normally valid?

☐ Three years after the date it was issued

☐ 10,000 miles

☐ One year after the date it was issued

☐ 30,000 miles

Some garages will remind you that your vehicle is due for its annual MOT test, but not all do. To ensure continuous cover, you may take your vehicle for its MOT up to one month before its existing MOT certificate runs out. The expiry date on the new certificate will be 12 months after the expiry date on the old certificate.

Mark one answer

What is a cover note?

☐ A document issued before you receive your driving licence

☑ A document issued before you receive your insurance certificate

☐ A document issued before you receive your registration document

☐ A document issued before you receive your MOT certificate

Sometimes an insurance company will issue a temporary insurance certificate called a cover note. It gives you the same insurance cover as your certificate but lasts for a limited period, usually one month.

12.25 — Mark one answer — HC p127, 134

You've just passed your practical test. You don't hold a full licence in another category. Within two years you get six penalty points on your licence. What will you have to do?

☐ Retake only your theory test

☐ Retake your theory and practical tests

☐ Retake only your practical test

☐ Reapply for your full licence immediately

If you accumulate six or more penalty points within two years of gaining your first full licence, it will be revoked. The six or more points include any gained due to offences you committed before passing your test. If this happens, you may only drive as a learner until you pass both the theory and practical tests again.

12.26 — Mark one answer — RES s2, HC p122

For how long is a Statutory Off-Road Notification (SORN) valid?

☑ Until the vehicle is taxed, sold or scrapped

☐ Until the vehicle is insured and MOT'd

☐ Until the vehicle is repaired or modified

☐ Until the vehicle is used on the road

A SORN allows you to keep a vehicle off-road and untaxed. SORN will end when the vehicle is taxed, sold or scrapped.

12.27 — Mark one answer — RES s2, HC p122

What is a Statutory Off-Road Notification (SORN)?

☐ A notification to tell DVSA that a vehicle doesn't have a current MOT

☐ Information kept by the police about the owner of a vehicle

☐ A notification to tell DVLA that a vehicle isn't being used on the road

☐ Information held by insurance companies to check a vehicle is insured

If you want to keep a vehicle untaxed and off the public road, you must make a SORN. It's an offence not to do so. Your SORN is valid until your vehicle is taxed, sold or scrapped.

12.28 — NI EXEMPT — Mark one answer — RES s2, HC p126

What's the maximum fine for driving without insurance?

☐ Unlimited

☐ £500

☐ £1000

☐ £5000

Driving without insurance is a serious offence. As well as an unlimited fine, you may be disqualified or incur penalty points.

12.29 — Mark one answer — RES s2, HC p122

Who's legally responsible for ensuring that a vehicle registration certificate (V5C) is updated?

- ☑ The registered vehicle keeper
- ☐ The vehicle manufacturer
- ☐ Your insurance company
- ☐ The licensing authority

It's your legal responsibility to keep the details on your vehicle registration certificate (V5C) up to date. You should tell the licensing authority about any changes. These include your name, address or vehicle details. If you don't do this, you may have problems when you try to sell your vehicle.

12.30 — Mark one answer — RES s2, HC p122

In which of these circumstances must you show your insurance certificate?

- ☐ When making a SORN
- ☐ When buying or selling a vehicle
- ☑ When a police officer asks you for it
- ☐ When having an MOT inspection

You must produce a valid insurance certificate when requested by a police officer. If you can't do this immediately, you may be asked to take it to a police station. Other documents you may be asked to produce are your driving licence and the vehicle's MOT certificate.

12.31 — Mark one answer — RES s2

Your vehicle must have valid insurance cover before you can do what?

- ☐ Make a SORN
- ☐ Sell the vehicle
- ☐ Scrap the vehicle
- ☑ Tax the vehicle

Your vehicle must have valid insurance cover before you can tax it. If required, it will also need to have a valid MOT certificate. You can tax your vehicle online, by phone or at certain post offices.

12.32 — Mark one answer — RES s2

Your vehicle needs a current MOT certificate. What will the MOT certificate enable you to do?

- ☐ Renew your driving licence
- ☐ Change your insurance company
- ☑ Tax your vehicle
- ☐ Notify a change of address

If your vehicle is required to have an MOT certificate, you'll need to make sure this is current before you're able to tax your vehicle. You can do this online, by phone or at certain post offices.

12.33

Mark one answer

RES s2, HC p120–122

Which of these is needed before you can legally use a vehicle on the road?

- ☑ A valid driving licence
- ☐ Breakdown cover
- ☐ Proof of your identity
- ☐ A vehicle handbook

Using a vehicle on the road illegally carries a heavy fine and can lead to penalty points on your driving licence. You must have

- a valid driving licence
- paid the appropriate vehicle tax
- proper insurance cover.

12.34

Mark one answer

RES s2

What must you have when you apply to renew your vehicle tax?

- ☑ Valid insurance
- ☐ The vehicle's chassis number
- ☐ The handbook
- ☐ A valid driving licence

You can renew your vehicle tax online, at post offices and vehicle registration offices, or by phone. When applying, make sure you have all the relevant valid documents, including a valid MOT test certificate where applicable.

12.35

Mark one answer

RES s2, HC p122

A police officer asks to see your documents. You don't have them with you. Within what time must you produce them at a police station?

- ☐ 5 days
- ☐ 7 days
- ☐ 14 days
- ☐ 21 days

You don't have to carry around your vehicle's documents wherever you go. If a police officer asks to see them and you don't have them with you, you may be asked to produce them at a police station within 7 days.

12.36

Mark one answer

RES s2, HC p122

When should you update your vehicle registration certificate?

- ☐ When you pass your driving test
- ☐ When you move house
- ☐ When your vehicle needs an MOT
- ☐ When you have a collision

As the registered keeper of a vehicle, it's up to you to inform DVLA of any changes in your details; for example, your name or address. You do this by completing and sending off the relevant section of the registration certificate.

You buy a second-hand motorcycle, which you want to ride immediately.

There are three days left on its **MOT** certificate.

You take your new motorcycle for its **MOT** test, which it fails as it needs some repair work.

For the repairs, you ride it to a garage a few miles away from the **MOT** centre.

A week later, you have the motorcycle retested. It successfully passes the second **MOT**.

You have the most basic type of insurance cover available.

12.1 What must you do before you can legally ride your motorcycle on the road?

Mark **one** answer

- ☐ Tax it and display a disc from the post office
- ☑ Tax it using the new keeper supplement
- ☐ Tax it with the V5C registration certificate
- ☐ Tax it using the last-chance warning letter

RES s2

12.2 When did the motorcycle pass its last MOT?
Mark **one** answer

- ☐ Almost six months ago
- ☑ Almost twelve months ago
- ☐ Almost two years ago
- ☐ Almost three years ago

RES s2 **HC** p121

12.3 Why could you ride your motorcycle to the garage?
Mark **one** answer

- ☐ It's allowed during daylight hours, but not at night
- ☐ It's allowed, but only until the vehicle tax expires
- ☐ It's allowed in order to get the motorcycle to a repairer
- ☐ It's allowed for a period of seven days after failure

HC p121

12.4 What's your type of insurance called?
Mark **one** answer

- ☐ Third policy
- ☐ Third practice
- ☐ Third party
- ☐ Third procedure

RES s2 **HC** p121–122

12.5 What does your insurance cover?
Mark **one** answer

- ☐ Damage to your vehicle
- ☑ Damage to other vehicles
- ☐ Injury to yourself
- ☐ All damage and injury

HC p121–122

Incidents, accidents and emergencies

In this section, you'll learn about

- what to do if your motorcycle breaks down
- how to ride safely in a tunnel, and what to do if you have an emergency
- what to do if you're the first to arrive at an incident
- first aid and how to help casualties at an incident
- reporting an incident to the police.

Incidents, accidents and emergencies

If you're involved in an incident on the road, such as your motorcycle breaking down or arriving first at the scene of a crash, knowing what to do can prevent a more serious situation from developing.

It's useful to carry a first aid kit, a warning triangle and a fire extinguisher for use in an emergency. This equipment could help to prevent or lessen an injury. You may be able to tackle a small fire if you have a fire extinguisher, but don't take any risks.

> Breakdowns

Knowing what to do if your motorcycle breaks down will help keep you safe, and avoid creating problems for other road users, such as traffic jams.

If a warning light shows on the instrument panel of your motorcycle, you may have a problem that affects the safety of the vehicle. If necessary, stop as soon as you can do so safely and check the problem.

HC p128

If a tyre bursts or you get a puncture while you're riding

- hold the handlebars firmly
- gently roll to a stop at the side of the road.

If you smell petrol while you're riding, stop and investigate as soon as you can do so safely. Don't ignore it.

If an emergency happens while you're on a motorway, try to get onto the hard shoulder and call for help from an emergency telephone. Marker posts show you the way to the nearest phone. An operator will answer and ask you

- the number on the phone, which will tell the services where you are
- details of yourself and your motorcycle
- whether you belong to a motoring organisation.

HC r270, 275 **RES** s16

Driver location signs can help you give the emergency services precise information about where you are. See this link for more details.

❯ **direct.gov.uk/prod_consum_dg/ groups/dg_digitalassets/@dg/@ en/documents/digitalasset/ dg_185820.pdf**

If you break down on a level crossing, get yourself, any passenger and your motorcycle off the crossing area immediately. If you can't move your motorcycle, phone the signal operator and follow any instructions given to you.

If you're waiting at a level crossing and the red light signal continues to flash after a train has gone by, you **MUST** wait, as another train may be coming.

HC r293, 299 **RES** s7 **KYTS** p27

If your motorcycle catches fire while you're riding, pull up as quickly and safely as possible. Get yourself and any passenger away from the motorcycle and then call the fire service.

HC p130 **RES** s11

Watch the Think! 'Van of Elvises' video to find out what to do if you break down on a motorway.

❯ **youtube.com/thinkuk**

> Warning others of a breakdown or incident

Use your hazard warning lights

- if you need to suddenly slow down or stop on a motorway or high-speed road because of an incident or hazard ahead; as soon as the traffic behind you has reacted to your hazard lights, you should turn them off
- when your vehicle has broken down and is temporarily obstructing traffic.

HC r116, 274

If you have a warning triangle, place it at least 45 metres (147 feet) behind your motorcycle. This will warn other road users that you've broken down. Never place a warning triangle on a motorway: there's too much danger from passing traffic.

HC r274 **RES** s16

If you're riding on a motorway and you see something fall from another vehicle, or if anything falls from your motorcycle, stop at the next emergency telephone and report the hazard to the police. Don't try to retrieve it yourself.

RES s16

> Safety in tunnels

You need to take extra care when riding in a tunnel because

- when you enter the tunnel, visibility is suddenly reduced
- the confined space can make incidents difficult to deal with.

Before riding through a tunnel, remove your sunglasses or sun visor if you're using them and make sure your dipped headlights are on. It's particularly important to keep a safe distance from the vehicle in front when riding in a tunnel, even if it's congested.

Look out for signs that warn of incidents or congestion.

If your motorcycle is involved in an incident or breaks down in a tunnel

- switch off the engine
- put your hazard warning lights on
- go and call for help immediately from the nearest emergency telephone point.

RES s8

Stopping at an incident

If you're the first to arrive at the scene of an incident or crash, stop and warn other traffic. Switch on your hazard warning lights. Don't put yourself at risk.

- Make sure that the emergency services are called as soon as possible.
- Ensure that the engines of any vehicles at the scene are switched off.
- Move uninjured people away from the scene.

HC r283 **RES** s16

A vehicle carrying dangerous goods will display an orange label or a hazard warning plate on the back. If a vehicle carrying something hazardous is involved in an incident, report what the label says when you call the emergency services. The different plates are shown in *The Official Highway Code*.

HC p117 **RES** s16

Helping others and giving first aid

Even if you don't know any first aid, you can help any injured people by

- keeping them warm and comfortable
- keeping them calm by talking to them reassuringly
- making sure they're not left alone.

HC p131–132 **RES** s16

Don't move an injured person if the area is safe. Only move them if they're in obvious danger, and then with extreme care. If a motorcyclist is involved, never remove their helmet unless it's essential in order to keep them alive, because removing the helmet could cause more serious injury. Always get medical help and never offer a casualty any food or drink, or a cigarette to calm them down.

`HC` p131–133 `RES` s16

There are three vital priorities

1. ensure a clear airway
2. check for breathing
3. try to stop any heavy bleeding.

If someone is unconscious, follow the **DR ABC** code.

Danger

Check for danger, such as approaching traffic, before you move towards the casualty.

Response

Ask the casualty questions and gently shake their shoulders to check for a response.

Airway

Check their airway is clear.

Breathing

Check for breathing for up to 10 seconds.

Compressions

If the casualty isn't breathing Using two hands in the centre of the chest, press down hard and fast – around 5–6 centimetres and about twice a second. You may only need one hand for a child (two fingers for an infant) and shouldn't press down as far.

If the casualty isn't breathing, consider giving mouth-to-mouth resuscitation.

Check and, if necessary, clear their mouth and airway.

Gently tilt their head back as far as possible.

Pinch their nostrils together.

Place your mouth over theirs. Give two breaths, each lasting one second.

Continue with cycles of 30 chest compressions and two breaths until medical help arrives.

Only stop when they can breathe without help. If the casualty is a small child, breathe very gently. Once the casualty is breathing normally, place them in the recovery position and check the airway to make sure it's clear. Keep checking, and don't leave them alone.

If they're bleeding, apply firm pressure to the wound. If the casualty is bleeding from a limb, raise it as long as it isn't broken. This will help reduce the bleeding.

People at the scene may be suffering from shock: signs include a rapid pulse, sweating and pale grey skin.

To help someone suffering from shock

- reassure them constantly
- keep them warm
- make them as comfortable as you can
- avoid moving them unless it's necessary
- make sure they're not left alone.

If someone is suffering from burns

- douse the burns thoroughly with cool non-toxic liquid for at least 10 minutes
- don't remove anything sticking to the burn.

> Reporting an incident

You **MUST** stop and give your name and address if you're involved in an incident. If there's damage to another vehicle, property or animal, report it to the owner. If you don't do this at the time, you **MUST** report the incident to the police as soon as is reasonably practicable, and in any case within 24 hours (immediately in Northern Ireland).

If another person is injured and you don't produce your insurance certificate at the time of the incident, you **MUST** report the incident to the police as soon as is reasonably practicable, and in any case within 24 hours (immediately in Northern Ireland).

HC r286, 287 RES s16

If another vehicle is involved, find out

- who owns the vehicle
- the make and registration number of the vehicle
- the other driver's name, address and telephone number and details of their insurance.

Following an incident (or at any other time), the police may ask you for

- your insurance certificate
- the MOT certificate for the motorcycle you're riding
- your driving licence.

HC r286, p122

Meeting the standards

At the scene of an incident, you must be able to

stop and park your machine in a safe place, if necessary

make sure that warning is given to other road users

give help to others if you can

where possible, record information about what you saw or the scene that you found. It may be helpful to take photographs and draw sketch plans.

You must know and understand

how to keep control of the machine, where possible, if it breaks down

how and when to use hazard warning lights

what the law says about stopping if you're involved in an incident that causes damage or injury to

- any other person
- another vehicle
- an animal
- someone's property

This includes what to do about

- stopping
- providing your details
- giving statements
- producing documents

how to contact the emergency services and how important it is to give them accurate information.

Notes

You can use this page to make your own notes or diagrams about the key points you need to remember.

Think about

- What should you do if your motorcycle breaks down on the motorway?
- How can you warn other road users if you've broken down on the road?
- If you're the first person to arrive at the scene of a crash, what should you do?
- If a motorcyclist is involved in the crash, should you remove their helmet?
- What does DR ABC stand for?
- If you're involved in an incident with another vehicle, what must you do?

Your notes

Things to discuss and practise with your trainer

These are just a few examples of what you could discuss and practise with your trainer. Read more about incidents, accidents and emergencies to come up with your own ideas.

Discuss with your trainer

- what it means if you see a driver displaying a 'help' pennant
- when you may and may not use your hazard warning lights
- what you should do if you arrive at the scene of a crash and find
  - an injured motorcyclist wearing a helmet
  - someone bleeding badly with nothing embedded in their wound
  - someone with a burn
  - someone who isn't breathing normally.

Practise with your trainer

Hopefully, you won't have the opportunity to practise what to do in the event of an incident or emergency during your lesson. Instead, practise with your trainer

- learning the rules relating to
  - breakdowns on all roads, including motorways
  - obstructions
  - incidents, eg warning signs and flashing lights
  - passing and being involved in a crash
  - incidents involving dangerous goods
  - which documents you'll need to produce if you're involved in a crash
  - incidents in tunnels.

Your motorcycle has broken down on a motorway. How will you know the direction of the nearest emergency telephone?

☐ By walking with the flow of traffic

☑ By following an arrow on a marker post

☐ By walking against the flow of traffic

☐ By remembering where the last phone was

If you break down on a motorway, pull onto the hard shoulder and stop as far over to the left as you can. Switch on your hazard warning lights (if fitted) and go to the nearest emergency telephone. Marker posts spaced every 100 metres will show you where the nearest telephone is.

When should you use the engine cut-out switch?

☑ To stop the engine in an emergency

☐ To stop the engine after a short journey

☐ To save wear on the ignition switch

☐ To start the engine if you lose the key

Most motorcycles are fitted with an engine cut-out switch. This is designed to stop the engine in an emergency and so reduce the risk of electrical sparks starting a fire.

You're riding on a motorway. The car in front switches on its hazard warning lights while it's moving. What does this mean?

☐ The driver is going to take the next exit

☑ There's danger ahead

☐ There's a police car ahead

☐ The driver is trying to change lanes

Drivers and riders may switch on their hazard warning lights to warn following traffic of an obstruction or danger ahead. This only applies on motorways and dual carriageways that are subject to the national speed limit. The hazard warning lights should be turned off again when it's clear the warning has been seen.

What will you be asked when you use the emergency telephone on a motorway?

☑ The number of the telephone you're using

☐ The number on your driving licence

☐ The name of your vehicle insurance company

☐ The route you were taking before the breakdown

Have information about your motorcycle and the number of the phone you're using ready before you call from an emergency telephone. For your own safety, face the traffic during the call.

13.5 | Mark one answer | RES s11, HC r116

You're on a motorway. When can you use hazard warning lights?

☐ When a vehicle is following too closely

☑ When you slow down quickly because of danger ahead

☐ When you're being towed by another vehicle

☐ When you're riding on the hard shoulder

Briefly using your hazard warning lights will warn the traffic behind you that there's a hazard ahead. Turn them off again when following drivers have seen and responded to your signal.

13.6 | Mark one answer | RES s16, HC r116, 274

You're riding through a tunnel. What should you do if your motorcycle breaks down?

☑ Switch on hazard warning lights

☐ Remain on your motorcycle

☐ Wait for the police to find you

☐ Rely on CCTV cameras seeing you

If your motorcycle breaks down in a tunnel, it could present a danger to other traffic. First switch on your hazard warning lights and then call for help from an emergency telephone point. Don't rely on being found by the police or being seen by a CCTV camera.

13.7 | Mark one answer | RES s11, HC r280

You're on a motorway. Luggage falls from your motorcycle. What should you do?

☑ Stop at the next emergency telephone and report the hazard

☐ Stop on the motorway and put on hazard warning lights while you pick it up

☐ Walk back up the motorway to pick it up

☐ Pull up on the hard shoulder and wave traffic down

If any of your luggage falls onto the road, pull onto the hard shoulder near an emergency telephone and call for assistance. Don't stop on the carriageway or attempt to retrieve anything.

Mark one answer

You're involved in a collision with another vehicle. Someone is injured and your motorcycle is damaged. What should you find out?

☐ Whether the driver owns the other vehicle involved

☐ Whether the other driver is licensed to drive

☐ The occupation of the other driver

☑ The other driver's vehicle insurance details

If you're involved in a collision where someone is injured, your first priority is to warn other traffic and call the emergency services. Make sure you have all the information you need before you leave the scene – such as the other driver's name, phone number and insurance details. Don't ride your motorcycle if it's unroadworthy.

Mark one answer

You see a car on the hard shoulder of a motorway with a 'help' pennant displayed. What does this mean?

☑ The driver is likely to be a disabled person

☐ The driver is first-aid trained

☐ The driver is a foreign visitor

☐ The driver is a rescue patrol officer

If a disabled driver's vehicle breaks down and they're unable to walk to an emergency phone, they're advised to stay in their car and switch on the hazard warning lights. They may also display a 'help' pennant in their vehicle.

Mark one answer

When are you allowed to use hazard warning lights?

☑ When stopped and temporarily obstructing traffic

☐ When travelling during darkness without headlights

☐ When parked on double yellow lines to visit a shop

☐ When travelling slowly because you're lost

You mustn't use hazard warning lights while moving, except to warn traffic behind when you slow suddenly on a motorway or unrestricted dual carriageway.

Never use hazard warning lights to excuse dangerous or illegal parking.

13.11   Mark one answer   RES s8, HC r126

You're going through a congested tunnel and have to stop. What should you do?

☐ Pull up very close to the vehicle in front to save space

☐ Ignore any message signs, as they're never up to date

☐ Keep a safe distance from the vehicle in front

☐ Make a U-turn and find another route

It's important to keep a safe distance from the vehicle in front at all times. This still applies in congested tunnels, even if you're moving very slowly or have stopped. If the vehicle in front breaks down, you may need room to manoeuvre past it.

13.12   Mark one answer   RES s11, HC r275

On a motorway, when should the hard shoulder be used?

☐ When answering a mobile phone

☐ When an emergency arises

☐ When taking a short rest

☐ When checking a road map

The hard shoulder should only be used in a genuine emergency. If possible, and if it's safe, use a roadside telephone to call for help. This will give your exact location to the operator. Never cross the carriageway or a slip road to use a telephone on the other side of the road.

13.13   Mark one answer   RES s16, HC p133

You arrive at the scene of a crash. Someone is bleeding badly from an arm wound. Nothing is embedded in it. What should you do?

☐ Apply pressure over the wound and keep the arm down

☐ Dab the wound

☐ Get them a drink

☑ Apply pressure over the wound and raise the arm

If possible, lay the casualty down. Check for anything that may be in the wound. Apply firm pressure to the wound using clean material, without pressing on anything that might be in it. Raising the arm above the level of the heart will also help to stem the flow of blood.

13.14
Mark one answer

RES s16, HC p132

At an incident, a casualty is unconscious. You need to check whether they're breathing. How long should you allow for this check?

☐ At least 2 seconds

☑ At least 10 seconds

☐ At least 1 minute

☐ At least 2 minutes

Once the casualty's airway is open, listen and feel for breath. Do this by placing your cheek over their mouth and nose, and look to see if their chest rises. This should be done for up to 10 seconds. If you cannot detect any breathing, you should begin compressions.

13.15
Mark one answer

RES s16, HC p133

Following a collision, someone has suffered a burn. The burn needs to be cooled. What's the shortest time it should be cooled for?

☐ 5 minutes

☑ 10 minutes

☐ 15 minutes

☐ 20 minutes

Check the casualty for shock and, if possible, try to cool the burn for at least 10 minutes. Use a clean, cool, non-toxic liquid, preferably water.

13.16
Mark one answer

RES s16, HC p132

A casualty isn't breathing normally. Chest compressions should be given. At what rate?

☐ 10 per minute

☑ 120 per minute

☐ 60 per minute

☐ 240 per minute

If a casualty isn't breathing normally, chest compressions may be needed to maintain circulation. Place two hands on the centre of the chest and press down hard and fast – around 5–6 centimetres and about twice a second.

13.17
Mark one answer

RES s16

A person has been injured. They may be suffering from shock. What are the warning signs to look for?

☐ Flushed complexion

☐ Warm dry skin

☐ Slow pulse

☑ Pale grey skin

The effects of shock may not be immediately obvious. Warning signs are rapid pulse, sweating, pale grey skin and rapid shallow breathing.

13.18 · Mark one answer · RES s16, HC p132

An injured person has been placed in the recovery position. They're unconscious but breathing normally. What else should be done?

- [ ] Press firmly between their shoulders
- [ ] Place their arms by their side
- [ ] Give them a hot sweet drink
- [x] Check their airway remains clear

After a casualty has been placed in the recovery position, make sure their airway remains open and monitor their condition until medical help arrives. Where possible, don't move a casualty unless there's further danger.

13.19 · Mark one answer · RES s16, HC r132

An injured motorcyclist is lying unconscious in the road. The traffic has stopped and there's no further danger. What should you do to help?

- [ ] Remove their safety helmet
- [x] Seek medical assistance
- [ ] Move the person off the road
- [ ] Remove their leather jacket

If someone has been injured, the sooner proper medical attention is given the better. Ask someone to phone for help or do it yourself. An injured person should only be moved if they're in further danger. An injured motorcyclist's helmet shouldn't be removed unless it's essential.

13.20 · Mark one answer · RES s11, HC r280

What should you do if you see a large box fall from a lorry onto the motorway?

- [x] Go to the next emergency telephone and report the hazard
- [ ] Catch up with the lorry and try to get the driver's attention
- [ ] Stop close to the box until the police arrive
- [ ] Pull over to the hard shoulder, then remove the box

Lorry drivers can be unaware of objects falling from their vehicles. If you see something fall onto a motorway, look to see if the driver pulls over. If they don't stop, don't attempt to retrieve the object yourself. Pull onto the hard shoulder near an emergency telephone and report the hazard.

13.21 · Mark one answer · RES s8

You're going through a long tunnel. What will warn you of congestion or an incident ahead?

- [ ] Hazard warning lines
- [ ] Other drivers flashing their lights
- [ ] Variable message signs
- [ ] Areas with hatch markings

Follow the instructions given by the signs or by tunnel officials. In congested tunnels, a minor incident can soon turn into a major one, with serious or even fatal results.

An adult casualty isn't breathing. To maintain circulation, compressions should be given. What's the correct depth to press for each compression?

☐ 1 to 2 centimetres

☑ 5 to 6 centimetres

☐ 10 to 15 centimetres

☐ 15 to 20 centimetres

An adult casualty isn't breathing normally. To maintain circulation, place two hands on the centre of the chest. Then press down hard and fast – around 5–6 centimetres and about twice a second.

You're the first to arrive at the scene of a crash. What should you do?

☐ Leave as soon as another motorist arrives

☐ Flag down other motorists to help you

☐ Drag all casualties away from the vehicles

☑ Call the emergency services promptly

At a crash scene you can help in practical ways, even if you aren't trained in first aid. Call the emergency services and make sure you don't put yourself or anyone else in danger. The safest way to warn other traffic is by switching on your hazard warning lights.

You're the first person to arrive at an incident where people are badly injured. You've switched on your hazard warning lights and checked all engines are stopped. What else should you do?

☑ Make sure that an ambulance is called for

☐ Stop other cars and ask the drivers for help

☐ Try and get people who are injured to drink something

☐ Move the people who are injured clear of their vehicles

If you're the first to arrive at a crash scene, the first concerns are the risk of further collision and fire. Ensuring that vehicle engines are switched off will reduce the risk of fire. Use hazard warning lights so that other traffic knows there's a need for caution. Make sure the emergency services are contacted; don't assume this has already been done.

You arrive at the scene of a motorcycle crash. The rider is injured. When should their helmet be removed?

☐ Only when it's essential

☐ Always straight away

☐ Only when the motorcyclist asks

☐ Always, unless they're in shock

Don't remove a motorcyclist's helmet unless it's essential. Remember they may be suffering from shock. Don't give them anything to eat or drink, but do reassure them confidently.

13.26

Mark one answer

RES s16, HC p132

You arrive at an incident. There's no danger from fire or further collisions. What's your first priority when attending to an unconscious motorcyclist?

☑ Check whether they're breathing

☐ Check whether they're bleeding

☐ Check whether they have any broken bones

☐ Check whether they have any bruising

At the scene of an incident, always be aware of danger from further collisions or fire. The first priority when dealing with an unconscious person is to ensure they can breathe. This may involve clearing their airway if you can see an obstruction or if they're having difficulty breathing.

13.27

Mark one answer

RES s16, HC p132

At an incident, someone is unconscious. What would your priority be?

☐ Find out their name

☐ Wake them up

☐ Make them comfortable

☑ Check their airway is clear

Remember this procedure by saying DR ABC. This stands for Danger, Response, Airway, Breathing, Compressions. Give whatever first aid you can and stay with the injured person until the emergency services arrive.

13.28

Mark one answer

RES s16, HC p131–132

You've stopped at an incident to give help. What should you do?

☑ Keep injured people warm and comfortable

☐ Give injured people something to eat

☐ Keep injured people on the move by walking them around

☐ Give injured people a warm drink

There are a number of things you can do to help, even without expert training. Be aware of further danger from other traffic and fire; make sure the area is safe. People may be in shock. Don't give them anything to eat or drink. Keep them warm and comfortable and reassure them. Don't move injured people unless there's a risk of further danger.

13.29

Mark one answer

RES s16, HC p132

There's been a collision. A driver is suffering from shock. What should you do?

☐ Give them a drink

☑ Reassure them

☐ Ask who caused the incident

☐ Offer them a cigarette

A casualty suffering from shock may have injuries that aren't immediately obvious. Call the emergency services, then stay with the person in shock, offering reassurance until the experts arrive.

13.30

You arrive at the scene of a motorcycle crash. No other vehicle is involved. The rider is unconscious and lying in the middle of the road. What's the first thing you should do at the scene?

☐ Move the rider out of the road
☑ Warn other traffic
☐ Clear the road of debris
☐ Give the rider reassurance

The motorcyclist is in an extremely vulnerable position, exposed to further danger from traffic. Approaching vehicles need advance warning in order to slow down and safely take avoiding action or stop. Don't put yourself or anyone else at risk. Use the hazard warning lights on your vehicle to alert other road users to the danger.

13.31

At an incident, a small child isn't breathing. To restore normal breathing, how should you breathe into their mouth?

☐ Sharply
☑ Gently
☐ Heavily
☐ Rapidly

If a young child has stopped breathing, first check that their airway is clear. Then give compressions to the chest using one hand (two fingers for an infant) and begin mouth-to-mouth resuscitation. Breathe very gently and continue the procedure until they can breathe without help.

13.32

At an incident, a casualty isn't breathing. What should you do while helping them to start breathing again?

☐ Put their arms across their chest
☐ Shake them firmly
☐ Roll them onto their side
☑ Tilt their head back gently

It's important to ensure that the airways are clear before you start mouth-to-mouth resuscitation. Gently tilt their head back and use your finger to check for and remove any obvious obstruction in the mouth.

13.33

At an incident, someone is suffering from severe burns. What should you do to help them?

☐ Apply lotions to the injury
☐ Burst any blisters
☐ Remove anything sticking to the burns
☑ Douse the burns with clean, cool, non-toxic liquid

Your priority is to cool the burns with a clean, cool, non-toxic liquid, preferably water. Its coolness will help take the heat out of the burns and relieve the pain. Keep the wound doused for at least 10 minutes. If blisters appear, don't attempt to burst them, as this could lead to infection.

13.34
Mark one answer
RES s16, HC p133

You arrive at an incident. A pedestrian is bleeding heavily from a leg wound. The leg isn't broken and there's nothing in the wound. What should you do?

☐ Dab the wound to stop bleeding

☐ Keep both legs flat on the ground

☐ Fetch them a warm drink

☐ Raise the leg to lessen bleeding

If there's nothing in the wound, applying a pad of clean cloth or bandage will help stem the bleeding. Raising the leg will also lessen the flow of blood. Don't tie anything tightly round the leg, as this will restrict circulation and could result in long-term injury.

13.35
Mark one answer
RES s16, HC p131–132

At an incident, a casualty is unconscious but breathing. When should you move them?

☐ When an ambulance is on its way

☐ When bystanders advise you to

☑ When there's further danger

☐ When bystanders will help you

Don't move a casualty unless there's further danger; for example, from other traffic or fire. They may have unseen or internal injuries. Moving them unnecessarily could cause further injury. Don't remove a motorcyclist's helmet unless it's essential.

13.36
Mark one answer
RES s16, HC p131–132

At an incident, it's important to look after any casualties. What should you do with them when the area is safe?

☐ Move them away from the vehicles

☐ Ask them how it happened

☐ Give them something to eat

☑ Keep them where they are

When the area is safe and there's no danger from other traffic or fire, it's better not to move casualties. Moving them may cause further injury.

13.37
Mark one answer
RES s16, HC p117

A tanker is involved in a collision. Which sign shows that it's carrying dangerous goods?

☐    ☑

☐   ☐

There will be an orange label on the side and rear of the tanker. Look at this carefully and report what it says when you phone the emergency services. Details of hazard warning plates are given in The Highway Code.

13.38
Mark one answer

HC r286, p122

You're involved in a collision. Afterwards, which document may the police ask you to produce?

☐ Vehicle registration document
☑ Driving licence
☐ Theory test certificate
☐ Vehicle service record

You must stop if you've been involved in a collision which results in injury or damage. The police may ask to see your driving licence and insurance details at the time or later at a police station.

13.39
Mark one answer

RES s16, HC p131

After a collision, someone is unconscious in their vehicle. When should you call the emergency services?

☐ Only as a last resort
☑ As soon as possible
☐ After you've woken them up
☐ After checking for broken bones

It's important to make sure that the emergency services arrive as soon as possible. When a person is unconscious, they could have serious injuries that aren't immediately obvious.

13.40
Mark one answer

RES s16, HC p133

A casualty has an injured arm. They can move it freely but it's bleeding. Why should you get them to keep it in a raised position?

☐ It will ease the pain
☐ It will help them to be seen more easily
☐ To stop them touching other people
☑ It will help to reduce the blood flow

If a casualty is bleeding heavily, raise the limb to a higher position. This will help to reduce the blood flow. Before raising the limb, you should make sure that it isn't broken.

13.41
Mark one answer

RES s16, HC p131

A collision has just happened. An injured person is lying in a busy road. What's the first thing you should do to help?

☐ Treat the person for shock
☑ Warn other traffic
☐ Place them in the recovery position
☐ Make sure the injured person is kept warm

The most immediate danger is further collisions and fire. You could warn other traffic by switching on hazard warning lights, displaying an advance warning triangle or sign (but not on a motorway), or by any other means that doesn't put you or others at risk.

13.42 — Mark one answer — RES s16, HC p132

At an incident, what should you do with a casualty who has stopped breathing?

- [ ] Keep their head tilted forwards as far as possible
- [x] Remove anything that's blocking their airway
- [ ] Raise their legs to help with circulation
- [ ] Try to give them something to drink

Unblocking the casualty's airway and gently tilting their head back will help them to breathe. They'll then be in the correct position if mouth-to-mouth resuscitation is required. Don't move a casualty unless there's further danger.

13.43 — Mark one answer — RES s16, HC p132

You're at the scene of an incident. Someone is suffering from shock. How should you treat them?

- [x] Reassure them confidently
- [ ] Offer them a cigarette
- [ ] Give them a warm drink
- [ ] Offer them some food

If someone is suffering from shock, try to keep them warm and as comfortable as you can. Don't give them anything to eat or drink but reassure them confidently and try not to leave them alone.

13.44 — Mark one answer — RES s16, HC p132

There's been a collision. A motorcyclist is lying injured and unconscious. Unless it's essential, why should you not usually attempt to remove their helmet?

- [ ] They might not want you to
- [ ] This could result in more serious injury
- [ ] They'll get too cold if you do this
- [ ] You could scratch the helmet

When someone is injured, any movement that isn't absolutely necessary should be avoided, since it could make the injuries worse. Unless it's essential to remove a motorcyclist's helmet, it's generally safer to leave it in place.

Case study practice – 13 Incidents, accidents and emergencies

You witness an incident involving a car and a motorcycle. The car driver isn't obviously injured but their skin has turned a grey colour, they're sweating and their breathing is rapid and shallow.

The motorcyclist is lying against the kerb with his helmet still on. He's conscious but very dazed, bruised and shocked.

You leave your own motorcycle standing on the road with the hazard warning lights on.

You call the emergency services and stay with both people involved in the incident until the services arrive.

You give your contact details to a police officer.

13.1 What condition is the car driver most likely to be suffering from?
Mark **one** answer

☐ Hunger
☐ Travel sickness
☐ Headache
☑ Shock

HC p132

13.2 Why should the helmet stay on for the time being?

Mark **one** answer

- ☐ Someone might steal the helmet if they take it off
- ☐ The helmet may get lost on the way to hospital
- ☑ Because removing it could cause further injuries
- ☐ The helmet will keep their head from getting cold

HC r283, p132

13.3 Why would you leave your motorcycle positioned in that way?

Mark **one** answer

- ☑ To warn following traffic of the hazard
- ☐ To ensure that the battery stays fully charged
- ☐ To highlight the incident for the emergency services
- ☐ To help you locate your motorcycle again later

RES s16 **HC** r283

13.4 How should you deal with the motorcyclist?

Mark **one** answer

- ☐ Offer them food
- ☐ Give them a drink
- ☑ Keep them warm
- ☐ Leave them alone

RES s16 **HC** p132

13.5 Why would you provide your details?

Mark **one** answer

- ☐ You were in a hurry to leave
- ☐ You witnessed the incident
- ☐ You wanted to be involved
- ☐ You left your licence at home

RES s16

Section fourteen
Motorcycle loading

In this section, you'll learn about

> how to carry loads safely on your motorcycle
> using a sidecar
> carrying a pillion passenger safely
> towing a trailer.

Motorcycle loading

Loading your motorcycle carefully will help to ensure that you can travel safely, whether your load is a passenger, a trailer or simply an overnight bag.

⊳ Keeping your motorcycle stable

As a rider, you need to make sure that your motorcycle isn't overloaded. Overloading can seriously affect the motorcycle's handling, especially the steering and braking.

`HC` r98 `RES` s14

You **MUST** securely fasten any load you're carrying before you start riding: it's an offence to travel with an insecure load.

A heavy or bulky load can make your motorcycle less stable.

When carrying a passenger or a heavy load on a motorcycle, you may need to adjust

- the tyre pressures
- the headlight aim
- the suspension.

RES s14

You should inflate your tyres to a higher pressure than normal

- when you're carrying a heavy load or pillion passenger
- if you're riding for a long distance on a dual carriageway or motorway at the speed limit for these roads.

Your motorcycle handbook should tell you the correct pressure for different circumstances.

RES s14, 15

> Sidecars

Before fitting a sidecar, you need to make sure that your motorcycle is suitable for use with a sidecar. The sidecar must be aligned correctly, otherwise your motorcycle will be difficult to control and is likely to be dangerous to ride.

When you ride for the first time with a sidecar fitted, keep your speed down and be careful when riding round bends and corners and at junctions. A motorcycle with a sidecar handles very differently from a solo motorcycle.

Remember that your stopping distance may also increase due to the extra weight of the sidecar.

RES s14

> Pillion passengers

A pillion passenger **MUST** wear a helmet that's correctly fastened. (This does not apply to a follower of the Sikh religion while wearing a turban.) They **MUST** sit astride the machine, facing forwards, on a proper passenger seat. Your motorcycle should have passenger footrests too.

You **MUST NOT** carry a pillion passenger unless

- you've passed a practical motorcycle test
- you have a full motorcycle licence for the category of motorcycle being ridden.

HC r83, 85 **RES** s14

Your pillion passenger needs to understand that they should lean with you when you lean the motorcycle over to steer around bends. If it's the first time the passenger has ridden, explain what to do and how to hold onto either your waist or the passenger grab rail.

Children should only be carried as pillion passengers when they can reach the handholds and footrests. They **MUST** also wear a helmet that's the right size and securely fastened, and sit properly on the pillion seat, facing forwards.

The extra weight of a passenger may change the way the motorcycle handles, so give yourself time to get used to it. The additional weight may also increase your stopping distance, so keep well back when following other traffic.

When you're riding with a passenger, think about their comfort and try to ride smoothly, avoiding harsh acceleration or braking.

Your passenger's clothing should be

- warm
- waterproof
- bright or reflective.

Passengers who wear protective motorcyclist clothing will gain protection from

- the weather
- the road surface, if they fall off the motorcycle.

Don't let your passenger wear a trailing scarf or belt, as this could become tangled in the rear wheel or drive chain and cause a serious incident.

RES s14

❯ Towing a trailer

To tow a trailer, you must have a full motorcycle licence and your motorcycle must have an engine capacity of more than 125 cc. A motorcycle trailer must be no wider than 1 metre (3 feet 3 inches). Remember that your stopping distance may increase due to the extra weight of the trailer.

If the trailer starts to swerve or snake as you're riding along

- ease off the throttle
- reduce your speed gradually to regain control.

There's a lower national speed limit for all vehicles towing trailers.

On a dual carriageway or motorway	Maximum speed 60 mph (96 km/h)
	A vehicle towing a trailer on a motorway that has more than two lanes **MUST NOT** be driven in the right-hand lane.
On a single carriageway	Maximum speed 50 mph (80 km/h)

HC r98, p40 **RES** s14

Find out more about towing a trailer at this website.

➲ **www.gov.uk**

Meeting the standards

You must be able to

make sure that a pillion passenger is seated legally, correctly and securely

make sure that loads are secure and distributed correctly, depending on the machine

allow for the effect that any extra load may have on how the machine handles.

You must know and understand

what to tell a passenger about how to behave when being carried on the machine

how to adjust the machine to allow for extra weight. For example, you may need to put more air in the tyres

how to change your riding to allow for extra weight; for example

- earlier braking
- use of lower gears.

> Notes

You can use this page to make your own notes or diagrams about the key points you need to remember.

Think about

- What sorts of load might you carry on your motorcycle that could affect its stability?
- When might you need to increase the tyre pressures?
- What would you need to tell a first-time pillion passenger about before you began riding?
- If you wanted to tow a trailer, what speed limits would you have to observe?

Your notes

Things to discuss and practise with your trainer

These are just a few examples of what you could discuss and practise with your trainer. Read more about motorcycle loading to come up with your own ideas.

Discuss with your trainer

- the effects that carrying a heavy load, such as panniers or a top box, might have on your riding
- the rules and advice for carrying a pillion passenger
  - your licence requirement
  - how a passenger should sit and behave on your motorcycle
  - what they should wear
  - the riding technique that you should use when carrying a passenger
- the techniques that you'll need to use and rules to follow when
  - riding with a sidecar
  - pulling a trailer.

Practise with your trainer

- the checks that you'll need to make when carrying a load
  - your tyre pressure
  - the preload on your shock absorbers
  - the angle of your headlights.

14.1

What should you do if a trailer you're towing swerves or snakes?

- ☑ Ease off the throttle and reduce your speed
- ☐ Let go of the handlebars and let it correct itself
- ☐ Brake hard and hold the brake on
- ☐ Accelerate until it stabilises itself

Don't be tempted to use harsh braking to stop swerving or snaking, as this could make things worse. You should reduce your speed gradually by easing off the throttle.

14.2

What should you be aware of when you ride a sidecar outfit for the first time?

- ☑ You need time to get used to it
- ☐ You'll be able to stop in a shorter distance
- ☐ You need to accelerate around bends
- ☐ You can approach corners without braking

A motorcycle with a sidecar, or a trike, will feel very different to ride than a solo motorcycle. It requires a specific technique, especially when cornering, with different methods used for right and left turns. Keep your speed down until you get used to the outfit, especially when negotiating bends and junctions.

14.3

What may you need to adjust when you're carrying a heavy load on your motorcycle?

- ☐ The footrests
- ☐ The gear lever
- ☐ The seat height
- ☑ The tyre pressure

Carrying extra weight, such as luggage or a pillion passenger, can affect the feel and handling of your motorcycle. If possible, some items may need to be adjusted to help overcome this. These adjustments include the aim of the headlights, the suspension settings, the tyre pressures and the mirrors.

14.4

What are the minimum test vehicle requirements for a motorcycle used to obtain a full category 'A' licence?

- ☐ Solo, with a maximum power of at least 25 kW (33 bhp)
- ☐ Solo, with a maximum power of at least 11 kW (14.6 bhp)
- ☐ Fitted with a sidecar, and with a maximum power of at least 35 kW (46.6 bhp)
- ☑ Solo, with a maximum power of at least 40 kW (53.6 bhp)

To obtain the full category 'A' on your driving licence, the motorcycle you use for your practical test must be a solo machine with a cylinder capacity of at least 595 cc and a power output of at least 40 kW (53.6 bhp).

14.5
Mark one answer RES s14

You're carrying a load on your motorcycle's luggage rack. What must you ensure?

☑ The load must be securely fastened

☐ The load must be unevenly balanced

☐ The load must be highly visible

☐ The load must be covered with plastic sheeting

Don't risk losing any luggage while riding: it could fall into the path of following vehicles and cause danger. It's an offence to travel with an insecure load.

14.6
Mark one answer RES s14, HC r83

What does a person need to do when they ride as a pillion passenger?

☐ Have a provisional motorcycle licence

☐ Be lighter than the rider

☐ Wear a motorcycle helmet

☐ Give signals for the rider

Pillion passengers must sit astride the motorcycle, on a proper passenger seat, and passenger footrests must be fitted. They must also wear a correctly fastened motorcycle helmet.

14.7
Mark one answer RES s14

What should a pillion passenger do while being carried on a motorcycle?

☐ Give the rider directions

☐ Lean with the rider when going around bends

☐ Take rear observation for the rider

☐ Give arm signals for the rider

When you ride with a pillion passenger, your motorcycle may feel unbalanced and its acceleration and braking distance may also be affected. Make sure your passenger knows they must lean with you while cornering. If they don't, they could cause the motorcycle to become unstable and difficult to control.

14.8
Mark one answer RES s14

When you're going around a corner, what should your pillion passenger do?

☐ Give arm signals for you

☐ Check behind for other vehicles

☐ Lean with you on bends

☐ Lean to one side to see ahead

A pillion passenger shouldn't give signals or look around for you – that's your responsibility as the rider. If your passenger has never been on a motorcycle before, make sure they know that they need to lean with you when going around bends.

Which of these may need to be adjusted when carrying a pillion passenger?

☐ Indicators

☐ Exhaust

☐ Fairing

☑ Headlights

Your headlights must be properly adjusted to avoid dazzling other road users. You'll probably need to do this when carrying a heavy load or the extra weight of a pillion passenger. You may also need to adjust the tyre pressures and the suspension.

What's the speed limit on a single carriageway road for a motorcycle towing a trailer?

☑ 50 mph

☐ 40 mph

☐ 60 mph

☐ 70 mph

When you tow a trailer, remember that you must obey the reduced speed limits of 50 mph on a single carriageway and 60 mph on a dual carriageway or motorway. Make sure that the trailer is hitched correctly and that any load in the trailer is secure. You should also bear in mind that your stopping distance may increase.

What can a heavy load in a motorcycle top box cause?

Carrying a heavy load in your top box could make your motorcycle unstable, because the weight is high up and at the very back of the machine.

☐ Improved stability

☑ Reduced stability

☐ Reduced tyre wear

☐ Improved braking

Who's responsible for making sure that a motorcycle isn't overloaded?

☐ The rider of the motorcycle

☐ The owner of the items being carried

☐ The licensing authority

☐ The owner of the motorcycle

Correct loading is the responsibility of the rider. Overloading a motorcycle can seriously affect the control and handling. It could result in a crash, with serious or even fatal consequences.

14.13   Mark one answer   RES s14

What should you do before fitting a sidecar to a motorcycle?

☐ Have the wheels balanced
☐ Have the engine tuned
☐ Pass the extended motorcycle test
☐ Check that the motorcycle is suitable

If you want to fit a sidecar to your motorcycle, check that the motorcycle is suitable and can cope with the extra load. Make sure that the sidecar is securely fixed and properly aligned. If your motorcycle was registered on or after 1 August 1981, the sidecar must be fitted on the left-hand side of the motorcycle.

14.14   Mark one answer   RES s14

You're using throwover saddlebags. Why is it important to make sure they're evenly loaded?

☐ Uneven loads can make the engine overheat
☐ Uneven loads can make the motorcycle uncomfortable
☑ Uneven loads can make the motorcycle unstable
☐ Uneven loads can make the battery overcharge

Panniers or saddlebags should be loaded so that you carry about the same weight in each bag. Uneven loading could make the motorcycle unstable, especially when cornering.

14.15   Mark one answer   RES s14

You're riding with a bulky tank bag. What could this affect?

☑ Your ability to steer
☐ Your ability to accelerate
☐ Your view ahead
☐ Your insurance premium

If your tank bag is too bulky, it could get in the way of your arms or restrict the movement of the handlebars.

14.16   NI EXEMPT   Mark one answer   RES s14, HC r85, p119

What requirement must you meet if you want to carry a pillion passenger on your motorcycle?

☐ You must hold a full car licence
☑ You must hold a full motorcycle licence
☐ You must be over the age of 21
☐ You must be over the age of 25

Before you can carry a pillion passenger, the law requires you to have a full licence for the category of motorcycle you're using.

14.17   Mark one answer   RES s14

When carrying a heavy load on your motorcycle, what may you need to adjust?

- ☐ Carburettor
- ☐ Fuel tap
- ☐ Seating position
- ☑ Tyre pressures

Take care if you're carrying a heavy load on your motorcycle. Try to carry the weight as low down as possible – ideally in panniers, with the weight evenly spread on each side. You may need to adjust your tyre pressures, your headlight aim and your rear shock-absorber preload setting.

14.18   Mark one answer   RES s14

You're carrying a pillion passenger. What should you do when you're following other traffic?

- ☐ Keep to your normal following distance
- ☐ Get your passenger to keep checking behind
- ☑ Keep further back than you normally would
- ☐ Get your passenger to signal for you

The extra weight of a passenger may increase your stopping distance. Allow for this when following another vehicle by increasing the separation distance.

14.19   Mark one answer   RES s14

When can you carry a child as a pillion passenger?

- ☐ When they're over 14 years old
- ☐ When they're over 16 years old
- ☐ When they can reach the floor from the seat
- ☑ When they can reach the handholds and footrests

Any passenger you carry – no matter how old they are – must be able to reach the footrests and handholds properly to remain safe on your machine. Also make sure they're wearing protective weatherproof clothing and a properly fitting helmet.

14.20   Mark one answer   RES s14

What should you check when you fit a sidecar to your motorcycle?

- ☐ That the sidecar has a registration plate
- ☐ That the sidecar is correctly aligned
- ☐ That the sidecar has a waterproof cover
- ☐ That the sidecar has a spare wheel

If the sidecar isn't correctly aligned with the mounting points, the outfit will be difficult to control and could be dangerous. Riding with a sidecar attached requires a different technique from riding a solo motorcycle. You should keep your speed down while learning this skill.

14.21 — Mark one answer — RES s14

How will riding a motorcycle and sidecar differ from riding a solo motorcycle?

- [ ] It will allow you to corner more quickly
- [ ] It will allow you to brake later for hazards
- [x] It will require a different riding technique
- [ ] It will improve your fuel consumption

You'll need to adapt your riding technique when riding a motorcycle fitted with a sidecar. The extra weight will affect the handling and may increase your overall stopping distance.

14.22 — Mark one answer — RES s14

You're carrying a pillion passenger. What should you adjust to allow for the extra weight?

- [ ] The preload on the front forks
- [x] The preload on the rear shock absorber(s)
- [ ] The balance of the rear wheel
- [ ] The front and rear wheel alignment

When carrying a passenger or other extra weight, you may need to make adjustments, particularly to the rear shock absorber(s), tyre pressures and headlight alignment. Check your vehicle handbook for details.

14.23 — Mark one answer — RES s14

What's the maximum width allowed for a trailer on a motorcycle?

- [ ] 0.5 metres (1 foot 8 inches)
- [ ] 1 metre (3 feet 3 inches)
- [ ] 1.5 metres (4 feet 11 inches)
- [ ] 2 metres (6 feet 6 inches)

When you're towing a trailer, you must remember that you may not be able to filter through traffic. Don't forget that the trailer is there, especially when riding round bends and negotiating junctions.

14.24 — Mark one answer — RES s14

What applies when you tow a trailer with your motorcycle?

- [ ] The motorcycle should be attached to a sidecar
- [ ] The trailer should weigh more than the motorcycle
- [ ] The trailer should be fitted with brakes
- [x] The trailer shouldn't be more than 1 metre (3 feet 3 inches) wide

To tow a trailer behind a motorcycle, you must have a full motorcycle licence and a motorcycle with an engine larger than 125 cc. Motorcycle trailers mustn't exceed 1 metre (3 feet 3 inches) in width.

14.25

You have a sidecar fitted to your motorcycle. What effect will it have?

- ☐ It will reduce the motorcycle's stability
- ☐ It will make the steering lighter
- ☑ It will increase the stopping distance
- ☐ It will increase the fuel economy

A sidecar will alter the handling considerably. Give yourself time to adjust to the different characteristics and allow a greater stopping distance.

14.26

How is a learner motorcyclist's licence restricted?

- ☑ They mustn't carry a pillion passenger
- ☐ They mustn't use the right-hand lane on dual carriageways
- ☐ They mustn't carry panniers on their motorcycle
- ☐ They mustn't ride faster than 30 mph

Learner motorcyclists aren't allowed to

- tow a trailer
- carry a pillion passenger
- use the motorway.

In addition, they must display red L plates (D plates in Wales) to the front and rear of the motorcycle.

14.27

What should you do if you want to tow a trailer behind your motorcycle?

- ☐ Display a 'long vehicle' sign on the back of the trailer
- ☐ Fit a larger battery to your motorcycle
- ☑ Hold a full motorcycle licence
- ☐ Use a motorcycle that has shaft drive

You may not ride a motorcycle towing a trailer if you only hold a provisional motorcycle licence.

When you tow a trailer, you need to be aware that lower speed limits apply and the trailer must be no more than 1 metre wide. The trailer's laden weight should be no more than 150 kg or two-thirds of the kerbside weight of the motorcycle – whichever is less.

14.28

What should your motorcycle have if you want to carry a pillion passenger?

- ☐ Passenger footrests
- ☐ A passenger communication system
- ☐ A passenger luggage box
- ☐ Passenger grab handles

When carrying a pillion passenger, you should explain to them that they must keep their feet on the footrests. Tell them not to give hand signals, lean away from the rider when cornering, fidget or move around. Also check that they aren't wearing anything long or loose that could get caught in the rear wheel or drive chain.

14.29
Mark one answer RES s14

What kind of items should you carry in a top box?

☐ Heavy items
☐ Personal items
☐ Emergency items
☑ Lightweight items

Carrying a heavy weight high up and at the very back of the motorcycle can cause problems in maintaining control, particularly when riding at speed. If you have heavy items to carry, it's better to carry them in panniers and keep the weight roughly the same on either side.

14.30
Mark one answer RES s2, HC r85

You hold a provisional motorcycle licence. Are you allowed to carry a pillion passenger?

☐ Only if the passenger holds a full licence
☑ Not at any time
☐ Not unless you're undergoing training
☐ Only if the passenger is under 21

You aren't allowed to carry a pillion passenger until you hold a full motorcycle licence. This gives you time to gain riding experience. Even when you've passed your test, don't carry a passenger if you aren't confident that you can do so safely. You're responsible for their safety.

14.31
Mark one answer RES s14

What may be seriously affected if you overload your motorcycle?

☐ The gearbox
☐ The weather protection
☑ The handling
☐ The battery life

Any load will affect the handling of your motorcycle by changing its centre of gravity. When using panniers, spread the weight evenly on each side. Avoid carrying heavy items in a top box, as this could make your steering dangerously light.

14.32
Mark one answer HC r124, 265

You're towing a small trailer on a busy three-lane motorway. What must you do if all the lanes are open?

☐ Not exceed 50 mph
☐ Not overtake
☐ Have a stabiliser fitted
☑ Use only the left-hand and centre lanes

The motorway regulations for towing a trailer state that you mustn't

- use the right-hand lane of a three-lane motorway unless directed to do so (for example, at roadworks or due to a lane closure)
- exceed 60 mph.

Case study practice – 14 Motorcycle loading

You and a friend are taking a road trip on your motorcycle.

You carefully connect up and check the loaded trailer. Your friend evenly packs the rigid panniers.

You go to the service station to buy fuel and make final checks.

Your journey takes you onto a three-lane motorway, where you travel at the speed limit when it's safe to do so. You increase the separation distance from the vehicle in front.

You don't use the right-hand lane.

14.1 Why do you check the trailer?

Mark **one** answer

☐ To make sure you haven't forgotten anything
☐ To make sure the paintwork isn't scratched
☑ To make sure the load is secure
☐ To make sure the colour matches the motorcycle

RES s14

14.2 Why would your friend pack the panniers in this way?

Mark **one** answer

- [ ] So that nothing rattles while you're riding
- [x] Uneven load distribution can affect balance
- [ ] So that you don't forget anything
- [ ] Even loads on each side look tidier

RES s14 **HC** r98

14.3 What's the speed limit for your motorcycle on this trip?

Mark **one** answer

- [ ] 40 mph
- [ ] 50 mph
- [x] 60 mph
- [ ] 70 mph

RES s14 **HC** r124

14.4 Why would you increase the separation distance?

Mark **one** answer

- [ ] The trailer might become detached from the motorcycle
- [ ] Your friend doesn't like you riding too close to other vehicles
- [ ] The motorway isn't very busy, so there's plenty of room
- [x] Stopping distance is increased on a fully loaded vehicle

RES s14

14.5 Why would you not use that lane?

Mark **one** answer

- [ ] Your trailer might cause buffeting and wind resistance
- [ ] That lane mustn't be used by vehicles with trailers
- [ ] You're not going in that direction
- [ ] You don't want to travel at a very high speed

HC r265

Case study
practice

Case study practice

Some of the questions within the test will be presented as a case study.

You'll be presented with a scenario – the case study – which will appear on the left-hand side of the screen. The scenario will be presented in a text format and may be accompanied by a supporting picture or diagram. As you move within the case study, the questions will appear, one by one, on the right-hand side of the screen, and you'll be asked to respond. You can re-read the scenario throughout the case study should you wish to do so.

A case study example is shown below and on the following pages.

In this section, you'll also find five mixed-topic, practice case studies similar to the ones in the actual test. Use these to help you prepare for the real thing.

Answers to all the case studies in this book are in section 16, Answers.

Candidate Name: (DVSA/DVA Trial Items)

Time Remaining: 10:30

Case Study

You decide to visit your friend, who lives about 20 miles away.

The journey will take you on various roads, including country lanes and A-roads.

You've been before, so you think you know the way. You also have a mobile phone with you, so you'll be able to ring for directions if you get lost.

During the journey, you go the wrong way and need to turn round. Later on, you decide to ring your friend to make sure you're still travelling in the right direction.

Mark one answer

To turn round after going the wrong way, you decide to make a U-turn in the road. What should you do before starting the U-turn?

- [ ] Give an arm signal as well as using indicators
- [ ] Signal so that other road users can slow down for you
- [ ] Look over your shoulder for a final check
- [ ] Select a higher gear than normal

Question 1 of 5

! Flag   **👓 Review Screen**   **Next ➡**

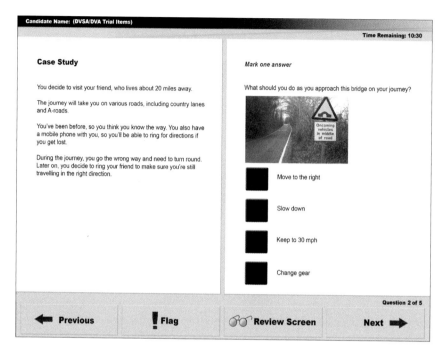

Case Study

You decide to visit your friend, who lives about 20 miles away.

The journey will take you on various roads, including country lanes and A-roads.

You've been before, so you think you know the way. You also have a mobile phone with you, so you'll be able to ring for directions if you get lost.

During the journey, you go the wrong way and need to turn round. Later on, you decide to ring your friend to make sure you're still travelling in the right direction.

Mark one answer

What should you do as you approach this bridge on your journey?

Oncoming vehicles in middle of road

☐ Move to the right

☐ Slow down

☐ Keep to 30 mph

☐ Change gear

Question 2 of 5

◀ Previous   ! Flag   👓 Review Screen   Next ▶

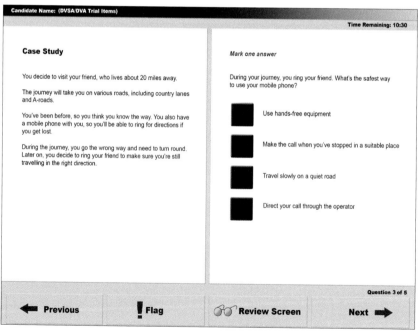

Case Study

You decide to visit your friend, who lives about 20 miles away.

The journey will take you on various roads, including country lanes and A-roads.

You've been before, so you think you know the way. You also have a mobile phone with you, so you'll be able to ring for directions if you get lost.

During the journey, you go the wrong way and need to turn round. Later on, you decide to ring your friend to make sure you're still travelling in the right direction.

Mark one answer

During your journey, you ring your friend. What's the safest way to use your mobile phone?

☐ Use hands-free equipment

☐ Make the call when you've stopped in a suitable place

☐ Travel slowly on a quiet road

☐ Direct your call through the operator

Question 3 of 5

◀ Previous   ! Flag   👓 Review Screen   Next ▶

452

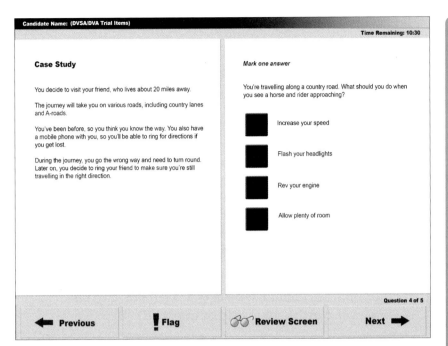

Case Study

You decide to visit your friend, who lives about 20 miles away.

The journey will take you on various roads, including country lanes and A-roads.

You've been before, so you think you know the way. You also have a mobile phone with you, so you'll be able to ring for directions if you get lost.

During the journey, you go the wrong way and need to turn round. Later on, you decide to ring your friend to make sure you're still travelling in the right direction.

Mark one answer

You're travelling along a country road. What should you do when you see a horse and rider approaching?

Increase your speed

Flash your headlights

Rev your engine

Allow plenty of room

Previous   Flag   Review Screen   Next

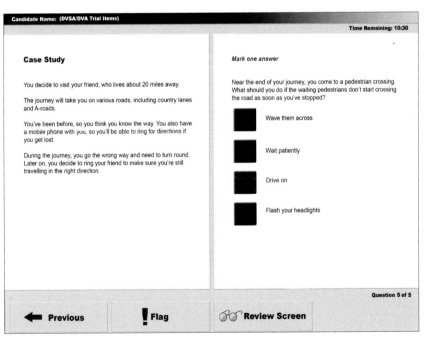

Case Study

You decide to visit your friend, who lives about 20 miles away.

The journey will take you on various roads, including country lanes and A-roads.

You've been before, so you think you know the way. You also have a mobile phone with you, so you'll be able to ring for directions if you get lost.

During the journey, you go the wrong way and need to turn round. Later on, you decide to ring your friend to make sure you're still travelling in the right direction.

Mark one answer

Near the end of your journey, you come to a pedestrian crossing. What should you do if the waiting pedestrians don't start crossing the road as soon as you've stopped?

Wave them across

Wait patiently

Drive on

Flash your headlights

Previous   Flag   Review Screen

Section fifteen Case study practice

You're taking your friend to collect their new motorcycle. They're already wearing the recommended helmet and clothing.

You reach a level crossing where the half-barriers are down. A train passes but the barriers stay down and the red lights continue to flash.

Further on, the road surface is cracked. You can see several potholes on your side of the road.

Later, there's a high-occupancy vehicle lane marked on the road and motorcycles are allowed to use it.

At the end of your journey you turn right into the motorcycle dealer's car park.

1   What might your friend be wearing?

Mark **one** answer

- ☑ Leather clothing, high-visibility waistcoat and white helmet
- ☐ Jeans, anorak, trainers and a light-coloured helmet
- ☐ Thick trousers, boots, high-visibility jacket and black helmet
- ☐ Tracksuit bottoms, high-visibility jacket and a dark helmet

RES s4 **HC** r86

2 What should you do at the level crossing?

Mark **one** answer

- ☐ Ride around the barriers as the lights may be faulty
- ☑ Wait, as another train will be coming
- ☐ Turn round and find an alternative route
- ☐ Immediately phone the signal operator and report a fault

RES s7 **HC** r293

3 What might you need to do on this road surface?

Mark **one** answer

- ☐ Ride in the gutter until you're past the affected area
- ☐ Dismount and quickly wheel the motorcycle past
- ☐ Ride along on the other side of the road for a while
- ☑ Slow down to ride over this patch of road

RES s8

4 How can you tell that you're allowed to ride in this lane?

Mark **one** answer

- ☐ The yellow sign shows a motorcycle
- ☐ The brown sign shows a motorcycle
- ☑ The blue sign shows a motorcycle
- ☐ The green sign shows a motorcycle

RES s7 **HC** r142 **KYTS** p140

5 What should you do just before turning into the car park?

Mark **one** answer

- ☑ Take a look over your right shoulder
- ☐ Take a look in the left-hand mirror
- ☐ Take a look over your left shoulder
- ☐ Take a look at the road ahead

RES s8

> Case study practice – B

You're going away for the weekend with a friend as pillion passenger and carrying your luggage in a trailer.

It's daylight and the weather is dry, but windy.

On the motorway, all three lanes are very busy. You avoid using the right-hand lane.

Later, there's a roundabout. You need to take the second exit, going straight on. There are two lanes on approach but no other road markings.

After the roundabout there are signs telling you that roadworks are being carried out further ahead.

1   What important check should you make before you set out?

Mark **one** answer

☑ Headlight aim

☐ Throttle cable

☐ Wheel alignment

☐ Seat position

RES s15 **HC** p98

456

2 What problem might you face under these weather conditions?

Mark one answer

☐ Being tired and very cold

☐ Being slowed right down

☐ Being overtaken by others

☑ Being blown off course

RES s12 **HC** r232–233

3 Why would you avoid the right-hand lane on the motorway?

Mark one answer

☐ Traffic travelling in the right-hand lane moves too fast

☐ You can't see road signs properly from the right-hand lane

☐ Vehicles with a trailer mustn't travel in the right-hand lane

☐ Only cars are allowed to travel in the right-hand lane

RES s11 **HC** r265

4 How should you approach the roundabout?

Mark one answer

☐ In the right-hand lane while signalling left

☑ In the left-hand lane without giving a signal

☐ In the left-hand lane while signalling right

☐ In the right-hand lane while signalling right

RES s9 **HC** r186

5 After the roundabout, what should you anticipate seeing?

Mark one answer

☐ Police officers

☐ Traffic wardens

☐ Crossing patrols

☑ Road workers

RES s8 **HC** r288

> Case study practice – C

> You're going on holiday. You'll be carrying heavy camping equipment in two bags.
>
> The first part of your journey is along a dual carriageway. The national speed limit applies.
>
> Later, you visit a garage, where you check your oil level.
>
> You leave your motorcycle to buy a snack at the shop.
>
> Near your destination, you follow a tractor along a country road.

1   Where should you carry the bags?

Mark **one** answer

- ☐ In a backpack
- ☐ In the tank bag
- ☑ In the panniers
- ☐ In the top box

RES s14

2   What's the speed limit on the first part of your journey?

Mark **one** answer

- ☐ 50 mph
- ☐ 60 mph
- ☑ 70 mph
- ☐ 80 mph

RES s7 **HC** r124, p40

3 Why might your check at the garage not be accurate?

Mark one answer

- ☑ Because the engine is warm
- ☐ Because the fuel is low
- ☐ Because your hands are cold
- ☐ Because your motorcycle is fully loaded

RES s15

4 What should you do when you go to buy a snack?

Mark one answer

- ☐ Leave your helmet and gloves on the seat
- ☑ Lock your motorcycle and remove the key
- ☐ Make sure you remove your helmet first
- ☐ Chain your motorcycle to a fuel pump

RES s8 **HC** p131

5 What should you do on the country road?

Mark one answer

- ☐ Ride closely behind the tractor to keep out of the wind
- ☐ Sound your horn to allow the tractor driver to hear you
- ☐ Flash your lights to allow the tractor driver to see you
- ☐ Drop back slightly so you can see the road ahead

HC r164

> Case study practice – D

On a summer day you plan to make an early start on a trip.

Before you leave, you're given some upsetting news over the phone.

It's a hot, sunny day and you think about what you should wear on your journey.

At the beginning of your trip, you're cut up by a driver at a roundabout.

Riding through town, you stop at a red traffic light behind a cyclist at an advanced stop line.

Later, you witness a crash between a car and another motorcycle.

1 **What should you do after your phone call?**

Mark **one** answer

☐ Make as early a start as you can

☑ Calm yourself down before you set off

☐ Start your journey but ride slowly

☐ Set off quickly to make up lost time

RES s1

2 What helmet should you wear on a day like today?

Mark **one** answer

- ☑ A brightly coloured helmet
- ☐ A dark full-face helmet
- ☐ A dark open-face helmet
- ☐ A lightweight cycling helmet

RES s4 **HC** r86

3 What should you do at the roundabout?

Mark **one** answer

- ☐ Catch up with the driver and complain
- ☐ Sound your horn twice at the driver
- ☐ Flash your headlights at the driver
- ☐ Keep calm and continue riding

RES s9 **HC** r147

4 What should you do when the traffic lights change to green?

Mark **one** answer

- ☐ Ride off quickly ahead of the cyclist
- ☑ Allow the cyclist plenty of room
- ☐ Follow closely behind the cyclist
- ☐ Ride around the cyclist to get in front

RES s10 **HC** r178, 212

5 What should you do at the crash scene?

Mark **one** answer

- ☑ Warn other road users of the danger
- ☐ Move the driver out of their vehicle
- ☐ Remove the motorcyclist's helmet
- ☐ Give the people involved a drink

RES s16 **HC** r283

> Case study practice – E

You're shopping for new clothing to wear while riding your motorcycle.

You're about to go on a camping holiday for two weeks.

Three days before you leave, you realise that your MOT certificate will expire while you're away.

On the day you leave, it's raining heavily.

You ride along a busy 'A' road, using the throttle rapidly and braking heavily.

You reach the scene of a crash between a cyclist and a car. The cyclist is unconscious but breathing and lying in the road.

1   What should you buy when out shopping?

Mark one answer

- [ ] Clothing that matches your motorcycle
- [ ] Clothing that's tight fitting
- [ ] Clothing that's loose and light
- [x] Clothing that keeps you warm and dry

RES s4

2 What should you do before your holiday?

Mark **one** answer

- ☑ Get your motorcycle through its MOT test
- ☐ Renew your vehicle tax immediately
- ☐ Tell your insurance company you're going away
- ☐ Tell DVLA you'll be away for two weeks

RES s2 **HC** p122

3 What should you be careful of on the day you leave?

Mark **one** answer

- ☑ Slippery roads
- ☐ Sticky tarmac
- ☐ Dry patches
- ☐ Level surfaces

RES s12

4 What will be the effect of riding in this way on the 'A' road?

Mark **one** answer

- ☐ Increased journey time
- ☐ Economical use of fuel
- ☑ Uneconomical use of fuel
- ☐ Decreased journey time

RES s17

5 What should you do for the cyclist?

Mark **one** answer

- ☐ Drag them to the side of the road
- ☐ Try to remove their cycle helmet
- ☑ Place them in the recovery position
- ☐ Administer chest compressions

HC p132

Section sixteen

Answers

> 1. Alertness

1.1	☐ Take a lifesaver glance over your shoulder
1.2	☐ A final rearward glance before changing direction
1.3	☐ Slow down before the bend
1.4	☐ Slow down or stop
1.5	☐ Extend the mirror arms
1.6	☐ When they're parked in a safe place
1.7	☐ As soon as the other vehicle passes you
1.8	☐ Look over your shoulder for a final check
1.9	☐ You'll lose concentration
1.10	☐ Slow down and stop if necessary
1.11	☐ Moving off
1.12	☐ Change direction
1.13	☐ Before changing lanes
1.14	☐ To give you the best view of the road behind
1.15	☐ A final rearward glance
1.16	☐ Never; you should always look for yourself
1.17	☐ Use your mirrors
1.18	☐ Mirrors don't cover blind spots
1.19	☐ Make a lifesaver check

1.20	☐ Check the width of the central reservation
1.21	☐ Make sure you know where all the controls and switches are
1.22	☐ Take a lifesaver glance over your left shoulder
1.23	☐ Take a lifesaver glance over your left shoulder
1.24	☐ Before moving into the left-hand lane
1.25	☐ Concentrate on what's happening ahead
1.26	☐ Look over your shoulder for a final check
1.27	☐ Slow down
1.28	☐ Approaching a dip in the road
1.29	☐ Overtaking traffic should move back to the left
1.30	☐ Ignore it
1.31	☐ To make you aware of your speed
1.32	☐ Be ready to stop
1.33	☐ Use the mirrors
1.34	☐ You'll allow the driver to see you in their mirrors
1.35	☐ To assess how your actions will affect following traffic

1.36 ☐ Stop and then move forward slowly and carefully for a clear view

2. Attitude

2.1 ☐ Slow down and prepare to stop

2.2 ☐ Well back, so that you can see past the vehicle

2.3 ☐ Slow down and be ready to stop

2.4 ☐ When the pedestrians have reached a safe position

2.5 ☐ Pull in when you can to let faster vehicles behind you overtake

2.6 ☐ Drivers at junctions ahead will be able to see you approaching

2.7 ☐ Because they're inexperienced

2.8 ☐ Give way to pedestrians already on the crossing

2.9 ☐ Another vehicle may be coming

2.10 ☐ Following another vehicle too closely

2.11 ☐ Your view ahead will be reduced

2.12 ☐ Four seconds

2.13 ☐ Slow down

2.14 ☐ Bomb disposal

2.15 ☐ Pull over as soon as it's safe to do so

2.16 ☐ Doctor's car

2.17 ☐ Tram drivers

2.18 ☐ Cycles

2.19 ☐ To alert others to your presence

2.20 ☐ In the right-hand lane

2.21 ☐ To help other road users know what you intend to do

2.22 ☐ Toucan

2.23 ☐ Allow the vehicle to overtake

2.24 ☐ When letting them know that you're there

2.25 ☐ Slow down and look both ways

2.26	☐ When checking your gap from the vehicle in front
2.27	☐ Steady amber
2.28	☐ Slow down, gradually increasing the gap between you and the vehicle in front

CASE STUDY PRACTICE – ANSWERS
Section 2 – Attitude
2.1 60 mph
2.2 Carefully, while increasing the distance from any vehicle in front
2.3 Slowly, leaving plenty of room
2.4 To allow you to see past the large vehicle
2.5 A doctor driving to an emergency

> 3. Safety and your motorcycle

3.1	☐ The rear wheel could lock
3.2	☐ To keep the machine roadworthy
3.3	☐ Carefully, until the shiny surface is worn off
3.4	☐ You'll be seen more easily by other road users
3.5	☐ Continue to wear protective clothing
3.6	☐ It helps other road users to see you
3.7	☐ To be seen better at night
3.8	☐ Touring
3.9	☐ Replace it
3.10	☐ 1 mm
3.11	☐ White helmet
3.12	☐ Stop as soon as possible and try to find the cause
3.13	☐ That they're correctly inflated

3.14	☐ The rear wheel could lock
3.15	☐ Slow gently to a stop
3.16	☐ It will have lower exhaust emissions
3.17	☐ Soapy water
3.18	☐ Stop as soon as possible and wipe it
3.19	☐ Boots
3.20	☐ Velcro tab
3.21	☐ Exhaust emissions
3.22	☐ Your wheel alignment
3.23	☐ Between 1 and 2 times
3.24	☐ The rear wheel alignment
3.25	☐ Worn steering-head bearings
3.26	☐ The motorcycle will be difficult to control
3.27	☐ Your suspension will be ineffective

3.28	☐ Incorrect rear wheel alignment	**3.48**	☐ It may be damaged
3.29	☐ Replace the tyre before riding the motorcycle	**3.49**	☐ A large bulge in the sidewall
3.30	☐ By checking the vehicle handbook	**3.50**	☐ By lubricating and adjusting them regularly
3.31	☐ Keep the cable oiled	**3.51**	☐ Better fuel economy
3.32	☐ Increased tyre wear	**3.52**	☐ A locked rear wheel
3.33	☐ Because it gives the best protection from the weather	**3.53**	☐ In poor visibility
		3.54	☐ When carrying a pillion passenger
3.34	☐ Use the steering lock	**3.55**	☐ Oil leaks
3.35	☐ Chain it to an immovable object	**3.56**	☐ Not on any occasion
3.36	☐ Leave it in a low gear	**3.57**	☐ Use the engine cut-out switch
3.37	☐ To stop the engine in an emergency	**3.58**	☐ Wear reflective clothing
3.38	☐ Maintain a reduced speed throughout	**3.59**	☐ Braking
		3.60	☐ Between 11.30 pm and 7.00 am in a built-up area
3.39	☐ Before a long journey	**3.61**	☐ It's powered by electricity
3.40	☐ Take it to a local-authority site	**3.62**	☐ To help the traffic flow
3.41	☐ Check out any strong smell of petrol	**3.63**	☐ To reduce traffic speed
		3.64	☐ When tyres are cold
3.42	☐ Wearing a brightly coloured helmet	**3.65**	☐ When its tyres are under-inflated
3.43	☐ When the helmet isn't fastened correctly	**3.66**	☐ Take it to a local-authority site
3.44	☐ When carrying a heavy load	**3.67**	☐ Harsh braking and accelerating
3.45	☐ Number plate	**3.68**	☐ Distilled water
3.46	☐ To stop the engine in an emergency	**3.69**	☐ Where the speed limit exceeds 30 mph
3.47	☐ Rear wheel alignment	**3.70**	☐ Keep engine revs low

3.71	☐ A faulty braking system
3.72	☐ Just above the cell plates
3.73	☐ Look at a map
3.74	☐ Use a route planner on the internet
3.75	☐ Print or write down the route
3.76	☐ You'll have an easier journey
3.77	☐ You're less likely to be delayed
3.78	☐ Your original route may be blocked

3.79	☐ Allow plenty of time for the trip
3.80	☐ Increased fuel consumption
3.81	☐ Brake fluid level

CASE STUDY PRACTICE – ANSWERS
....

Section 3 – Safety and your motorcycle

3.1 Getting cold

3.2 It makes you easier to see

3.3 It helps to improve your safety

3.4 To give you an unobstructed view behind

3.5 1 mm across three-quarters of the tread breadth and all around

❯ 4. Safety margins

4.1	☐ When you're riding with a passenger
4.2	☐ Use both brakes
4.3	☐ Ease off the throttle
4.4	☐ Consider whether your journey is essential
4.5	☐ They help other road users to see you
4.6	☐ When visibility is 100 metres (328 feet) or less
4.7	☐ When visibility is poor
4.8	☐ They'll make it harder to see unlit objects
4.9	☐ The brakes
4.10	☐ Slowly, in a low gear

4.11	☐ Using dipped-beam headlights
4.12	☐ Keep your visor or goggles clear
4.13	☐ The painted lines may be slippery
4.14	☐ Wear reflective clothing
4.15	☐ Wear suitable clothing
4.16	☐ Wear reflective clothing
4.17	☐ When it's raining
4.18	☐ Loose gravel
4.19	☐ Traffic could be turning here
4.20	☐ Heavy braking

4.21	☐ Ease off the throttle smoothly
4.22	☐ Ride slowly, braking lightly
4.23	☐ Switch on your dipped headlights
4.24	☐ The time gap when following another vehicle in good conditions
4.25	☐ The painted area
4.26	☐ When you overtake a large vehicle
4.27	☐ A bus may have left patches of oil
4.28	☐ 38 metres (125 feet)
4.29	☐ Ten times
4.30	☐ Passing pedal cyclists
4.31	☐ To improve your view of the road
4.32	☐ Go slowly while gently applying the brakes
4.33	☐ The tyre grip
4.34	☐ On an open stretch of road

4.35	☐ 96 metres (315 feet)
4.36	☐ 73 metres (240 feet)
4.37	☐ Drop back to regain a safe distance
4.38	☐ 53 metres (175 feet)
4.39	☐ 36 metres (118 feet)
4.40	☐ 38 metres (125 feet)
4.41	☐ Increase your distance from the vehicle in front
4.42	☐ Reduce your speed and increase the gap in front
4.43	☐ Choose an appropriate lane in good time

CASE STUDY PRACTICE – ANSWERS

Section 4 – Safety margins

4.1 Tyre pressures and headlight aim
4.2 It would be difficult to hold a steady course
4.3 They would try to avoid cracks and holes
4.4 More slowly
4.5 Check over your right shoulder for overtaking vehicles

> 5. Hazard awareness

5.1	☐ Your concentration will be impaired
5.2	☐ By signalling with your right arm
5.3	☐ Find a way of getting home without riding
5.4	☐ Poor judgement
5.5	☐ At all times when riding

5.6	☐ Your judgement of speed will be worse
5.7	☐ Tinted
5.8	☐ When riding on a motorway, to warn traffic behind of a hazard ahead
5.9	☐ To help prevent hearing damage

5.10	☐ Stick to non-alcoholic drinks
5.11	☐ Your insurance may become invalid
5.12	☐ To check for overtaking vehicles
5.13	☐ Ask your doctor
5.14	☐ When your motorcycle has broken down and is causing an obstruction
5.15	☐ A soft road surface
5.16	☐ On a large goods vehicle
5.17	☐ The cyclist crossing the road
5.18	☐ The parked car (arrowed A)
5.19	☐ Slow down and get ready to stop
5.20	☐ Doors opening on parked cars
5.21	☐ The road will bend sharply to the left
5.22	☐ Slow down and allow the cyclist to turn
5.23	☐ The view is restricted
5.24	☐ Buses
5.25	☐ Lorry
5.26	☐ Stop behind the line, then edge forward to see clearly
5.27	☐ Ignore the error and stay calm
5.28	☐ They'll take longer to react to hazards
5.29	☐ A school crossing patrol

5.30	☐ Yes, regular stops help concentration
5.31	☐ Stop before the barrier
5.32	☐ Be prepared to stop for any traffic
5.33	☐ Wait for the pedestrian in the road to cross
5.34	☐ Only consider overtaking when you're past the junction
5.35	☐ Be prepared to give way to large vehicles in the middle of the road
5.36	☐ They give a wider field of vision
5.37	☐ Approach with care and pass on the left of the lorry
5.38	☐ Stay behind and don't overtake
5.39	☐ The bus may move out into the road
5.40	☐ A school bus
5.41	☐ Children running out between vehicles
5.42	☐ The cyclist may swerve into the road
5.43	☐ Stop and take a break
5.44	☐ At a reduced speed
5.45	☐ Because of the level crossing
5.46	☐ To enable you to change lanes early
5.47	☐ Traffic in both directions can use the middle lane to overtake

5.48	☐ A disabled person's vehicle
5.49	☐ Stop
5.50	☐ People may cross the road in front of it
5.51	☐ Approaching a junction
5.52	☐ Poor judgement of speed

❯ 6. Vulnerable road users

6.1	☐ So your view ahead isn't obstructed
6.2	☐ Give them plenty of room
6.3	☐ Be ready to slow down and stop
6.4	☐ Keep calm and be patient
6.5	☐ Slow down gradually to increase the gap in front of you
6.6	☐ Be prepared to stop
6.7	☐ The rider may be blown across in front of you
6.8	☐ Allow the person to finish crossing
6.9	☐ At junctions
6.10	☐ To check for any overtaking traffic
6.11	☐ Revving your engine
6.12	☐ They lack experience and judgement
6.13	☐ Overestimating their own ability

6.14	☐ You must not wait or park your motorcycle here
6.15	 ☐
6.16	☐ Give way to them
6.17	☐ Pedestrians
6.18	☐ They may be overtaking on your right
6.19	☐ Cyclists can use it
6.20	☐ By displaying a 'stop' sign
6.21	☐ On the rear of a school bus or coach
6.22	☐ A route for pedestrians and cyclists
6.23	☐ They're deaf and blind
6.24	☐ Be patient and allow them to cross in their own time
6.25	☐ Be careful; they may misjudge your speed

6.26	☐ Give the cyclist plenty of room
6.27	☐ Bicycle
6.28	☐ They're harder to see
6.29	☐ Motorcycles can easily be hidden behind obstructions
6.30	☐ So that the rider can be seen more easily
6.31	☐ Drivers often do not see them
6.32	☐ Stay behind
6.33	☐ To check for traffic in their blind area
6.34	☐ Motorcyclist
6.35	☐ Give them plenty of room
6.36	☐ Wait patiently because they'll probably take longer to cross
6.37	☐ Reduce speed until you're clear of the area
6.38	☐ To allow a clear view of the crossing area
6.39	☐ On a school bus
6.40	☐ Any direction
6.41	☐ Stay behind until the moped has passed the junction
6.42	☐ Stay well back
6.43	☐ Be patient and prepare for them to react more slowly
6.44	☐ Be patient, as you expect them to make mistakes

6.45	☐ Pedestrians
6.46	☐ Be aware that their reactions may be slower than yours
6.47	☐ Hold back until the cyclist has passed the junction
6.48	☐ In any direction
6.49	☐ They'll have a flashing amber light
6.50	☐ Just before you turn left
6.51	☐ The vehicle is slow moving
6.52	☐ With-flow cycle lane
6.53	☐ Slow down and be ready to stop
6.54	☐ To ensure children have a clear view from the crossing area
6.55	☐ Watch out for pedestrians walking in the road
6.56	☐ Allow extra room in case they swerve to avoid potholes
6.57	☐ Cycle route ahead
6.58	☐ The cyclist is slower and more vulnerable
6.59	☐ Prepare to slow down and stop
6.60	☐ The pedestrian is deaf
6.61	☐ Cyclists and pedestrians
6.62	☐ To allow cyclists to position in front of other traffic
6.63	☐ The cyclist might swerve

6.64	☐ Go very slowly
6.65	☐ You're approaching an organised walk
6.66	☐ By taking further training

❯ 7. Other types of vehicle

7.1	☐ Keep well back
7.2	☐ They can't steer to avoid you
7.3	☐
7.4	☐ The large vehicle can easily hide an overtaking vehicle
7.5	☐ Stay well back and give it room
7.6	☐ Wait behind the long vehicle
7.7	☐ Keep well back
7.8	☐ To get the best view of the road ahead
7.9	☐ Watch carefully for pedestrians
7.10	☐ Drop back until you can see better
7.11	☐ Drop back further

7.12	☐ Allow it to pull away, if it's safe to do so
7.13	☐ Keep well back until you can see that it's clear
7.14	☐ Cars
7.15	☐ Slow down and be prepared to wait
7.16	☐ Don't overtake as you approach or at the junction
7.17	☐ 8 mph
7.18	☐ It will take longer to pass one

8. Road conditions and motorcycle handling

8.1	☐ Check that the neutral lamp shows when the ignition is switched on	8.19	☐ When the motorcycle is upright and moving in a straight line
8.2	☐ Slow down and be ready to stop	8.20	☐ The condition of the tyres
8.3	☐ Anticipate the actions of others	8.21	☐ When your motorcycle is broken down on the hard shoulder
8.4	☐ Braking too hard	8.22	☐ Leave parking lights on
8.5	☐ Ride slowly in as high a gear as possible	8.23	☐ Close the throttle and roll to a stop
8.6	☐ At all times	8.24	☐ By a rainbow-coloured pattern on the road surface
8.7	☐ Check that your lights are working	8.25	☐ Tar banding
8.8	☐ On firm, level ground	8.26	☐ Apply the front brake just before the rear brake
8.9	☐ Keep your speed down	8.27	☐ Braking
8.10	☐ In the centre of your lane	8.28	☐ The steel rails can be slippery
8.11	☐ From the left and apply the front brake	8.29	☐ Release and reapply the brakes
8.12	☐ Practise off-road with an approved training body	8.30	☐ Fuel spilt on the road
8.13	☐ It will reduce your control of the motorcycle	8.31	☐ Wheelspin when accelerating
8.14	☐ Slow down	8.32	☐ Release both brakes together
8.15	☐ It can become unusually slippery	8.33	☐ Apply both brakes smoothly
8.16	☐ Cornering too fast	8.34	☐ Place both feet on the ground
8.17	☐ Apply the front brake just before the rear brake	8.35	☐ It will be slippery
8.18	☐ You'll upset your balance		

8.36	☐ When you're cornering
8.37	☐ When you're in a one-way street
8.38	☐ It will be doubled
8.39	☐ Beware of bends in the road ahead
8.40	☐ When oncoming traffic prevents you turning right
8.41	☐ **Humps for ½ mile**
8.42	☐ Slow traffic down
8.43	☐ Red
8.44	☐ Alert you to a hazard
8.45	☐ Leave plenty of time for your journey
8.46	☐ Make sure you don't dazzle other road users
8.47	☐ Slow down and stay behind
8.48	☐ To make you aware of your speed

8.49	☐ There would be a different surface texture
8.50	☐ Stop at a passing place
8.51	☐ To prevent the motorcycle sliding on the metal drain covers
8.52	☐ Your brakes will be soaking wet
8.53	☐ It's more difficult to see what's ahead

CASE STUDY PRACTICE – ANSWERS

Section 8 – Road conditions and motorcycle handling

8.1 The extra weight can affect your balance

8.2 Lean with you when going round bends

8.3 Headlights

8.4 Edge forward slowly until you can see clearly

8.5 You'll need more room in which to stop safely

9. Motorway riding

9.1 ☐ Only in an emergency

9.2 ☐ In the left-hand lane

9.3 ☐ Adjust your speed to the speed of the traffic on the motorway

9.4 ☐ 50 cc

9.5 ☐ The left-hand lane

9.6 ☐ 70 mph

9.7 ☐ Continuous high speeds increase the risk of your motorcycle breaking down

9.8 ☐ Give way to traffic already on the motorway

9.9 ☐ 70 mph

9.10 ☐ Any vehicle

9.11 ☐ A vehicle towing a trailer

9.12 ☐ It allows easy location by the emergency services

9.13 ☐ Gain speed on the hard shoulder before moving out onto the carriageway

9.14 ☐ On a steep gradient

9.15 ☐ They're countdown markers to the next exit

9.16 ☐ Between the central reservation and the carriageway

9.17 ☐ White

9.18 ☐ Green

9.19 ☐ In the direction shown on the marker posts

9.20 ☐ To build up a speed similar to traffic on the motorway

9.21 ☐ Face the oncoming traffic

9.22 ☐ Red

9.23 ☐ Left

9.24 ☐ Keep a good distance from the vehicle ahead

9.25 ☐ In the left-hand lane

9.26 ☐ Obey all speed limits

9.27 ☐ Cars driven by learner drivers

9.28 ☐ Look much further ahead than you would on other roads

9.29 ☐ Keep in the left-hand lane

9.30 ☐ Overtaking

9.31 ☐ Stopping in an emergency

9.32 ☐ Move to the left and reduce your speed to 50 mph

9.33 ☐ When you're signalled to do so by flashing red lights

9.34 ☐ Move to another lane

9.35 ☐ Keep to the left-hand lane unless overtaking

9.36 ☐ When in queues and traffic to your right is moving more slowly than you are

9.37 ☐ In cases of emergency or breakdown

9.38	☐ Stop and direct anyone on a motorway
9.39	☐ You shouldn't travel in this lane
9.40	☐ The hard shoulder can be used as a running lane
9.41	☐ To reduce congestion
9.42	☐ You must obey the speed limits shown
9.43	☐ Your overall journey time will normally improve
9.44	☐ When signs direct you to
9.45	☐ Variable speed limits
9.46	☐ In an emergency or breakdown
9.47	☐ 70 mph

9.48	☐ Well away from the carriageway
9.49	☐ Stop and wait
9.50	☐ The hard shoulder is for emergency or breakdown use only
9.51	☐ Use all the lanes, including the hard shoulder
9.52	☐ At the nearest service area

CASE STUDY PRACTICE – ANSWERS

Section 9 – Motorway riding

9.1   Steering and braking
9.2   All traffic should do so unless they're overtaking
9.3   Four seconds
9.4   Temporary maximum speed advised
9.5   300 yards

❯ 10. Rules of the road

10.1	☐ To check for cyclists
10.2	☐ Tram lane
10.3	☐ Parking for solo motorcycles
10.4	☐ Use mirrors and shoulder checks
10.5	☐ You can't park there, unless you're permitted to do so
10.6	☐ Pull into a passing place on your left
10.7	☐ So you can see approaching traffic

10.8	☐ Watch for vehicles emerging from side roads
10.9	☐ Wait for the green light
10.10	☐ Headlight deflectors
10.11	☐ 125 cc
10.12	☐ 60 mph
10.13	☐ When signalled to do so by a police officer
10.14	☐ National speed limit applies
10.15	☐ 70 mph
10.16	☐ By street lighting

10.17	☐ 30 mph
10.18	☐ End of minimum speed
10.19	☐ Stay behind the tractor if you're in any doubt
10.20	☐ Long lorry
10.21	☐ At any time
10.22	☐ Waiting restrictions
10.23	☐ When you're in a one-way street
10.24	☐ Overtaking or turning right
10.25	☐ Continue in that lane
10.26	☐ On either the right or the left
10.27	☐ Indicate left before leaving the roundabout
10.28	☐ Long vehicle
10.29	☐ When your exit road is clear
10.30	☐ When oncoming traffic prevents you from turning right
10.31	☐ A police officer
10.32	☐ Stop to let them cross and wait patiently
10.33	☐ Cyclists and pedestrians
10.34	☐ Wait for pedestrians on the crossing to clear
10.35	☐ To pick up or set down passengers
10.36	☐ Keep the other vehicle to your right and turn behind it (offside to offside)

10.37	☐ Children may run out from between the vehicles
10.38	☐ Give way to oncoming traffic
10.39	☐ To overtake slower traffic
10.40	☐ No-one has priority
10.41	☐ 10 metres (32 feet)
10.42	☐ At or near a bus stop
10.43	☐ Carry on waiting
10.44	☐ No-waiting zone ends
10.45	☐ Obey the speed limit
10.46	☐ You can be easily seen by others
10.47	☐ Wait until the road is clear in both directions
10.48	☐ 60 mph
10.49	☐ Park with parking lights on
10.50	☐ Approaching a concealed level crossing
10.51	☐ A traffic officer
10.52	☐ Signal left just after you pass the exit before the one you're going to take

CASE STUDY PRACTICE – ANSWERS

Section 10 – Rules of the road

10.1	Blue and white
10.2	Stop and wait until the green light shows
10.3	Take a look over your right shoulder
10.4	To slow down the traffic
10.5	Circular

> 11. Road and traffic signs

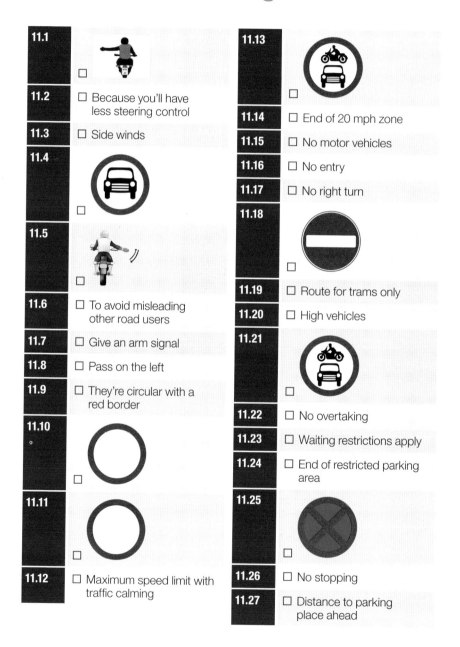

11.1	
11.2	☐ Because you'll have less steering control
11.3	☐ Side winds
11.4	
11.5	
11.6	☐ To avoid misleading other road users
11.7	☐ Give an arm signal
11.8	☐ Pass on the left
11.9	☐ They're circular with a red border
11.10	
11.11	
11.12	☐ Maximum speed limit with traffic calming

11.13	
11.14	☐ End of 20 mph zone
11.15	☐ No motor vehicles
11.16	☐ No entry
11.17	☐ No right turn
11.18	
11.19	☐ Route for trams only
11.20	☐ High vehicles
11.21	
11.22	☐ No overtaking
11.23	☐ Waiting restrictions apply
11.24	☐ End of restricted parking area
11.25	
11.26	☐ No stopping
11.27	☐ Distance to parking place ahead

11.28	☐ Vehicles may park fully on the verge or footway
11.29	☐ Give priority to oncoming traffic
11.30	☐ You have priority over vehicles coming towards you
11.31	☐
11.32	☐ Stop
11.33	☐ Minimum speed 30 mph
11.34	☐ Pass either side to get to the same destination
11.35	☐ Route for trams
11.36	☐ Give an instruction
11.37	☐ On a one-way street
11.38	☐ Contraflow bus lane
11.39	☐ Tourist directions
11.40	☐ Tourist attraction
11.41	☐ To give warnings
11.42	☐ T-junction
11.43	☐ Risk of ice
11.44	☐ Crossroads
11.45	☐ Roundabout
11.46	☐ Road narrows
11.47	☐ Cycle route ahead
11.48	☐

11.49	☐
11.50	☐ Give way to trams
11.51	☐ Humps in the road
11.52	☐
11.53	☐ End of dual carriageway
11.54	☐ Side winds
11.55	☐ Danger ahead
11.56	☐ Hold back until you can see clearly ahead
11.57	☐ Level crossing with gate or barrier
11.58	☐ Trams crossing ahead
11.59	☐ Steep hill downwards
11.60	☐ Water across the road
11.61	☐ No through road on the left
11.62	☐ No through road
11.63	☐
11.64	☐
11.65	☐ The right-hand lane is closed

11.66	☐ Contraflow system
11.67	☐ Lane for heavy and slow vehicles
11.68	☐ You must stop and wait behind the stop line
11.69	☐ Stop at the stop line
11.70	☐ When your exit from the junction is blocked
11.71	☐
11.72	☐ Traffic lights out of order
11.73	☐ Nobody
11.74	☐ Level crossings
11.75	☐ No parking at any time
11.76	☐ To pass a road maintenance vehicle travelling at 10 mph or less
11.77	☐ You're approaching a hazard
11.78	☐ On road humps
11.79	☐
11.80	☐ Visibility along the major road is restricted
11.81	☐ Give way to traffic from the right
11.82	☐ Flash the headlights, indicate left and point to the left
11.83	☐ Stop at the stop line
11.84	☐ The driver intends to turn left

11.85	☐ On a motorway slip road
11.86	☐ Change to the lane on your left
11.87	☐ Temporary maximum speed 50 mph
11.88	☐ Right-hand lane closed ahead
11.89	☐ The number of the next junction
11.90	☐ As an overtaking lane
11.91	☐ On the right-hand edge of the road
11.92	☐ At slip-road entrances and exits
11.93	☐ Leave the motorway at the next exit
11.94	☐ End of motorway
11.95	☐
11.96	☐ 60 mph
11.97	☐ End of restriction
11.98	☐ A diversion route
11.99	☐ A mandatory speed-limit change ahead
11.100	☐ Compulsory maximum speed limit
11.101	☐ Carry on with great care
11.102	☐ Give an arm signal
11.103	☐ No motorcycles
11.104	☐ Pass the lorry on the left

11.105	☐ Move into another lane in good time
11.106	☐ To warn others of your presence
11.107	☐ When another road user poses a danger
11.108	☐ No parking on the days and times shown
11.109	☐ Quayside or river bank
11.110	☐
11.111	☐ Hazard warning
11.112	☐ To prevent queuing traffic from blocking the junction on the left
11.113	☐ It separates traffic flowing in opposite directions
11.114	☐ To warn you of their presence
11.115	☐ 20 mph
11.116	☐ Trams must stop
11.117	☐ At a mini-roundabout
11.118	☐ Pull up on the left
11.119	☐ Red alone
11.120	☐ Leave the motorway at the next exit
11.121	☐ Stop even if the road is clear
11.122	☐

11.123	☐ Mini-roundabout
11.124	☐ Two-way traffic crosses a one-way road
11.125	☐ Two-way traffic straight ahead
11.126	☐ Hump bridge
11.127	☐
11.128	☐ Direction to park-and-ride car park
11.129	☐ Wait for the green light
11.130	☐ Just before a 'give way' sign
11.131	☐ Wait
11.132	☐ Direction to emergency pedestrian exit
11.133	☐
11.134	☐ With-flow bus and cycle lane
11.135	☐
11.136	☐ Zebra crossing ahead
11.137	☐

11.138	☐
11.139	☐
11.140	☐ All traffic is going one way
11.141	☐ Red and amber
11.142	☐ Tunnel ahead

CASE STUDY PRACTICE – ANSWERS

Section 11 – Road and traffic signs

11.1   Where the joining side roads are slightly offset from each other
11.2   Regulatory
11.3   Blue with white arrow
11.4   Green
11.5   All the time

> 12. Essential documents

12.1	☐ The make and model
12.2	☐ Any Driver and Vehicle Standards Agency (DVSA)-approved training body
12.3	☐ That the motorcycle is insured for your use
12.4	☐ Three years
12.5	☐ The registered keeper's name
12.6	☐ When your permanent address changes
12.7	☐ Injury to others
12.8	☐ Third-party only
12.9	☐ The year of first registration
12.10	☐ To make sure your motorcycle is roadworthy
12.11	☐ A valid compulsory basic training (CBT) certificate

12.12	☐ When you have a medical condition that affects your riding
12.13	☐ Reapply for your provisional licence
12.14	☐ Carrying a pillion passenger
12.15	☐ 125 cc
12.16	☐ Yes, you need L plates while learning with a qualified instructor
12.17	☐ When the rider holds a full licence for the category of motorcycle they're riding
12.18	☐ Two years
12.19	☐ A valid certificate of insurance
12.20	☐ A full motorcycle licence
12.21	☐ You must have a full motorcycle licence

12.22	☐ You'll have to pay the first £100 of any claim
12.23	☐ One year after the date it was issued
12.24	☐ A document issued before you receive your insurance certificate
12.25	☐ Retake your theory and practical tests
12.26	☐ Until the vehicle is taxed, sold or scrapped
12.27	☐ A notification to tell DVLA that a vehicle isn't being used on the road
12.28	☐ Unlimited
12.29	☐ The registered vehicle keeper
12.30	☐ When a police officer asks you for it

12.31	☐ Tax the vehicle
12.32	☐ Tax your vehicle
12.33	☐ A valid driving licence
12.34	☐ Valid insurance
12.35	☐ 7 days
12.36	☐ When you move house

CASE STUDY PRACTICE – ANSWERS

Section 12 – Essential documents

12.1 Tax it using the new keeper supplement
12.2 Almost twelve months ago
12.3 It's allowed in order to get the motorcycle to a repairer
12.4 Third party
12.5 Damage to other vehicles

❯ 13. Incidents, accidents and emergencies

13.1	☐ By following an arrow on a marker post
13.2	☐ To stop the engine in an emergency
13.3	☐ There's danger ahead
13.4	☐ The number of the telephone you're using
13.5	☐ When you slow down quickly because of danger ahead
13.6	☐ Switch on hazard warning lights

13.7	☐ Stop at the next emergency telephone and report the hazard
13.8	☐ The other driver's vehicle insurance details
13.9	☐ The driver is likely to be a disabled person
13.10	☐ When stopped and temporarily obstructing traffic
13.11	☐ Keep a safe distance from the vehicle in front

13.12	☐ When an emergency arises
13.13	☐ Apply pressure over the wound and raise the arm
13.14	☐ At least 10 seconds
13.15	☐ 10 minutes
13.16	☐ 120 per minute
13.17	☐ Pale grey skin
13.18	☐ Check their airway remains clear
13.19	☐ Seek medical assistance
13.20	☐ Go to the next emergency telephone and report the hazard
13.21	☐ Variable message signs
13.22	☐ 5 to 6 centimetres
13.23	☐ Call the emergency services promptly
13.24	☐ Make sure that an ambulance is called for
13.25	☐ Only when it's essential
13.26	☐ Check whether they're breathing
13.27	☐ Check their airway is clear
13.28	☐ Keep injured people warm and comfortable
13.29	☐ Reassure them
13.30	☐ Warn other traffic
13.31	☐ Gently

13.32	☐ Tilt their head back gently
13.33	☐ Douse the burns with clean, cool, non-toxic liquid
13.34	☐ Raise the leg to lessen bleeding
13.35	☐ When there's further danger
13.36	☐ Keep them where they are
13.37	☐
13.38	☐ Driving licence
13.39	☐ As soon as possible
13.40	☐ It will help to reduce the blood flow
13.41	☐ Warn other traffic
13.42	☐ Remove anything that's blocking their airway
13.43	☐ Reassure them confidently
13.44	☐ This could result in more serious injury

CASE STUDY PRACTICE – ANSWERS

Section 13 – Incidents, accidents and emergencies

13.1 Shock
13.2 Because removing it could cause further injuries
13.3 To warn following traffic of the hazard
13.4 Keep them warm
13.5 You witnessed the incident

14. Motorcycle loading

14.1	☐ Ease off the throttle and reduce your speed
14.2	☐ You need time to get used to it
14.3	☐ The tyre pressure
14.4	☐ Solo, with a maximum power of at least 40 kW (53.6 bhp)
14.5	☐ The load must be securely fastened
14.6	☐ Wear a motorcycle helmet
14.7	☐ Lean with the rider when going around bends
14.8	☐ Lean with you on bends
14.9	☐ Headlights
14.10	☐ 50 mph
14.11	☐ Reduced stability
14.12	☐ The rider of the motorcycle
14.13	☐ Check that the motorcycle is suitable
14.14	☐ Uneven loads can make the motorcycle unstable
14.15	☐ Your ability to steer
14.16	☐ You must hold a full motorcycle licence
14.17	☐ Tyre pressures
14.18	☐ Keep further back than you normally would
14.19	☐ When they can reach the handholds and footrests
14.20	☐ That the sidecar is correctly aligned
14.21	☐ It will require a different riding technique
14.22	☐ The preload on the rear shock absorber(s)
14.23	☐ 1 metre (3 feet 3 inches)
14.24	☐ The trailer shouldn't be more than 1 metre (3 feet 3 inches) wide
14.25	☐ It will increase the stopping distance
14.26	☐ They mustn't carry a pillion passenger
14.27	☐ Hold a full motorcycle licence
14.28	☐ Passenger footrests
14.29	☐ Lightweight items
14.30	☐ Not at any time
14.31	☐ The handling
14.32	☐ Use only the left-hand and centre lanes

CASE STUDY PRACTICE – ANSWERS

Section 14 – Motorcycle loading

14.1 To make sure the load is secure
14.2 Uneven load distribution can affect balance
14.3 60 mph
14.4 Stopping distance is increased on a fully loaded vehicle
14.5 That lane mustn't be used by vehicles with trailers

➤ 15. Case study practice

Case study on pages 451–453

1 Look over your shoulder for a final check
2 Slow down
3 Make the call when you've stopped in a suitable place
4 Allow plenty of room
5 Wait patiently

Case study practice A

1 Leather clothing, high-visibility waistcoat and white helmet
2 Wait, as another train will be coming
3 Slow down to ride over this patch of road
4 The blue sign shows a motorcycle
5 Take a look over your right shoulder

Case study practice B

1 Headlight aim
2 Being blown off course
3 Vehicles with a trailer mustn't travel in the right-hand lane
4 In the left-hand lane without giving a signal
5 Road workers

Case study practice C

1 In the panniers
2 70 mph
3 Because the engine is warm
4 Lock your motorcycle and remove the key
5 Drop back slightly so you can see the road ahead

Case study practice D

1 Calm yourself down before you set off
2 A brightly coloured helmet
3 Keep calm and continue riding
4 Allow the cyclist plenty of room
5 Warn other road users of the danger

Case study practice E

1 Clothing that keeps you warm and dry
2 Get your motorcycle through its MOT test
3 Slippery roads
4 Uneconomical use of fuel
5 Place them in the recovery position

WIN
AN UNFORGETTABLE EXPERIENCE DAY

WORTH £200*

TSO, DVSA's official publishing partner, is offering you the chance to WIN an unforgettable experience day of your choice worth £200*

With hundreds of days on offer, there's something for everyone – from a relaxing spa weekend to the thrill of an exhilarating driving experience.

To enter, visit www.surveymonkey.com/s/WINNERBIKE
and answer this question correctly:

What is the minimum motorcycle engine size allowed on a motorway?

The winner will be selected at random from all entrants who answered the question correctly. Closing date: 31 March 2017.

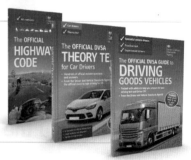